Hegel, Heidegger, and the Ground of History

Hegel, Heidegger, and the ground of History

Michael Allen Gillespie

The University of Chicago Press · Chicago & London

MICHAEL ALLEN GILLESPIE is assistant professor of political science at Duke University

The University of Chicago Press, Chicago 60637
The University of Chicago Press, Ltd., London

© 1984 by The University of Chicago
All rights reserved. Published 1984
Printed in the United States of America

93 92 91 90 89 88 87 86 85   5 4 3 2

Library of Congress Cataloging in Publication Data

Gillespie, Michael Allen.
    Hegel, Heidegger, and the ground of history.

    Based on the author's thesis.
    Bibliography: p.
    Includes index.
    1. History—Philosophy—History—19th century.
2. History—Philosophy—History—20th century.   3. Hegel,
Georg Wilhelm Friedrich, 1770–1831.   4. Heidegger, Martin,
1889–1976.   I. Title.
D16.8.G535   1984   901   84-2472
ISBN 0-226-29376-9

To my parents,
Charles and Eileen Gillespie

Contents

Preface

What is history? The importance and scope of this question for our times is only vaguely and then only imperfectly understood. Despite this lack of comprehension, and whether we like it or not, we dwell in the midst of this question, only rarely, if ever, experiencing it as a question but continually confronted with and challenged by its various answers. The question itself permeates all of our thinking about ourselves and our civilization, but it would be erroneous to assume that its importance is therefore merely theoretical—or to believe that the theoretical and spiritual, however distinguished from the practical and material, can in this case be completely or even largely dissociated from them, or that the political and economic well-being of man and his civilization is not inextricably bound up with his reflective consideration of himself, his political circumstances, and the state of his civilization.

There are two great intellectual forces in the modern world, science and history, and while they often seem mutually antagonistic they are in fact fundamentally complementary. Modern science determines the causal laws that govern the motions of matter but, in contradistinction to ancient science, eschews teleology and thus any determination of human ends. While it may thus present humanity with supreme knowledge of the mechanism of nature and open up the possibility for the technological conquest of the natural world and indeed of human nature itself, it does not and in principle it cannot tell us what we ought to do or how we ought to live. It is this question that history answers.

History of course is not modernity's only answer to this question. Empiricism for example answered this question with the doctrine of natural rights; rationalism discovered a solution in rational theology; humanism and classicism looked to ancient concepts of virtue and individuality; and transcendental idealism turned to teleological judgment and art. Moreover, many of these notions still exercise considerable force on contemporary thought and the political institutions that this thought informs. The continued importance of natural rights in the American context is only one example of this. Despite this importance, however, these other forms of thought have generally been unable to resist the encroachments of various forms of historical understanding. Gradually and often imperceptibly they have been permeated and overwhelmed by history. Even we Americans who in many ways have been least receptive to historical thinking find ourselves surprisingly dependent upon it. Despite our predisposition for scientific explanations, we seldom ask about what is simply true, or good, or just, or beautiful but rather about historical truth, or the judgment of history, or historical causes, or roots in history. We are concerned with the historical situation, with social progress, with human and technological development, with the process of industrialization and modernization, even characterizing those peoples and cultures which have not yet been wholly caught up in this process as underdeveloped or, charitably, developing. While this is still a far cry from the thorough historicism of the continental tradition, it is perhaps an ominous indication of the general tendency of our thought.

In the ancient world the consideration of humanity and its institutions fell within the purview of poetry or mythology and philosophy. Both claimed to comprehend not merely man but both man and the cosmos, and thus to establish man's place and duty in a cosmological hierarchy. In our world the task of such reflection upon human ends and duties has been assumed by history. For antiquity rhetoric was the chief form of practical and especially political deliberation: the wisdom of philosophy, which contemplated the general and necessary, was turned to a consideration of the particular and possible in and through rhetoric. In our times this classical function of rhetoric has been superseded or supplanted by propaganda, which implements the ideologically determined laws of history, and by public policy, which employs the knowledge gleaned by natural science to determine the most efficient means for the transformation of man and nature in accordance with historically determined social and technological goals.

Nowhere, however, is the importance and depth of the question about the nature and ground of history more evident than in the debate about its answer. Unfortunately, this debate is not merely the concern of learned men and societies, nor is it contested only with words: the debate about the nature and ground of history has become ideological and revolutionary; it has become bellicose and cataclysmic. The greatest event of our times, the Second World War, in whose unperceived shadow we stand, was in principle an internecine struggle about the nature of history. The current state of international tension is no less the result of the conviction and fervor of some and the perplexity and paralysis of others about the answer to this question.

As depressing as these reflections may be, they certainly would be made more bearable by the prospect of an unequivocal answer to the question of history or the dissolution of history itself as a way of understanding. But who today can soberly hope for such an answer or such a dissolution? Our thinking, our speaking, and our activity are so suffused with and dependent upon history and historical categories that any thought of such a transformation must be rejected by anyone who seriously considers the matter. In fact, such consideration must convince one that the influence of history upon our thinking and our lives is neither speedily nor steadily diminishing but rather continually increasing. History is and remains decisive for human life and thought, and the question of history thus becomes all the more important. We cannot forget and we dare not neglect this question: the truth, the value, the consistency, and the function of all historical concepts and hence the justice or propriety of their practical application is dependent upon a true or adequate answer to it. Without such an answer or the dissolution of the question itself, we are undoubtedly consigned to a debate between the convinced and the perplexed, with the ever-increasing danger of a new but nonetheless "final solution." It is in this very real sense that the incipient world technological civilization, in which we place all our hopes and find all our fears, is essentially bound up with this question.

But what if the question itself is inappropriate, if the question itself has misguided us? What if, however useful the means, the ends of modern civilization which history reveals are simply false, or worse, that this civilization has no ends, no purpose, no meaning? In view of these possibilities, a concrete questioning about the nature and ground of history is apparently necessary as a prolegomenon to any serious attempt to determine the ultimate importance of history to and for humanity, and hence to and for politics.

It is the purpose of this work to raise this question through an examination of the thought of Hegel and Heidegger. If not the first, Hegel's philosophic system was undoubtedly the most comprehensive attempt to understand man and existence as historical. It was, moreover, the culmination of the entire Western philosophic tradition and the source of almost all succeeding thought about history. While not the last, Heidegger's investigations were surely the most significant recent examination of history. His thought also is, or at least claims to be, an, if not *the*, alternative to Hegel's and indeed to the whole Western tradition. Through the examination of the thought of these two thinkers we may thus be able to gain a decisive insight into the question of history.

Chapter 1 attempts to demonstrate the necessity for asking about the ground of history through a consideration of the conceptual development of history. History for us is ambiguous: it is on one hand the totality of human events, and on the other the account of these events. For the ancients and early moderns history meant the account of events which were thought to be intrinsically capricious. Since the Enlightenment, however, history has come to be identified with the events themselves. This is the result of a fundamental transformation of our understanding of man and the relationship of nature and convention. For the Greeks, history like poetry and philosophy aimed at revealing the eternal in the actual, i.e., the underlying natural truth that appeared in and through the conventional actions of men. It thus supported and was bound up with the polis. The decline and dissolution of the polis in the Roman and Christian worlds led to the degeneration of history and its ultimate subordination to Scripture. While the modern concept of history develops on this ancient model, it comes to depend increasingly upon the modern view of man as a free and self-conscious being. History in this sense comes to be understood as the progressive unfolding of rational freedom and purpose in opposition to a degenerate and merely mechanical nature. This notion rests upon a reversal of the ancient view of the relation of nature and convention, which certainly in part is due to Christianity. History for modernity thus becomes the progressive liberation of man from the tyranny of nature. The course of the development of the concept of history from the Enlightenment to the French Revolution, Idealism, the Historical School, Marxism, nihilism, historicism, and existentialism is only the increasing radicalization of this initial premise that ends, however, not in the complete liberation and perfection of man but in relativism, fanaticism, and world war. In light of this development it is thus necessary to call history into question. The question about history in this sense leads to the question of the ground of history, the question whether history is or can be anything at all.

Chapter 2 considers the origin of the question of the ground of history and attempts to show how this question arose for Hegel. Although the question of the ground was already central to ancient philosophy, the consideration of the ground of history only begins with Rousseau and arises in his *Second Discourse* in response to the question of the relationship of the political and the natural. Humanity is characterized by its ability to free itself from and oppose itself to nature in and through the political. History for modernity, as it appears in Rousseau, is the account of the progress of man to self-consciousness and freedom. The relationship of self-consciousness and freedom to nature and its laws, however, is not considered by Rousseau, and it is consequently difficult to discern the ground of their interaction. It is precisely this question, however, that Kant addresses in the Third Antinomy of Pure Reason.

According to Kant, both universal natural necessity and freedom are necessary and also antinomious, since every event must have a prior cause, and yet, unless there is a first and hence free cause, the series will always be incomplete and the laws of nature thus never sufficiently grounded. Kant solves this antinomy by showing that the contradiction is not in the world but in consciousness, positing two distinct and independent realms, the phenomenal realm of nature and the noumenal realm of freedom.

Hegel's conception of history is a direct response to the Third Antinomy and Kant's problematic solution to it. This problem for Hegel, however, is not merely theoretical but also practical. In fact, the antinomy of freedom and natural necessity as it appears in the French Revolution and English bourgeois society was apparently the immediate impetus for his thought. In Hegel's view Kant solved the antinomy only by making consciousness itself contradictory and therefore unintelligible. Hegel, however, accepts this contradiction and makes it the basis of his system. Antinomy becomes dialectic.

Chapter 3 is a consideration of the phenomenological ground that Hegel presents as the answer to the question of the ground of history. It is primarily an examination of the "Introduction" to the *Phenomenology* in which Hegel outlines his project and discusses his methodology. In his view history is, on one hand, the development of the knowledge of the objective or natural world. This is phenomenology as the appearing of knowledge of the phenomenal. As such, it is the account of the development of consciousness to absolute knowledge. On the other hand, history is the experience of consciousness itself, i.e., of the subject as it comes to an ever-deeper and fuller knowledge, not about the natural world but about itself. The experience of consciousness is thus the process by which man comes to complete self-consciousness and unity with himself. Insofar as this development is the development of consciousness it is dialectical, and insofar as it is the development of self-consciousness it is speculative. Together the dialectical and the speculative constitute the fullness of the absolute and the essence of science. This is Hegel's new understanding of consciousness as spirit and the absolute that is the basis for the reconciliation of the subjective and the objective, and therefore of freedom and natural necessity. This reconciliation in turn is the ground Hegel establishes for history.

Chapter 4 examines Hegel's discussion of the character of this phenomenological ground within the concrete history of man's political and spiritual development and its foundation in the science of logic. In his lectures on the *Philosophy of History* Hegel attempts to show that the process of the development of consciousness and self-consciousness that he described in the *Phenomenology* is identical with the concrete history of humanity as the interaction and reconciliation of freedom and nature within the political realm. In the *Phenomenology* Hegel considers each of these moments separately, as the development of consciousness, spirit, and the absolute. From the perspective of completed science as it appears in the *Philosophy of History*, however, this development can be understood in its unity and truth as the concrete history of humanity.

However, even if Hegel successfully demonstrates the unfolding of the phenomenological ground in and as concrete history, he still has to concede that the entire system is based on contradiction. It would thus seem that at least prima facie it must be irrational. Hegel attempts to meet this objection and establish a true ground for history and consciousness in his *Science of Logic*. What is, according to Hegel, is contradictory *and* unitary, the whole is the identity of identity and nonidentity. Being and nothing understood statically are opposites; understood in and as the process of becoming they are identical. The dialectical process thus has a speculative unity. The question arises, however, whether this dialectical logic is itself comprehensible or whether it is only a logical illusion which justifies underlying moral and political predispositions. Even granting that Hegel may be correct, the ground of history as it appears in his work thus remains fundamentally mysterious. The chapter consequently ends with a critique of Hegel's answer to the question of the ground of history and his thought as a whole.

Chapter 5 is a consideration of Heidegger's reevaluation of history as Being and the consequences of this reevaluation for ethics and politics. The failure of Heidegger's initial attempt to show that Being is time or history leads him to a critique of subjectivity and modernity. Modernity as the realm of subjectivity is also in Heidegger's view the realm of alienation. This alienation in turn engenders a desire for reconciliation. Modern man's attempt to reconcile himself with the world by objectifying it through science and historiography in order to subordinate it to the categories of subjectivity leads, however, only to nihilism as it appears in unfettered world technology, ideological politics, and world war.

In Heidegger's view nihilism is not merely the consequence of modernity but is rooted in the metaphysical essence of the West as such. It is in fact the result of the history or destiny of Being that begins with the pre-Socratics and ends with Marx, Nietzsche, and modern technology. For Heidegger this history is the consequence of a growing concealment and forgetfulness of the mysterious beginning of the West in an original experience of Being. This withdrawal of Being in favor of being which is the essence of this history reaches its conclusion in nihilism which denies Being altogether in favor of being.

While nihilism thus seems to betoken the total degradation of man, Heidegger wants to see it as the highest revelation of Being itself and hence as the ground for an authentic ethical, political, and spiritual life. Such a new understanding depends upon the recognition that Being is utterly different than all beings, that it appears consequently as nothing, and that this nothing is the aporia or question that is the beginning of all thought and therefore of all ontology. Understood in this manner Being appears in its truth not as a what but as a how, not as eternity but as history or destiny. The unfolding of the West, then, is fundamentally determined by the revelation and conceal-ment of Being.

The solution that Heidegger sees to the problem of nihilism thus lies not with man but with Being. The nothingness of nihilism may foreshadow a new revelation of Being as destiny, but this cannot be brought forth by man. For man at the end of modernity, and that means at the end of Western civilization itself, there remains only a preparatory waiting that steps back out of technology and ideology, out of science and metaphysics, into the question or abyss of Being in hopes of a new revelation. This chapter, and the work as a whole, concludes with a critique of the problems and dangers of Heidegger's project and a consideration of its consequences for ethics and politics.

This study was made possible in large part by several generous grants from the Deutscher Akademischer Austauschdienst (DAAD) which sup-ported my work at the Hegel Archives and the Ruhr Universität in West Germany. I would like to thank the DAAD and the director of the Hegel Archives, Otto Pöggeler, for their support and encouragement of my work. I would also like to thank the many friends and teachers who have helped me find my way through the labyrinth of German thought. I am especially grateful to Joseph Cropsey, Paul Ricoeur, Nathan Tarcov, and Ruth Grant for their thoughtful criticism of the manuscript, and to Sharon Wachel and Queen Ward for typing it. This study must in consequence of its insuffi-ciency be but a poor recompense to the kindness of so many, yet I hope that it may serve as an adequate occasion for my thanks.

1
The Question of History

What is *history*? Such an important question ought to have a straightforward and unambiguous answer. This, however, is not the case. As we understand it today, history has two different but related meanings: it is on one hand the totality of events, the *res gestae*, that constitute the unfolding of human civilization, and on the other the account or report of these events, the *historia rerum gestarum*. Thus, even on the most rudimentary level, we encounter ambiguity. How are we to understand history? Is it fundamentally the whole of events of which a posteriori an account is given, or is it only in and through the account that these events become history? Does history, in other words, have an objective reality, or is it only a story that has a relationship to events and perhaps even in some sense gives them meaning but that is not in or of the events themselves?

This ambiguity is in fact only a reflection of a deeper disagreement. In antiquity and even in early modernity history was understood as the *historia rerum gestarum*, while the events themselves were thought to be governed not by rational or causal laws but by an incomprehensible destiny. Since the Enlightenment, however, the opinion that history is the human actuality or *res gestae*, which historians merely describe or reconstruct, has grown and solidified. To come to terms with this ambiguity and the question of history, it is thus necessary to examine the debate about the nature of history itself.

History originated with the Greeks and was closely related in their view to philosophy and poetry. Indeed, at first these three were hardly distinguished from one another: the earliest philosophers often wrote in verse and apparently called their works histories. Nor is this very surprising, since the word itself derives from the same root—*eidenai*, 'to know (through having seen)'—as the philosophic term *eidos, idea*, 'form'. This close relationship is likewise evident in its early usage, where it generally means 'witnessing', 'knowing', or 'enquiring'. Heracleitus, for example, used the term to describe the thought of Hesiod, Pythagoras, Xenophanes, and Hecateus, clearly suggesting a sort of knowing that is akin to both philosophy and poetry.[1]

In the fifth century, however, the conception of history became more specific and differentiated. History for Herodotus still meant 'enquiry,' but his was an enquiry only into human affairs.[2] The same might be said of Thucydides, although he did not use the word 'history', since it was a foreign word in classical Attic. On this basis Aristotle characterized history as a story or account of human affairs.[3] Fastening on a different aspect of the original conception of history, Plato and Theophrastus understood it as natural history or enquiry into nature, i.e., as the science that "brings the flowing to a stand-still."[4] While history was still the general name for the enquiry into and account of the motions of nature and the actions of men, a clear and decisive divergence into two genres, natural history and political history, was thus already apparent in the fourth century and led to the later isolation of natural history as a specialized discipline separated from political history. Despite this divergence, however, the original meaning of history and its close attachment to philosophy and poetry were not lost. The historian was the witness or judge of events, and as such his activity depended upon his having seen or at least having enquired of those who had seen the events in question.[5] Such seeing was rudimentary not just to history, however, but to all the ways of knowing. For example, it was just such a desire 'to know through having seen' (*eidenai*) that characterized poetry and that Aristotle described as peculiarly and naturally human and philosophic.[6] History was thus in a fundamental way bound up with philosophy and poetry and along with them constituted the essence of Greek thought.

Reality for the Greeks is a conjunction of the actual and the eternal. The transience of human life and the deeds of men, in their view, can only be understood in conjunction with the eternity of the gods and nature. The gods exist in a realm beyond both death and change and are the embodiment of individual immortality and perfection, while nature is the realm of constant change which is governed by a teleology that produces the eternal repetitions of the heavens and the species. Time in this sense is, as Plato's Timeaus asserts, the moving image of eternity. By contrast, man is a lamentably finite being. He is chiefly characterized by death, and his deeds are even more fleeting than his life. He is lifted up for a moment onto "the coasts of light" to struggle for preeminence and contemplate the radiant beauty of nature and the gods only to be crushed by these gods for their sport or to be devoured by a dark and omnivorous destiny. In contrast to the orderliness of nature, human affairs are governed by chance, subject to such sudden and unpredictable reversals that even the most powerful men and the greatest empires are never secure. All that is certain is that everything that has come to be will also pass away, that today's victor will on some tomorrow lay in the dust under the heel of a new master upon whom fortune has momentarily smiled.

Both the goal and the limit of human striving are thus established by the eternal.[7] Man constantly seeks but can never attain immortality. He is of course vouchsafed the species-immortality of nature, but this does not satisfy him since it is something he shares with all other life. He desires the individual immortality of the gods, but this is beyond him, and the hubris that characterizes the attempt to attain it is the worst of all crimes and is met with the most terrible of all punishments. To know thyself for the Greeks is thus to know that you are not a god, and to do everything in measure is to act as a mortal man rather than as an immortal god. Despite these limitations man is granted a certain sort of immortality, an immortality that lies between the immortality of nature and that of the gods, between the species and the individual. This middle ground is the polis.

The polis is the place of human life, and those who live outside it, as Aristotle maintained, are for the Greeks either beasts or gods. Man is the *zōon politikon*, the political animal, and whatever immortality is granted him as a man must be bound up with the polis. This immortality, however, cannot simply be due to the eternity of the polis itself, for every polis, as the *Iliad* made apparent and as every Greek well knew, had at one time come into being and would just as certainly pass away. Thus it is not the eternality of the polis that is the source of human immortality. Human immortality is rather bound up with the polis because the polis is the place of speech, the place in which the eternal is brought to light in the actual through speech. As the *zōon politikon* man is the *zōon logon echon*, the speaking or rational animal, and thus has access to and in a sense can participate in that which transcends him.

Although there are many different forms of speech in the polis, philosophy, poetry, and history are the highest because they most clearly reveal the eternal. According to Aristotle, philosophy aims at the revelation of the necessary, while poetry is concerned with the possible and history with the actual.[8] Philosophy in his view thus explains what, for example, virtue and vice are in themselves, while poetry presents us with images of virtuous and vicious men, as they necessarily would be if they were. History, in contradistinction to both, is a putting into words of what has been seen in human affairs, for it is only thus that events last; it is only thus that they are remembered and have meaning. As Epictetus remarked, it is not through the deeds of men but through the words about these deeds that we are moved.[9] History for the Greeks does not explain the logical development of events, because there is no such logical development, but rather makes static and thus comprehensible the highest moments of the ephemeral. These moments are the highest, however, because they most clearly reveal what is essential and eternal in human life. History thus calls back to memory what has been seen, not in order to describe or reconstruct actuality but to open up the eternal for man. The eternality that history reveals, however, does not depend upon the eternality of the written or oral record of events. Historical events are not eternal because they are remembered but are remembered because they reveal the eternal. They are thus eternal in the same sense that Achilles' deeds are eternal—because they embody what is true about man everywhere and always. History in this sense reveals the source of *human* immortality.[10]

History, however, like philosophy and poetry, does not aim merely at the revelation of the eternal but also at the preservation of the polis. All three thus have both a theoretical and a practical goal, although philosophy and poetry often find it difficult to reconcile these two goals and tend rather to uncover an abyss between the conventional and the natural, or between the affairs of men and those of gods. Indeed, from a political point of view, philosophy and poetry tell man more often what he is not than what he is, emphasizing his mortality to indicate the source of his immortality. History, on the contrary, reveals the eternality of explicitly political actions, and consequently it guarantees an undying fame for the virtuous and valiant and an undying opprobrium for the vicious and cowardly, thus motivating men to sacrifice their ephemeral pleasures, their wealth, and even their lives in the service of the polis. In this way history sets the polis at the center of Greek life and immortalizes those deeds that are conducive to its preservation and glory. Such an immortalization of the actual, however, is only possible because the eternal shines forth out of the events themselves. This does not mean that the Greeks believed that the actual is the eternal. On the contrary, actuality and eternity in their view are for the most part fundamentally severed. There are, however, occasions when the shape of actuality approaches that of eternity, i.e., when the eternal appears in and as the actual. It is such occasions that the historian immortalizes and through them that he approaches the truth of philosophy and poetry. Thus, Thucydides, for example, could write a work "for all time," because he had before him the "greatest war of all time." Even in such a case, however, he did not merely describe the actual but also recomposed the speeches of the various orators to bring out what was appropriate to the occasion. The historian in this sense chooses an event or action that most clearly reveals or embodies what is essential or eternal in human life and reworks it in whatever way is necessary to bring out the truly real element in it.

It is precisely for such distortions, however, that we moderns often criticize ancient historians and question whether their work is really history. In this light it is often asserted that they were unable to develop a true historical science because they lacked a sense of history or of actuality, or because they had only a rudimentary or primitive conception of scientific methods, or that they were too encumbered with a mythological past to recognize the true causal connections between events.[11] While all of these assertions may in some sense be correct, they fundamentally misconstrue the Greek conception of history. The truth is not that the Greeks were unable to develop a historical science but that they did not want to, that their methodology was different than our own because their end was different than our own. History for the Greeks does not provide a logical and complete explanation of the actual, which is in their view impossible, but strives to reveal the eternal in the actual and thus to provide the ground for human immortality. The events themselves and the connection between them, which are of such importance to us today, are only significant for the Greeks insofar as the eternal is present in these events and can be extracted and preserved in words, i.e., only insofar as the glorious deeds of valiant men can be preserved from the oblivion that the necessity of their deaths would otherwise entail.

History thus recognizes and immortalizes the deeds that preserve and glorify the polis and, as such, is only possible in the context of the polis, for only in such a relatively small community are individual deeds significant. It is thus not surprising that the degeneration of the polis and the degeneration of history go hand in hand. This first became evident in the late Roman Republic when the political demand for glorification subverted the philosophic demand for truth in history. History was no longer written by those outside the regime "for all time" but by those involved in public affairs for the political necessities of the moment. In this way history became merely a rhetorical tool. As with all tools, however, it is still possible to distinguish a good and a bad use. Caesar, for example, wrote excellent accounts of his wars in Gaul, which, however, aimed only at his own aggrandizement. Cicero, on the contrary, sought to preserve history's service to the state. History in his view is a branch of rhetoric that makes use of embellishments but also stresses the moral lessons of the story.[12] In this manner Livy, for example, consciously sacrificed the truth on many occasions for the sake of Roman glory and the preservation of examples of martial virtue for emulation. History as the unity of theoretical and practical wisdom is dissolved in favor of the practical. While it may retain a certain nobility, its higher philosophic character and thus its connection to the eternal are thereby lost.

Even this political task of history, however, disappeared with the destruction of the polis under the Empire. With the dissolution of the polis all men became, as Aristotle had earlier maintained, either gods or beasts, either divine and all-powerful emperors or private citizens with rights but no duties, with property but no capacity to perform noble deeds. In this context history degenerated into universal history on one hand and biography on the other. Universal history arose as the accumulation and coordination of the individual histories of the previously independent states that had been absorbed into the Empire and aimed at providing a basis of understanding for commerce and interchange. The ethical and political purpose that Cicero had still recognized as belonging to history thus came to an end.

History was consequently reduced to little more than a tool of economics and administration that relied entirely upon the accounts of others and made no pretense to the contemplation and evaluation of contemporary events. Such an evaluation, however, was carried out in a different form: history became biography.

For the Greeks history was concerned with the noble actions of men in the context of the polis. The dissolution of the various cities into the universal Empire, however, put an end to noble deeds, since no ordinary citizen could ever play a truly significant role in so great a state. Indeed, the only persons capable of truly noble or ignoble deeds were the emperors, but they rose so far above their fellows that they were deemed divine and their actions could consequently be neither praised nor blamed according to human standards. It is thus hardly surprising that history should give way to biography and that the demand upon history for rhetorical glorification and flattery should supersede and dissolve the political demand for virtue and public spiritedness. This is already evident in the dissolution of the distinction of history and drama in late Hellenistic art as well as in Tacitus and the late Roman biographers.[13] The way to history as a fictional story almost certainly follows from this dissolution.

Concomitant with the degeneration of Greek and Roman history under the Empire was the rise of Christian history. This new form of history was the result of the confrontation of Jewish or Christian thought with the work of the ancient historians. The first Christian histories, to be sure, relied almost exclusively on the accounts of ancient Judaism and the lives of Christ and the Apostles, but it would be a mistake to see the origin of this sort of history in the so-called historicism of the Old or New Testament. There is in fact no word in ancient Hebrew for history, and the concept is foreign to ancient Jewish thought.[14] Christian history was rather the result of the encounter of theology and history. Confronted with the accounts of a glorious pagan antiquity, the Christian historians had to find some means of demonstrating that the actions and characters described by the pagan historians could in no way rival those described in Scripture in order to wean men from the ancient models of the good or noble life. Their task was not simply to deny classical antiquity but to subordinate it to the Christian world view.[15]

This synthesis of Christian theology and ancient history brought about a decisive and fundamental change in the conception of history itself. The original Greek sense of history as *witness* remains in Christian history, but it is no longer the knowledge of what is seen but the knowledge of God through the witness of the Apostles. History which had sought the eternal in the actual thus becomes the revelation of the eternal as such, the witness to the hidden truth or meaning of events as a whole, which comes to light and hence visibility in and through the Word, i.e., in and through Christ. History thus comes to rest not upon seeing or contemplation, i.e., not upon the immediate experience and apprehension of the eternal, but upon the authority and through the mediation of Scripture, i.e., through the Word itself. Thus history for Christianity is not the *enquiry* into or the account of events with a view to extracting and immortalizing noble deeds but the *faith* in the single event, the kairos, that reveals the hitherto hidden truth and order in all creation.

All Christian history in this sense is written *sub specie aeternitatis*. Time is no longer understood as the realm of transience, governed by caprice or destiny, but the unfolding of eternity backwards and forwards out of the moment of creation, i.e., out of the kairos in which Christ comes into the world. This single event is thus the key to all creation, since every other event follows from it and is only comprehensible in terms of it. History in this sense becomes prophetic, for just as the Old Testament prophets were able to foresee the coming of Christ by means of divine inspiration, so on the basis of this new dispensation the significance of the entire past and the entire future becomes comprehensible.

Henceforth it was not the experience of the eternal in the actual but the revelation of the eternal in Scripture that was the measure of all things. The fidelity to the original witness that characterized ancient history, however, remained and was in fact intensified in no small part because the witness was conceived as divine or at least divinely inspired. The importance of the immediately seen and thus of man, however, was thereby correspondingly diminished. Man, who is in any case a poor and untrustworthy witness in comparison to God, is rendered even less trustworthy by original sin, which, according to Christian dogma, produces a necessary blindness in man's soul. Moreover, the significance of all other events is infinitesimal in comparison to *the* event and can hardly be worth observing or recording. Consequently, Scripture is always more important in understanding events than an enquiry into the events themselves.

Scripture also determines the substance of history.[16] Since history is an account of God's purposes with man from creation to Parousia, it is universal or ecumenical. It is the history of all men. This does not of course mean that all men are equally important: they are distinguished by their relationship to God. Christian history is thus the account of the struggle of believers with nonbelievers, of the city of God with the city of the pagans. Both, however, are understood as agents of divine will and the struggle itself as the trial of faith that will determine salvation. Even the outcome of this struggle is foretold in Scripture. In this sense, Christian history teaches the same lesson as Scripture—that it is not noble deeds or wisdom but faith, not worldly success but the proximity to God that is the source of human immortality. In this manner Christian history offers a bulwark against the lure of the ethical and political life portrayed by the ancient historians. Christian history is fundamentally a meditation on the relationship of God and man and aims not at political stability or glory but at the propagation of the faith, not at the discovery of the eternal in the actual but at the demonstration of the actual as the unfolding of the eternal and the determination of its completion in the prediction of the Parousia.

With Christianity, history, as the Greeks and Romans understood it, comes to an end. History for the ancients is that form of speech which reveals what is essential and thus eternal in the actual affairs of men. For Christianity, however, the eternal appeared only once in the actual and thereafter transcends it. The glittering immediacy of the eternal that shone forth out of the actual for the ancient poets, philosophers, and historians retreats into the darkness of a transcendent reality that can be attained and understood only through the mediation of revelation. As a result, history almost entirely disappears in the Middle Ages.[17] Even chronicles and annals are rare and then are often little more than lists of popes and emperors. Medieval man understood time on the basis of eternity and found it difficult to believe that merely temporal differences could be very significant. Man lived at the end of time and sought only to determine the proximity of his translation into eternity. The tension between the actual and the eternal that had characterized antiquity was thus resolved in favor of the eternal by Christianity, and history consequently became superfluous.

The relevance of history for human life only again became apparent in modernity. Early modernity, however, still understood history on the ancient model as the *historia rerum gestarum*, and it was not until the middle of the eighteenth century that it was understood as the *res gestae*.[18] In the fifteenth century, for example, it was held to be a close neighbor of rhetoric and poetry, and in 1651 Hobbes still considered it "the register of the *knowledge of fact*" and divided it into the two classical genres, natural and political history.[19] History for early modernity was thus still only a literary form and not in or of the events themselves. Although such Renaissance historians as Machiavelli recognized the ability of man to influence his own destiny, they were still convinced that history was not ultimately governed by reason or purpose but by fortune.

How then did history, which had always been understood as the *historia rerum gestarum*, come to be understood as the *res gestae*? We who are so accustomed to think of history in this way perceive nothing so extraordinary in this transformation and are perhaps only surprised that the ancients themselves failed to recognize such an obvious truth. They, however, would certainly have found such a notion as ludicrous as the idea that there was an actual or objective realm of philosophy or poetry. This is thus no mean or insignificant transformation, nor is it easily understood. It is clear, however, that it is peculiarly bound up with modernity itself.

Modernity is characterized by the rejection of traditional authorities and the articulation of a new standard of truth. In contradistinction to antiquity, which discovered the truth in the blossoming of the eternal in the actual, and Christianity, which believed it had found the truth in the revelation of an eternal and transcendent God, modernity finds truth in man himself as a conscious and self-conscious being. Modernity is thus characterized by consciousness and recognizes as real only that which arises through consciousness, either through observation or introspection. Consciousness thus becomes the standard of truth for modernity.

Consciousness is not mere thinking. On one hand it is the awareness or sensation of objects, and on the other it is self-consciousness, i.e., the consciousness of consciousness that characterizes the subject. Consciousness is thus not merely the empirical consciousness in the head of a subject but the twofold of subjectivity and objectivity, or in Descartes' terms of the *res extensa* and the *res cogitans* that constitutes the fullness of reality for modernity. Both the extensive realm of nature and the inner realm of the human self arise out of and rest upon consciousness, which consequently supplies the standard of truth for each realm. Only that which man can see and ascertain through observation or introspection is real, and everything else is merely a projection of the imagination. The proper study for man is consequently not the exegesis of Scripture but the study of nature and the human soul.

Early modernity concentrated its attention on nature, and modern natural science which seeks to determine the causes of events and ultimately to manipulate nature for the benefit of man was the result. The investigation of human nature takes place within this same horizon as empirical psychology, which attempts to determine the causes of human as opposed to merely natural motion. Man in this view is motivated by passions induced by natural objects. Certain passions, however, are more powerful and decisive than others, e.g., the desire for self-preservation, or a ceaseless striving for power after power. On the basis of such an understanding the early moderns believed they could determine principles of natural justice or right: if happiness arises out of the satisfaction of the passions, they reasoned, justice must consist in the greatest possible satisfaction of the passions of each consistent with the satisfaction of all. As a minimum, government must provide for the security of all and allow everyone the opportunity to satisfy his desires. This is, of course, the basis of modern individualism and liberalism and the modern doctrine of natural right. In this manner nature seemed to early modernity to present man with an eternal standard of right or justice against which he could judge human actions and evaluate the legitimacy of political institutions.

This modern doctrine of natural right, however, rests upon a weak foundation, for it is not nature that is the final standard for modernity but man, and not natural necessity that is determinative but human freedom. As self-consciousness, man is not merely in himself but also for himself, i.e., he is not simply subject to the universal law of natural causation but he rises above it to the realm of freedom. To be free in this sense means to be free from the laws of nature, from the bondage to one's passions. This freedom is thus not license or caprice but the freedom to live according to rational laws. To be free is thus to be rational. To be rational, though, means to be self-conscious in the fullest sense, to rise above the state of merely reactive consciousness into the state of complete self-consciousness where I = I. To be rational in this sense means to be self-identical and not contradictory, to be an I or a subject as opposed to a not-I or object. Freedom is thus the liberation from nature and natural desire, from all tyranny of objectivity. The recognition of subjectivity, however, is likewise the recognition that all men are subjects who ought not to be treated as objects, i.e., as something merely natural, and who must therefore be freed from the tyranny of natural desire. Such a liberation, however, can only be achieved if both man and nature are subordinated to the laws of reason, if nature is subjectivized. The modern conception of man as a free and rational subject thus undermines natural right and gives birth of the notion that nature itself must be overcome.

Despite its assault upon Christianity, modernity thus in a sense completes the Christian project.[20] As self-consciousness, man stands between the actual and the eternal. He is connected to the actual by consciousness or sensation and to the eternal by self-consciousness or reflectivity. It is introspection, however, that is decisive. Luther, for example, argued that individuals can know the highest truths, i.e., the truths about God, through conscience, i.e., through the introspective examination of their own souls. For Leibniz, in a similar fashion, it is the essence of apperception or self-consciousness that in thinking of itself it also thinks being, substance, and God.[21] This does not mean that for modernity man *is* God—although the culmination of this aspect of modernity in Nietzsche's conception of the overman comes close to such an assertion—but rather that man is the agent of the absolute or eternal in the actual. The freedom that arises out of self-consciousness thus imposes a fundamental obligation upon man to rise above nature and natural desires and transform both in accordance with the laws of reason. The task of man, as modernity understands it, is thus set by his unique access to the eternal—he must realize the Kingdom of God in this vale of tears by subordinating a fundamentally brutish nature to the humane laws of reason.

This notion of the unfolding of human freedom and reason in opposition to nature gave birth to the idea of progress. Progress in this sense is the process by which man conquers and transforms nature. This transformation, however, presupposes the development of consciousness to self-consciousness and the consequent liberation of man from nature. In modernity's view such a development is the result of experience, i.e., of trial and error, which is embodied in memory and transmitted through education. Progress is thus the consequence of the cumulative experience of mankind. The proof of this idea of progress for modernity was the manifest superiority of modern natural science and the liberation of man through modern morality and politics. Francis Bacon, for example, saw the discoveries of

Columbus and Copernicus as a demonstration of the superiority of modernity to antiquity, and Voltaire drew the obvious, although in many respects ludicrous, conclusion that young people leaving school in his own time knew more than the philosophers of antiquity.[22] Previously, human development had been an unconscious progress from mere consciousness and the slavery of natural desire to self-consciousness and the freedom of self-determination. With the advent of a self-conscious humanity and the recognition of human freedom, however, this development need no longer necessarily be accidental and plodding but could be directed and accelerated by the conscious application of reason.

There were dangers, however, that lurked within the idea of progress that modernity did not at first perceive. The ancients, among others Lucretius, recognized progress within the realm of convention in the increasing perfection of the arts, but this conventional or technical progress was limited by and subordinate to the order of nature in their view. The modern conception of progress, however, envisions the conquest and consequent subordination and transformation of nature by human freedom armed with a supreme knowledge of nature's secrets and a highly developed technology. The idea of progress thus represents an inversion of the ancient relationship of nature and convention and, indeed, is only a fuller expression of the essential truth of modernity, that man and not nature or God is the measure and master of all things.[23] The significance of this doctrine for human life, however, only becomes fully apparent in the Enlightenment.

Human conduct for the ancients was regulated by convention which established the standards of right and wrong and of praise and blame for human actions. These standards often varied from city to city. Because of this the Greek conventionalists argued that there were no standards beyond the customs of the city. The mainstream of Greek philosophic thought, however, resisted this notion and argued that the mere variation of conventions did not lead to relativism because the various conventions could all be judged against nature. The notion of the superiority of nature to convention thus formed the basis for the ancient conception of natural right. The modern form of this doctrine, however, rests on much less certain ground because of the reversal of nature and convention, which appears in the idea of progress. The unfolding of the essence of modernity thus effectively undermines nature and natural rights, since it makes evident the truth that was always implicit in modernity, that in matters of human conduct man must look not to nature but to human freedom as it manifests itself in conventions to know what he ought to do.

Such a doctrine, however, is constantly in danger of becoming a mere conventionalism or subjectivism. If man can only look to himself to discover the standards for his actions, he constantly runs the danger of mistaking current prejudices and opinions for the truths of reason, or of simply identifying *what is* with *what ought to be*. What is thus apparently necessary is a rational standard for evaluating convention. Modernity's ultimate answer to this question is history.

Early modernity and the early Enlightenment were primarily concerned with natural or political science and empirical psychology and had serious doubts about history. This was hardly accidental. These sciences rested upon the immediate experience and observation of man and nature, and their results could be ostensively verified or ascertained. History, on the contrary, depended upon memory, which is less certain than sense-experience, and upon authorities, whose judgment could not be evaluated or trusted. It thus did not seem to meet the standards of a legitimate science. Voltaire, who was himself a historian, doubted for example that historical sources before the Renaissance could be trusted. For the early Enlightenment history was at best but *une fable convenue*, which might reinforce the truths of reason but really had no independent authority of its own.

The growth of the idea of progress and the collapse of nature as a standard for human conduct, however, gave rise to the modern conception of history. Whereas nature had hitherto seemed to form a rational whole in comparison to the irrationality and caprice of human affairs, the discovery of rational human freedom that transcended nature led, on one hand, to the recognition of the incompleteness or insufficiency of nature and, on the other hand, to the realization of the basic rationality of human affairs. Modernity thus came to conceive of the unfolding of human freedom in and as progress as the basic truth of actuality. It was this new conception of human affairs as a rational development that led to the notion of history as the *res gestae*.[24]

This modern conception of history first appeared in the latter half of the eighteenth century in the work of Vico, Montesquieu, Voltaire, Gibbon, Herder, Turgot, Condorcet, and others.[25] While only a few of these writers examined history as a whole, they were all anxious to demonstrate the reality of progress that was responsible for the superiority of modernity to antiquity. History in this sense, though, is not merely the history of man but the history of the unfolding of the eternal in and through man; and the end or goal of history is the complete conquest and rationalization of nature, the perfect institutionalization of a secularized and fundamentally logical city of God. This recognition of a rational end to historical development fills the moral and political vacuum left by the collapse of the doctrine of natural right. History presents a rational standard that lifts man above mere conventionalism or capricious subjectivism because it allows man to judge all conventions in terms of their state of progress toward the perfectly just society which is the rational end of history.

The doctrine of historical progress, however, not only establishes standards of justice and right by which to measure conduct and political institutions but also creates a goal or destination for humanity and a concomitant historical duty or moral imperative. The conscious recognition of the hitherto unconscious development of history and of its necessary goal or end leads to the obligation, as Condorcet for example understood it, to accelerate historical development and thus to shorten man's way to perfection.[26] In this way the idea of historical progress ends in a doctrine of acceleration and mobilization. All man's efforts must be turned toward this goal, and all resistance is understood as the consequence of naturally self-interested and irrational passions, which must consequently be beaten down. In this view the recalcitrant must be forced to be free and all men obliged to obey the law of universal reason that is the necessary ground of human perfection. The rise of history thus leads man not to social reformation within the confines of an expansive liberalism but to millenarianism and revolution.

The French revolutionaries were possessed by this vision of a rational state and driven by the moral imperative of what they perceived as their historical duty to seek its institutionalization. The revolutionaries, to be sure, were attempting to remedy real injustices, but their remedy was chiliastic. They recognized that violence was evil but believed that revolutionary violence, directed by a true understanding of universal history and universal rights, could put an end to all evil and establish a rational society of universal *liberté, égalité*, and *fraternité*. Revolutionary violence thus was justifiable as the evil that put an end to all evil, that freed man finally from the tyranny of his natural impulses. The bright beginnings of the Revolution, however, ended not in universal justice but in the Terror and in European war. The attempt to establish the millennium brought about the rule of violence and death. This led to a general reconsideration of the Revolution and the conception of history and rights that lay at its heart.

There were, of course, those who attempted to redeem the idea of revolution from the failure of the Revolution. They argued that the Revolution failed not because of an innate human irrationality that appeared when all traditional constraints were removed but because the time was not ripe, or because the Revolution was subverted to the selfish interests of a new but nonetheless nefarious oligarchy, or because the Revolution had not been radical or ruthless enough and as a result the old ruling class had been able to mount a successful resistance that turned man back at the very gates of paradise. They argued in short that the failure of the Revolution was not a failure of principle but merely the result of accident or circumstance and that consequently revolution was still the necessary and legitimate means to a just and rational society.

In view of the fanaticism and violence that often accompanies such a philosophy of revolution, it is not surprising that many of those who were staunch supporters of the idea of progress nonetheless here parted company with the revolutionaries and attempted to formulate a theory of history that demonstrated the necessity of progress but denied the concomitant necessity of revolution. The articulation of such a theory has been the self-appointed task of the Anglo-French historical tradition.

In general this tradition deviates little from the Enlightenment conception of historical progress through the scientific conquest and subordination of nature. Instead of revolution, however, this tradition favors the application of the methodology of natural science to the historical or social sciences to produce a rational basis for public policy and reform. Despite this general abhorrence of revolution, however, it is not at all clear that this tradition sufficiently guards against it. Indeed, insofar as it accepts the idea of progress and acceleration, it is difficult to see how it can reject revolution except on grounds of general or private utility. There is, however, no principled barrier here to revolution, and this tradition is thus constantly in danger of falling away from the liberalism and moderation that it professes. The Anglo-French tradition therefore does not really present an alternative to the Enlightenment idea of progress and revolution. This in part is certainly because of its devaluation of nature in favor of freedom and reason. The end of history is consequently always utopian, always a negation of nature and therefore also of human nature. What is necessary is a more fundamental and more thorough consideration of the ground of the relationship of nature and freedom. This task was first undertaken by German Idealism.

German Idealism, especially in its culmination in the thought of Hegel, represents the first, the fullest, and perhaps the most profound attempt to come to terms with the meaning of history. Idealism had already accepted the Enlightenment doctrine of historical progress before the Revolution and even supported the Revolution at its beginning, but in light of its disastrous conclusion found it necessary to reconsider both history and progress. The result was a new view of historical progress based on a new understanding of the relationship of man and nature. Early modernity had given precedence to nature and natural law while the late Enlightenment had recognized human freedom and revolution as decisive. Idealism attempted to reconcile these two elements in a new understanding of reality. Nature, according to Idealism, does not dictate laws to animalistic man, nor does man stand as the absolute master of nature. Both are necessary to one another and are reconciled in consciousness and reason. History thus is no longer understood as the total liberation of man and the utter subordination of nature but as the dialectical process of their reconciliation. The end of history is thus not a self-positing humanity free from all natural constraints but a humanity whose freedom is coincident with a rational nature. History itself is thus conceived not as a linear development or the mere accumulation of knowledge but as the dialectical development of consciousness. History thus repeatedly leads man into contradiction and guides him to his goal only by first misguiding him through every possible error. It is, therefore, impossible to extrapolate from the present on the basis of mere calculative reason in order to predict the future because such a prediction is always only a universalization of the present and that means the universalization of one particular error. Consequently, any revolution that seeks to establish total or radical human freedom is necessarily misguided.

Hegel, however, claims that history has come to its end and fulfillment in his own time and that it is possible to retrospectively survey the totality of historical development and to know absolutely. This knowledge is not, however, the basis for a revolutionary transformation or fundamental reformation of society and leads in fact only to the completion of the basic changes that have already occurred. Idealism thus ends in the notion of acceptance and reconciliation.

Like Idealism, Romanticism turned against the Revolution. Romanticism, however, adopted a radically different tack. Modernity, as we have seen, is characterized by consciousness, by the duality of subjectivity and objectivity. German Idealism attempted to reconcile the subjective and the objective, i.e., human freedom and nature, on the basis of a new understanding of consciousness. The Anglo-French tradition, in contrast, thought that the objective, i.e., what is seen and experienced, was decisive. Romanticism, on the other extreme, discovered the truth not in the observation or consciousness of objects but in the self-consciousness or introspection of the subject, not in the motions of the stars but in the motions of the human heart.

For Romanticism, man has access to the eternal and therefore to the truth, not through rational calculation or understanding but through feeling. Reason, in contrast, isolates man in his individuality, alienating him from God, nature, and his fellow human beings, thus undermining the unity and harmony of traditional life. The consequence of such enlightenment in the Romantic view is alienation and revolution. In the political realm, the Romantic attack upon the Enlightenment was led by the Historical School under the leadership of Savigny, Ranke, and others.[27] The Enlightenment understood man as fundamentally individual and sought to establish a political system to guarantee individual natural or human rights. Such a universal individualism, however, undermines the community, which arises out of traditional customs and laws. According to the Historical School, however, such a traditional community is the true center of human life and the basis of all individual development. The attack by the Historical School upon the Enlightenment and the Revolution thus does not turn against history or against rights per se but only against their universality, i.e., against reason. The result is a conception of national or regional histories which attempt to glorify and strengthen the community. History for the Historical School is not a linear or dialectical development of human freedom and universal reason but a garden of many different flowers, each with its own peculiar character and needs. One set of rights thus could not satisfy all men, and so it is necessary to isolate and articulate specific English, French, or German rights through an investigation of the histories and traditions of the various peoples themselves.[28]

Such a conception of localistic or nationalistic history did indeed establish a bulwark against millenarianism and provide a basis for traditional community, but the cost was high. This view of history gave rise on one hand to a Romantic nationalism that has thrust itself forward in various and often bellicose forms, and on the other to a cultural relativism that regards all standards as idiosyncratic and circumstantial. Both of these were unfortunately exacerbated by the inability of the Historical School itself to construct a convincing system of specifically national rights. Indeed, almost every conception of right proved to have *some* historical justification, thus allowing almost any doctrine, however perverse or alien, to parade under the banner of nationalism or *Volk* and fortify its own fanaticism with an ardent patriotism.

The collapse of philosophy and especially metaphysics after 1848 and the consequent growth in the stature and influence of natural science gave rise to the notion that history should also be a positive science. This led, in turn, to a partial rapprochement of the Anglo-French and German traditions. This was especially evident in the movement within the Historical School toward a more positivistic science of history. Sybel, a student of Savigny and Ranke, argued, for example, that history was superior to philosophy not merely because it was concerned with the nation rather than mankind as a whole but also because it dealt with facts rather than reason and hence was more compatible with natural science. The result of this development was the increasing identification of historical with mechanical causation and the development of a historical logic analogous to the logic of the natural sciences.

While this application of scientific methodology to the study of history enormously increased its range and explanatory power, it did so only by sacrificing any claim to determine standards for human conduct. Science and scientific history in this view are concerned with facts, not values. This conception of history consequently found its philosophical home in the neo-Kantian separation of science and morality, which allowed it to neglect the question of values with a good conscience in the name of science. This value-free historical or social science thus only "solves" the question of values by abdicating all responsibility, with the assertion that values arise in some general but undefinable way out of concrete historical situations. This, however, is nothing more than a return to the conventionalism that history was meant to overcome.

With the failure of this neo-Kantian or positivistic science of history to answer the question of values and provide a ground for the interaction of nature and freedom, thought turned back to a reconsideration of Hegel who had articulated a conception of history based upon the reconciliation of nature and freedom and of facts and values. Indeed, the further development of the conception of history in essence has been nothing other than an ever-increasing radicalization of the Hegelian position. Few of course have accepted Hegel uncritically, but even those who have rejected him remain within the Hegelian horizon.

The first and certainly most politically significant of these Hegelians was Marx. In Marx's view there is no distinction between history and nature or facts and values. In this respect he remains within the Idealist horizon. His thought, however, takes a distinctly materialist turn. History in his view is the "interpretation of things as they actually are and have occurred" and consequently "every profound philosophical problem dissolves into an empirical fact."[29] The *historia rerum gestarum* is thus merely the reflection of the truly real *res gestae*. Actual history, however, is understood not as the reconciliation of human freedom and nature but as the concrete development of the means of production that will ultimately allow man to master nature and establish a realm of perfect human freedom and creativity. In this sense Marx returns to the Enlightenment idea of progress. This doctrine in his hands, however, is radicalized even further through the subordination of philosophy to history. Whereas the Enlightenment and Idealism had both recognized that philosophy is prior to history, i.e., that the eternity of reason first makes the actual comprehensible, Marx believed that history as the *res gestae* determines the character of all philosophy. Philosophy for Marx is ideology, and far from revealing the truth about man and values only reveals the prejudices and desires of a particular age and class. Marx, however, does not thereby fall into relativism. History gives man direction. Indeed, it alone is the source of truth and it alone can tell us what we ought to do: it is "our one and all."[30]

History directs man by indicating what is to come next, thus presenting him with a moral imperative to join the avant-garde and prod his slower-moving contemporaries into action. But since history is dialectical, its ultimate goal only appears on the threshold of its actual completion. Marx, like Hegel, recognizes an absolute moment in which the whole course of history and its final destination become apparent. In contradistinction to Hegel, however, this knowledge arises in Marx's view before the actual completion of history and thus serves not so much as an explanation but as an instigation to action. Marx, however, radicalizes the Enlightenment idea of revolutionary acceleration. For the Enlightenment, revolution may be necessary if all efforts at reform fail; for Marx, revolution is an inevitable and unavoidable aspect of progress. Marx thus views revolution not as a lamentable necessity but as a positive duty, not as a course that man can enter upon only with a heavy heart and deep distrust but as the most noble and glorious of human deeds.

In contrast to Marx, Nietzsche rejects the Hegelian notion of history as a rational process and characterizes it instead as the process of unreason or nihilism. For Nietzsche, as for Schopenhauer and Kierkegaard, it is not history but eternity that is the source of truth and the standard or guide for human conduct. The eternity to which he turns, however, is fundamentally restless. The attempt "to press onto becoming the character of being" likewise necessarily presses the character of becoming onto being. Thus the entire distinction of actuality and eternity disappears for Nietzsche—there is no eternity apart from the eternal repetition of the actual. Moreover, the fundamental antagonism in the actual is not overcome or reconciled as it is in Hegel and Marx because there is no end of history. Contradiction is eternal. The result is an absolutized relativism or perspectivism that understands every theory as the expression of an age, and history as the struggle of equally perspectival world views for predominance. Herewith any idea of a rational historical development and hence a rational determination of values is put to rest, and all that is left of the historical task is a fatalism that tells man to "be hard" and guarantees him only death and defeat. Here is the same propensity to glorify struggle that we saw in Marx, but in Nietzsche's case it is not the struggle for a rational end but only the expression of the eternal struggle that lies at the heart of actuality. Man is thus only what he makes himself, his highest task is to attain power, to create something magnificent through struggle, and "everything is permitted." Relativism thus becomes a creative nihilism that continually creates meaning then again destroys it. Man is radically free and the truth is the product of his creative freedom, but this freedom no longer aims at the institutionalization of reason. The consequences of this conception of nihilism for history are drawn by historicism and existentialism.

Historicism, as developed by Dilthey and Croce, represents an explicit appropriation and further radicalization of Hegel's thought.[31] It began with the assumption that history is not merely one realm of being but all reality and that there is nothing behind or beneath or above history, not even a restless eternity of becoming such as Nietzsche supposed. What is real is life-experience, and this cannot be explained either by natural science or introspection but only by history. Man's understanding of history, however, is really only a self-understanding that never escapes the present. Man has no eternity of nature, no end determined by historical development, not even a restless eternity turning round in its incomprehensible cycles, but only the moment of his life in terms of which to judge himself, his deeds, and his political institutions.

Such a doctrine, however, finds it hard to avoid relativism and nihilism. Dilthey and later Weber thought that it was possible to recognize the recurrence of certain archetypes and on this basis to construct a science of the human spirit (*Geisteswissenschaft*), and Mannheim attempted to show that the perspectival character of knowledge did not necessarily undermine values because values arise out of social reality. Such a view, however, seems to assume that most human beings are not affected by theoretical discourse and will not notice that what they take to be absolutes are in fact merely the projections of momentary necessities, or that human beings can live contented lives despite the recognition that their standards have no basis other than their own subjective desires and judgments. Historicism in fact assumes that men can live without reference to *the* good as long as they have *a* good, however ephemeral or contradictory, to guide their actions. Such a view, however, undermines all moral obligation and only more securely attaches men to the dictates of their own passions and desires. The realm of historicism is the realm of unrestricted subjectivity and absolutized relativism. It leads either to paralysis or caprice, to the despairing recognition that God and all ideals are dead, or to the realization that "everything is permitted."

It was not the philosophy of Nietzsche or historicism, however, that shook the optimism of modernity but the First World War, which left the idea of progress that had reigned since the Enlightenment buried beside its other victims in Flanders' fields. The collapse of the idea of progress, however, did not lead to a rejection of history but only opened the way for even more radical and politically more bellicose forms of historical thought. The very premise of the peace was in fact an outgrowth of Romantic nationalism. If nationalist aspirations were the cause of the War, men reasoned, then their satisfaction would serve as the basis of the peace. Marxism, on the contrary, understood the War as the necessary consequence of capitalist competition and saw the way to peace and justice not in nationalism or a general social progress but in a revolutionary transformation of society. The First World War in this sense dispirited the liberalism that understood history as a process of rational technical and political development and turned men's aspirations toward ideologies that offered radical solutions through revolutionary action.

Hegel understood his age as the end of history and looked back upon historical development as the process of reconciliation that culminated in rational states and absolute knowledge. For Nietzsche this path had become the path of nihilism that led man not to reason or God but to the recognition that God is dead and that all forms of knowledge and political life are only ghost bridges thrown over unfathomable abysses. The First World War seemed to many to have blown away all the gossamer imaginings of modern man and to have opened up the hard truth of his destiny beyond all his shattered illusions. It thus led to a fundamental reconsideration of history and modernity, and indeed of the West itself, that sought a way out of the rubble in which modern man suddenly found himself. Troeltsch saw this crisis as the result of the defective character of the modern natural rights teaching and proposed a return to the ancient interpretation of natural rights.[32] Spengler, on the contrary, saw this as the fateful and inescapable setting of the West and suggested that men accept their destiny. Existentialism finally considered this crisis as the necessary consequence of the spiritual presuppositions of the West and urged even more radically that men reject Western civilization as a whole. This rejection, however, is itself based upon a further radicalization of historicism.

Existentialism, especially as developed by Heidegger, begins with the premise of historicism that actuality is life-experience, but it attempts to retrieve life from an utter historicization through a reconnection to the eternal. This reconnection is achieved through a phenomenological or existential analysis of life-experience that strives not to ground history in being or reason or to press becoming with the character of being but to demonstrate that being itself is history or time. In this manner, existentialism claims to go beyond all metaphysics and thus beyond the West itself, which understands being always only metaphysically as eternal presence. It is in fact this metaphysical understanding of eternity and not historicism that existentialism believes is the source of nihilism. The solution to nihilism, therefore, is not a rejection of history and a return to ancient thought, which is only an earlier and less-developed form of nihilism, but the recognition that being or eternity is itself history or time. Being is thus not presence, not any sort of thing but nothing, the abyss or chaos out of which everything is born, the fate that establishes the character and the horizon for all things.

All historical forms or epochs are in this view unique revelations of being that spring up out of the abyss and that hence cannot be predicted or even entirely understood but only recognized and accepted as the fateful sending of being. Man always finds himself thrown into a world with a particular horizon that determines both the character and limits of his knowledge and action. His task is the resolute acceptance of a fate revealed in a moment of vision or a radical choice, a leap into *engagement* or commitment that has no basis in reason, history, or experience but arises out of the recognition that mere deliberation is absurd and that the basis for choice can only be understood by those who are already committed by their deeds.

It would seem that existentialism, then, is nothing other than radical nihilism, the final and most abysmal stage in the historicization of human life. Hegel discovered the truth of history in dialectical reason, Nietzsche in the eternal repetitions of becoming, historicism in becoming itself, and existentialism finally in nothing. Whether existentialism is truly nihilism, however, depends upon the character of this nothing. If it is merely the absolute negation of everything, which leaves only a chaotic and meaningless actuality, then existentialism is indeed the most extreme form of historicism and nihilism. If, however, this nothing is in truth the manifestation of the eternal in the actual, which gives everything else form and meaning without ever taking on form or becoming meaningful itself, then existentialism offers an alternative to historicism, modernity, and indeed to the West itself. Existentialism, however, carries us beyond good and evil and indeed beyond reason. Consequently, we cannot determine whether this beyond is superrational or subrational. While existentialism thus indicates a way out of the crisis of modernity it directs us only to a dark staircase and does not tell us whether it leads upward to the light or downward into an even more monstrous night.

All of these attempts to come to terms with nihilism and the crisis of the West, however, were lost like lifeboats in the oblivion of a heavy sea as the second and greatest storm of our century, the Second World War, carried traditional European civilization, which had already been seriously battered by the First World War and the Depression, to the bottom. Neither Spengler's pessimism, nor Troeltsch's suggestion that man set sail for the calmer waters of the Aegean, nor even the urgings of existentialism that man flee into the storm to find the sun could convince more than a few of their fellow voyagers. It was, rather, two other forms of historical thought, Romantic nationalism and Marxism, that struggled for control of the ship, and it was their vehemence and fanaticism that finally destroyed it.

Nietzsche had predicted that the wars of the future would be conflicts not of interest but of principle and that men would consequently exterminate their fellows not from a mere love of destruction or natural cruelty but from a religious zeal as missionaries of new moralities. The Second World War was a testimony to his foresight, for it was in principle nothing other than a disagreement about the nature of history. While the Romantic and revolutionary nationalism of the Nazis and Fascists, which grew out of the nationalistic history of the Historical School and the thought of Nietzsche, understood history as a struggle of nations and races that had to end in the predominance of the superior Aryan race, Marxism believed its essence was class struggle that could only end with the triumph of the proletariat. Thus, not only were they both characterized by particular conceptions of history but these views likewise determined their historical duty and fostered an ideological fervor and fanaticism that propelled them into war.

The Second World War, however, does not seem at first glance to have produced as great a shock as the First. There was no sense of a setting of the West, no lost generation, no outbreak of existential anxiety and despair. In fact, it seemed at its end as if a new day had begun, as if Orpheus-like man had finally returned from the underworld. But in fact the real effect of the Second World War was only more subtle, more concealed, and hence more dangerous. Its inhumanity was simultaneously unimaginable and mundane. No one could grasp its enormity, and each particular incident, however horrible and perverse, became insignificant and trivial in comparison with the whole. The War thus evoked a tremendous anxiety that prevented man from coming to terms with its horror and drove him instead into the future as the secure harbor of his hopes and the bastion against his fears.

The question of history, however, was not settled by the War but only made less visible and therefore more difficult to comprehend. Romantic nationalism and Marxism in fact resurged after the War, sometimes singly, sometimes united in movements of national liberation, sometimes even fortified by an existentialism that finds truth in struggle and death.[33] Far from shaking the trust that these movements place in history, the War only strengthened their convictions and intensified their missionary zeal.

In contrast, liberalism found little in its own conception of history to provide a bulwark against the convictions of its adversaries. While originally based upon the conception of natural rights, modern liberalism has come increasingly to identify its communal and political task with economic, social, and technical progress. Its claim to superiority is not merely that it better secures human freedom but that it is also the most efficient way to universal prosperity and happiness. This idea of progress, which derives from the Enlightenment via the Anglo-French historical tradition, was, however, peculiarly transformed by the two World Wars and their aftermath. The hopefulness of a world that had overcome such horrors found the fulfillment of its dreams in the growth of prosperity in America and the startlingly swift recovery of Western Europe and Japan. The future seemed an open road to the social justice of a great society. It is apparent, however, that we are unable to accept this progress with the pure optimism of the nineteenth century. This is hardly accidental: each step toward prosperity is also one step nearer annihiliation—our increasing ability to please ourselves has been matched only by our increasing ability to destroy ourselves. We thus greet the future with a deep and unperceived schizophrenia.[34] In the face of a committed Marxism and in the shadow of nuclear destruction we strive to see only a sunny future but are repeatedly thrown into despair: unwilling to peer into the night, we are tormented by our own lengthening shadows.

As the question of history becomes more and more urgent, we thus become increasingly unwilling or unable to confront it. Despite the decisive role that history plays in almost all aspects of our lives, the question of history tends to disappear. The conviction of Marxism, which allows no questioning of received doctrine, and the anxiety of liberalism, which shies away from such a questioning, have swallowed up the question in a scholarly oblivion.

History has, to be sure, been rejected or depreciated by many. Neopositivism, for example, denies that history is anything more than a story and characterizes historicism as superstition.[35] According to this view the chief question about history is whether it is a sort of explanation or merely a kind of narration.[36] This attack upon history and historicism, however, fails to take seriously the claims made for history, and its refutation scarcely amounts to more than the assertion that history fails to meet the standards of objectivity and causation characteristic of natural science.[37] History cannot, however, merely be rejected: it forms such an integral part of our lives and our world that a mere rejection serves only to conceal its real importance and thus to becloud our vision as we attempt to circumvent an abyss.

What is thus necessary is a fundamental reconsideration of the question of history. Whether we like it or not our world has come to conceive of history as the human actuality. It is thus all the more perplexing and disheartening that we are unable to articulate a conception of history that can consistently sustain human dignity. This failure might well prompt one to abandon history altogether and turn instead to the apparently less problematic and clearly less dangerous notion of antiquity that the human actuality is not determined by history but by chance or fate, which operates within the wide parameters of nature. This ancient view rests upon the denial that history is the *res gestae*. Such diverse schools of thought as historicism, existentialism, and neopositivism have in different ways come to more or less this conclusion. Actual "history," as they understand it, is little more than a capricious or at best fateful concatenation of events such as antiquity described. The crucial difference between the ancient view and these contemporary notions, however, is that we today have no cosmology or theology to fall back upon that can give meaning to our lives. God is dead or at least "distant in the moment of need," and nature is a mere mechanical causality whose only end is entropy. For modernity the purpose of human life arises not out of religion or nature but only out of human reason and freedom. To conclude that history, which is the actualization of this rational freedom, is chaos is thus to surrender to nihilism.

History cannot be simply rejected nor at least in its present state can it be simply accepted or affirmed. Thus history must be either transcended or given a rational ground. To transcend history it is first necessary, however, to demonstrate that history is not the human actuality, that it is not a *res* and that there is consequently no *res gestae*. To establish a rational ground for history, on the contrary, it is necessary to demonstrate the reality of such a *res*. The question about the *res* or whatness of history, however, is nothing other than the question of the ground of history. Thus the first step in any attempt to deal with the problem of history for human life and thought is the consideration of the question of the ground of history. It is to this question that we must turn.

2
The Question
of the Ground
# of History

As we have seen, the question "What is history?" asks whether history is the human actuality or merely the product of human imagination, i.e., whether it is the *res gestae* or only the *historia rerum gestarum*. Modernity has come to the conclusion that it is the human actuality. The attempt to explain and ground history as the *res gestae*, however, has proven more difficult than modernity at first suspected and has led to a continual radicalization of the concept of history. History, which the Enlightenment believed was at best only a support for natural reason, increasingly has come to supplant reason as the definitive interpretation of human life and the natural world. The philosophical development that occurs under the names Hegel, Savigny, Marx, Nietzsche, Dilthey, and Heidegger represents the increasing and ultimately utter historicization of Western life and thought. Moreover, this process is driven forward not by the success of history in explaining human life but by its failure: just as men have sought to cure the ills of democracy with more democracy, so they have sought to cure the ills of history with more history. This cure, however, has left the patient if not fatally weakened at least thoroughly confused and frightened. It is thus not accidental that in our times we note an ever more vehement and partisan attachment to particular conceptions of history on one hand and a total rejection of history as the *res gestae* on the other. Both the unthinking acceptance and unreflective rejection of history arise from the same source—the chaos and confusion that the historicization of human life and thought has produced.

History, however, cannot be merely accepted or rejected. For better or worse it is an integral and inescapable part of our lives. What is necessary, then, is not action but thought, not acceptance or rejection but reflection.

Thinking, however, is not the mere comparison of dogmatic assertions that, for example, puts Aristotle and Nietzsche onto a philosophic or ethical balance and discovers that one is weightier than the other. Thinking means rather a willingness to dwell in questions and aporiae, to suspend both action and belief, and to follow the bleak path from one perplexity to another, in the recognition that what is good can only be fully or adequately determined on the basis of what is true. In the present case that means suspending judgment about history, either for or against it, until we can determine what history is.

What then is history? For our times this question has become the question of the ground of history, the question whether history is or can be a *res*, i.e., a what or a being. The question "What is *history*? thus becomes "*What* is history?" as the question of the whatness of history, and that means before all else the question whether history can be a what at all. Only when this question about the ground and possibility of history has been answered does the question about its particular character arise, and only on the basis of an adequate answer to the question of the ground can the question about the nature of history be answered.

The what-question is *the* philosophic question and differentiates philosophy from poetic mythology, which asks about the who, and modern science and technology, which asks about the how. It has its origin in, and is the hidden impetus of, the thought of the Greeks. Their answer to this question took many forms, but these might be summarized as nature or, more abstractly, as being. This answer, however, is not an answer in the ordinary sense of the term but rather the highest and most perplexing aporia. In face of the question "What is being?" Aristotle concludes, "Being is what is."[1] The ultimate mysteriousness of the ground is thus neither solved nor dissolved. It is, rather, embodied and concealed in this answer, which is not a mere tautology that puts an end to thinking but an expression of the fundamental perplexity that everywhere and always gives rise to thinking.

Philosophy for antiquity begins with questions and is a continuing and ever-deepening questioning that ends in the consideration of first causes and principles that are themselves perplexing and mysterious and apparently have no demonstration. They are first not because they are the most certain but because they are the most aporetic; they are that which is everywhere at hand and yet utterly impenetrable and incomprehensible. Philosophy and questioning come to an end in the consideration of these firsts precisely because they no longer direct questioning beyond themselves; they are themselves forms that are naturally whole and indivisible and hence beautiful. These forms themselves cannot be analyzed; they can only be contemplated. Thus, questioning leads to *sophia*, to wisdom, for in the contemplation of the highest aporia, the beautiful form, philosophy, the love and pursuit of wisdom, attains its end and becomes wisdom. Ancient philosophy is thus in the most literal sense *skeptical*, questioning *and* contemplative, interrogating nature without destroying the natural, falling into neither the abyss of endless reflection nor the superficiality of mere observation.[2]

The question of the ground of history, however, does not arise for the Greeks because history for them is merely the *historia rerum gestarum*, the art that strives to capture what is eternal and thus memorable in the actual affairs of men. History in their view is thus not a *res* or being about which one could even ask such a question. Indeed the question of the ground of history would have made no more sense to them than the question of the ground of poetry or philosophy. For modernity, on the contrary, the question of the ground of history has become increasingly important as history has replaced nature as the predominate explanation of actuality. This growing predominance of history has also continually undermined the ground that the Greeks discovered in the unchanging and increasingly revealed not the beauty and mystery of irreducible forms but the leering face of the abyss.

In part this is certainly because modernity seeks the ground not in nature but in man. Man for the Greeks was one part of nature; for modernity nature is one realm of human consciousness. Hence, the ground can hardly be something merely natural. This becomes particularly apparent when we consider causality. For antiquity causality is essentially teleological. The motions of nature and the activities of men are conceived for example by Aristotle as a continual striving for perfection and completion. The measure of this perfection and thus the principle or ground (*aition*) that governs change is the natural form.[3] It is this eternal and unchanging moment in nature that, for example, guides the craftsman when he fashions his product. He is merely the immediate or efficient cause, that through which the thing comes to be. Modernity, on the contrary, eschews a teleological explanation of causality and recognizes instead only a mechanical or efficient causality. The ground of motion or change is thus not found in the natural end or form but in the preceding state of motion. Each preceding state, however, is itself something caused and thus cannot serve as the final ground. Even an infinite sequence of causes offers no real solution to this enigma. Modernity resolves this problem with the principle of sufficient reason, i.e., with the notion that the series of causes is rational because it is whole.[4] The wholeness of this whole, however, depends upon a first, uncaused cause. Such a cause, though, cannot be something merely natural and must in fact transcend nature. This transcendent cause modernity discovers in a divine or human freedom that arises out of self-consciousness or reason.

Insofar as reason becomes the measure of reality, however, the scriptural assertion of divine and human freedom or spontaneity becomes untenable, and freedom, especially in the form of history or the doctrine of progress, itself requires a ground. As modern man liberates himself from nature by subordinating nature to the imperatives of his own will, he is forced to assume the burdens that nature previously bore. Thus he is somewhat dismayed to discover that his destruction of the independence of nature has left him nowhere to stand, no firm ground on which to plant his overburdened feet, and he is finally compelled to ask about the ground of his own freedom and that means about the ground of history. The unfolding of Western thought from Rousseau to Kant to Hegel is the working out of this question.

The Question of the Ground of History in Rousseau and Kant
as the Antinomy of Freedom and Natural Necessity

Although preceded by Vico's *New Science* (1725), Rousseau's *Discourse on the Origin and Foundations of Inequality among Men* (1755) is the real beginning of the consideration of the question of history and its ground, for while Vico's work was little known outside southern Italy until the nineteenth century, Rousseau's *Second Discourse* touched off a debate that occupied European thought for the rest of the eighteenth and much of the nineteenth century. In his first work, the *Discourse on the Arts and Sciences*, Rousseau had questioned the idea of progress and thus the whole notion of history as the development of humanity and concluded that the development of the arts and sciences had not fostered human excellence but had in fact produced only human degradation. The value of the whole historical process was thus called into question. The *Second Discourse* is Rousseau's attempt to explain how this disaster came about. It is thus a consideration of the essence and ground of the historical development itself.

The source of degradation and degeneration in the second *Discourse* is inequality. Rousseau thus believes it necessary "To mark in the progress of things the moment when, right succeeding violence, nature was subordinated to law; to explain by what succession of miracles the strong could resolve themselves to serve the weak, and the people to purchase an ideal repose at the price of real felicity."[5] In contradistinction to Aristotle, Rousseau does not seek the source of inequality in nature. Nor for that matter does he find it in convention. Nature is characterized by equality and convention is based upon inequality. The question for Rousseau becomes how convention itself arises out of and in opposition to nature. The answer to this he discovers in man and his history.

In turning away from both nature and convention Rousseau turns toward man, toward *human* being as the source and ground of all being. Although in some sense natural, man is also above or apart from nature. Moreover, insofar as man is natural, he is apparently nonpolitical, for the political or conventional is not a natural growth but the product of free choice. Insofar as man is political he is thus unnatural. The origin of inequality and the essence of history thus lie in man's transcendence over or fall from nature

into the political. The crucial question is thus not about nature or politics
but about man and his history. The determination of the origin of inequality
and the essence of history thus requires not the study of nature or convention but of man himself as he arises out of nature and passes into convention, of man as a self-reflecting being.

> . . . for how can one know the source of inequality among men if
> one does not commence to know them themselves? and how
> will man finally come to see himself as nature has formed him
> through all the changes that the succession of times and things
> must have produced in his original constitution, and to unravel
> that which he retains of his proper foundation from that which
> the circumstances and his progress have adjoined to or changed
> in his primitive state?[6]

The essence of history appears in Rousseau's view in and through man's
self-examination and thus in and through his contemplation of the transformations of the human soul. History is in a very literal sense psychology,
the logic of the soul, and it is only in the introspective self-examination of
the soul, i.e., only in and through self-consciousness, that the original state
of the soul and the reason for its transformations can be determined. The
logic or essence of history is thus the logic of the successive transformations
of soul, and the foundation or ground of history is not in nature or being
per se but in *human* nature, or better *human* being, as it is revealed in and
by self-consciousness in introspection.[7]

   This logic or character of the human soul, of its passions and thoughts, is
the logic of history as the process of the development or degeneration of
humanity. History as psychology is sociology. The actual or factual history of
mankind is not in question in the *Second Discourse*. Rather, Rousseau writes
the *essential* history of humanity; he does not strive for the factual accuracy
of historical scholarship but seeks through hypothetical or conditional
reasoning to give the account or the logic of the character or essence of man
and history as the journey of soul from the freedom and basic equality of the
state of nature, "which exists no longer, which perhaps did not exist, which
probably will never exist," to the slavery and inequality of civil society, from
"love of self (*amour de soi*) . . . a natural sentiment" to "pride (*amour
propre*) . . . a sentiment which is relative, artificial, and born in society," from
one state of soul to another.[8] The *Second Discourse* is thus the description of
history as the soul's coming to consciousness of itself, i.e., becoming what it
always, at least potentially, was and is, self-consciousness, and hence the
description of the loss of its *natural* unity and ground. The savage, according to Rousseau, lives within and in unity with himself, as simple or natural
soul or consciousness; social man lives constantly outside of himself, as
self-consciousness, not in the natural unity and individuality of soul but in
the diremption or alienation of his particular self from his general or social
consciousness.[9]

The question of the *essence* of history for Rousseau is thus the question of the twofold of the natural and conventional as it appears in the human soul. The decisive and characterizing moment of the soul and hence of history is the differentiation of these two states. It is this moment that distinguishes the natural from the political and destroys what in Rousseau's view constitutes the unity and real happiness of the soul. "The first who, having enclosed a piece of earth, thought to say, '*This is mine,*' (*Ceci est à moi*) and found men simple enough to believe him was the true founder of civil society."[10] The decisive moment of human history as the spiritual history of humanity is itself an act of soul, namely, the assertion of a part of the world as mine. This assertion is complex. It is the assertion of the distinction of world and I and the concomitant assertion of (a part of) the world as mine, as for or *to me*, as being (with respect) to me (*est à moi*), which itself presupposes the distinction of you (he, she, it) and I (and therefore mine and yours) and we and they (and consequently ours and theirs). This event is in truth the advent of self-consciousness. Self-consciousness distinguishes world and I and reunifies them as being-to or having and hence as property and ownership. Self-consciousness, however, also destroys the unity of the soul itself. The I is not individual and indivisible natural soul but the particular self which is necessarily bound up with the *we* and hence with the political.

This decisive moment of all history is thus the separation of man from nature and the diremption of the soul into a particular *self* or I and a social *consciousness*. The nature from which man is alienated is his own human nature, which itself was immediately related to nature as a whole. As self-consciousness man is related only mediately, i.e., only through custom and language, to nature. Moreover, self-*consciousness* is not something that belongs to any single self but that in which all selves take part—it is the opinions and beliefs, the customs and conventions of political society. It is general or universal and as such it *is* the political.[11] As general, it is outside of or transcends any one self and hence is generally conscious or aware of each single self as a part of its own generality, i.e., it is the perception and estimation of each by all. Self-*consciousness* is thus *self*-consciousness, the social or general consciousness and estimation of each self, of each I, you, he, etc., and hence the ground and determination of what is *proper* to each self, of what is its *own*, and thus the source and ground of *property* and inequality. History is the history of human being, of the transformation of natural soul into social or political self-consciousness and the subsequent development of this state. The actual events of history are past and remain conjectural but the truth of history is in the human soul, in the unfolding of *its* possibilities. Thus, while the immediate cause of any particular historical event may be accidental, the course or direction of events as a whole is necessary.[12]

The status of the soul with respect to nature, however, is ambiguous. Rousseau suggests that man is in some sense natural, but it is precisely that which Rousseau attributes to him as natural, i.e., freedom and perfectibility, that distinguish him from nature. In exercising his "natural" capacities and removing himself from nature man destroys his own "natural" unity. Soul in nature is isolated from other soul. Its only thought is of its own existence and preservation. It is the whole. Nature itself, however, is or presents difficulties for this soul in the shape of droughts, overpopulation, etc., that give rise to scarcity, forcing the soul to exercise its freedom, i.e., its ability to oppose nature, and in perfecting itself to raise itself above or out of nature and the difficulties of nature. The soul is driven back upon itself and its own freedom into a kind of reflection and the recognition of the humanity of other men. In the moment the soul becomes social it loses its independence and unity. Through language, the family, and the polis the diremption of its self and consciousness is continually augmented. Through the exercise of its own "natural" faculties the soul separates itself first from nature and then from itself. The soul becomes self-consciousness.[13]

This history of the spiritual development or degeneration of man is thus intertwined with nature but ultimately independent of natural necessity. The soul is affected by natural necessity but ultimately is dependent upon itself. Here, though, Rousseau's questioning apparently reaches an end. The question of the relationship between human being and nature is not raised. If human being is grounded in nature and hence is itself something natural, how can it be free or perfectible and hence above or removed from nature? Is human being that moment of nature in which nature transcends itself, or is human being itself something supernatural? Both of these alternatives are problematical. If there is freedom and hence purposive causality in nature, how can there be anything like natural laws or, for that matter, any unity to nature at all? If, on the other hand, human being is not natural, how can nature have any effect upon it? Yet is it more satisfying to accept what seems to be the only alternative, namely, that human being is *both* natural and supernatural? Thereby, we may preserve the consistency of nature and natural law and the unproblematic interaction of man and nature but only by making human being itself incomprehensible. If human being is both natural and not natural, how can it be a unity? This is perhaps even more perplexing than the other alternatives. What is then the relation of human being, i.e., of *freedom* and perfectibility and therefore the political, to *nature* and natural necessity?

This is not an idle question but the decisive question with which Idealism begins and in a sense ends. For Kant this question appears in and as the Third Antinomy of Pure Reason, which forms the philosophical center of his *Critique of Pure Reason*. Kant had already considered the antinomy in his dissertation in 1770 and wrote in a letter to Garve late in life:

> Not the investigation of the existence of God, of immortality, etc.
> but the antinomy of pure reason was the point from which I
> began: "The world has a beginning—: it has no beginning, etc.,
> to the fourth [!?] There is freedom in human being,—against:

there is no freedom and everything is natural necessity"; it was this that first woke me from my dogmatic slumber and drove me to the critique of reason itself to dissolve the scandal of the contradiction of reason with itself.[14]

An event or the experience of an event according to Kant can only be rational, and hence sufficiently grounded, if it derives causally from previous events or experiences and if the sequence of events or experiences is itself complete and hence necessary or grounded in a first or necessary cause. Kant apparently believed that he had proven the causal consistency of events or experiences in the Second Analogy, but this fulfilled only the first condition of rationality. The question of the consistency and sufficiency of events *as a whole* is the topic of the Third Antinomy.

According to Kant, what reason establishes or sets (*setzt*) as true is a law (*ein Gesetz*). Reason thus is inherently thetic (from the Greek *tithēmi*, 'I set') and thereby establishes *nomoi*, laws or conventions, and is hence nomothetic, law-giving.[15] Reason is not merely thetic, however, for it does not merely set or establish laws at random but sets or puts laws together with one another; reason as thetic is thus also synthetic. This putting together of laws that it has established brings reason into conflict with itself, for it discovers that two laws which it has established as true contradict one another and hence that its synthesis is in fact an antithesis. Reason as both nomothetic and antithetic becomes antinomious.

The Third Antinomy is the antinomy of causality, which arises when reason tries to grasp the causal character of the world as a whole. On one hand, it seems that there must be a free causality in addition to a causality in accordance with the laws of nature because without such transcendental freedom causality itself can never be complete or sufficiently determined, since there can by definition be no first or final cause, hence no end to the series of causal determinations, and therefore no true or complete knowledge of the originating cause. This is the Thesis position that Kant identifies with rationalism. The Antithesis position, i.e., the position of empiricism, is that there is only natural causality and no causality through freedom. If there were transcendental freedom, according to the Antithesis, then there would be a cause that was itself uncaused and this would overturn the fundamental presupposition of causality, i.e., that there is an unbroken chain of cause and effect, and hence causality itself would be self-contradictory. The proof of each position thus follows from the refutation of the other and results in the disheartening conclusion that there can be no natural causality and therefore no natural laws without freedom but also that there can be no natural law with freedom, that both positions are thus mutually necessary *and* mutually contradictory. Kant's answer to this problem is transcendental idealism.

According to Kant, the Thesis and the Antithesis can only be conceived in relation to one another. Transcendental freedom is essentially the denial of the universality of natural necessity, just as the universality of the law of nature is the denial of a free causality. Both positions exist and, according to Kant, can only exist as the constituent elements of an antithesis. Their synthesis is thus fundamentally dialectical and antinomious. The ground of the antinomy thus lies in reason itself, for reason as thetic is also architectonic, and as such seeks to extend its understanding and the categories of understanding beyond the experience of the finite to the infinite.[16] Reason attempts to form a system for the infinite with finite forms and thus becomes dialectical and antinomious, since the infinite transcends all finite categories and can only be indicated by a *negation* of the finite. Consequently, it is reason itself that entangles itself in contradiction.

As architectonic reason, however, also seeks to solve or dissolve the antinomies, not merely because the disharmony is aesthetically or logically displeasing but because the consideration of the antinomy makes rational activity impossible and life itself ultimately unbearable. Human thought or consciousness finds itself in a quandary or aporia when it considers its relation to events as a whole, for in reflecting upon itself and its place in the order of things consciousness understands itself on one hand as free and causative and on the other as merely a necessary moment of the natural causal process. It thus appears to itself in *self-consciousness* as *both* absolutely free *and* absolutely determined.

It is precisely this problem that is the impetus of Kant's transcendental idealism, and it is with a view to grounding morality and clarifying the natural condition that he seeks to resolve this question. Kant believed that he had already demonstrated in the Transcendental Aesthetic that all that we experience has no grounded existence outside of our own thoughts, i.e., that we do not perceive or experience the things-in-themselves but only that which *appears* within the forms of our consciousness, i.e., within space and time. Hence, events as a whole cannot transcend the limits of consciousness.

The antinomy arises, according to Kant, not because the world is itself antinomious but because finite human reason tries to transcend its own limits and obtain speculative knowledge of the infinite. The solution to the antinomy of freedom and natural necessity thus involves the recognition of the inherent limits of human understanding. Kant concludes that the contradiction can be resolved if we recognize two separate but possibly isomorphic realms of reason, a phenomenal realm of appearances governed by the scientific laws of nature and a noumenal realm of the things-in-themselves governed by the moral law of freedom, i.e., a realm of pure reason and a realm of practical reason. According to Kant, a causal determination through nature and a causal determination through freedom are thus at least hypothetically possible insofar as these two realms are truly isomorphic. The antinomy in his view thus only appears to be a contradiction within the world when in fact it is only a reflection of the underlying structure of consciousness or reason itself. The two realms of reason thus reflect the two capacities of consciousness. The apparent contradiction of freedom and natural necessity is thus resolved in Kant's view in and by transcendental idealism, which recognizes the duality of the phenomenal and noumenal realms as a reflection of the underlying truth and unity of consciousness or reason itself.

The problem that arose in Rousseau's conception of the essence of history as the question of the relationship of natural necessity and freedom is thus apparently solved in transcendental idealism. But is Kant's solution sufficient? Does transcendental idealism provide a real ground for the reconciliation of the natural and the spiritual, or the phenomenal and the noumenal? Kant solves the antinomy by demonstrating that the contradiction is not in the real world but in consciousness. But does this not make consciousness itself contradictory? The suspicion arises that Kant's solution is in fact only a deeper and more trenchant problem. He seems to have saved science and morality only by sacrificing man, to have preserved the unity of the world by giving up the unity of consciousness. Kant consequently does not solve but only radicalizes the problem we discovered in Rousseau. Thus, while he may have opened up a "revolution in the way of thinking," he did not find the way to bring it to a close. He did, however, establish the horizon for a solution, and it was within this horizon that speculative idealism sought to construct a new world and thus to bring the Kantian revolution to its conclusion.

Hegel's Reception of the Antinomy: The Revolution of Freedom and the Tyranny of Natural Desire

It was the failure of transcendental idealism that gave birth to perhaps the most profound and certainly the most comprehensive attempt to understand and articulate the historicality of man, his institutions, and his world, i.e., speculative idealism. The work of Fichte, Schelling, and Hegel has long been recognized as an outgrowth and a transformation of Kantian transcendental idealism. While the work of Fichte and Schelling in large part antedates that of Hegel and certainly had a decisive influence upon his reception of Kantian philosophy, Hegel was nonetheless the most important of Kant's heirs, first because of the innate depth and breadth of his thought, and second because of its unambiguous importance for the political and intellectual constellations of the nineteenth and twentieth centuries.

In the preface to his first published work, *The Difference of Fichte's and Schelling's System of Philosophy* (1801), Hegel locates the common origin of speculative idealism in the reception of the spirit although not the letter of Kant's transcendental idealism: "Kantian philosophy made it necessary that its spirit be separated from the letter and the pure speculative principle be lifted out of the rest which belongs to rationalizing reflection or which can be used by it."[17] According to Hegel, it was with a view to redeeming the spiritual element within Kantian philosophy and reconciling its internal contradictions that the renewal of philosophic speculation was necessary.

"Diremption is the source of the need of philosophy and as the culture of the age the dependent and given side of the form."[18] The need of philosophy arises when that which is received as tradition is *entzweit*, literally 'in-twoed' or more commonly 'bifurcated,' 'estranged,' or 'dirempt.' Humanity always exists within a tradition, within the shadow of its past—each generation is constrained, although not determined, by the limits and forms of the world into which it is born. Whatever changes are brought about are necessarily in and in reaction to something that is. So long as this received tradition is unproblematic, so long as harmony and unity prevail over discord and contradiction, there is no need of philosophy—which is not to say that in such ages there is no philosophy but only that there is no social or spiritual necessity for a new form of philosophy. Only when humanity is torn by contradiction, by division and alienation, is there truly a need of philosophy.

"To overcome such solidified contradictions is the single interest of reason."[19] Reason is judgment and therefore synthesis, the putting or setting together of different elements and thus the establishment of a reconciliation between these elements within a unity that transcends and encompasses them. Reason thus has an interest, i.e., a connective function among or between beings, in overcoming and subordinating the contradictions that arise between objects, concepts, laws, etc., and hence in reunifying what is bifurcated or alienated. Reason thus assumes both difference and unity and cannot sacrifice either. Consequently it must not dispute the actual contradictions that do arise but rather demonstrate both their necessity and the necessity of the unity that is the ground of their compatibility.

When this overarching unity disappears and the unifying force in human life diminishes, then philosophy becomes necessary to reestablish the harmony and unity in the order of things. This conception of the beginning or source of philosophy is essential to speculative idealism. For Hegel and his age philosophy had become necessary because the religion "in which man raises himself above all alienation and in the realm of grace sees the freedom of the subject and the necessity of the object disappear" was no longer a sufficient unifying force.[20] Hitherto all contradictions had been reconciled in God and his grace. The ground of this reconciliation, however, was destroyed by the incorporation and transformation of religion into modern philosophy. Philosophy thus needed to discover a new ground and reconciliation for the prevailing antagonisms and contradictions. In Hegel's case this meant, for the contradiction of freedom and nature that he saw, on one hand, in the opposition of the French Revolution and English bourgeois society and, on the other hand, in the diremption in German spiritual life that manifested itself in transcendental idealism.

Although philosophically rooted in the reception and transformation of transcendental idealism, the decisive and directing impetus for Hegel's thought was the French Revolution and to a somewhat lesser extent the English industrial revolution.[21] The tale of Hegel, Hölderlin, and Schelling dancing around a freedom tree to celebrate the outbreak of the French Revolution has been properly discounted by modern scholarship, but it is nonetheless illustrative of what was undoubtedly Hegel's initial enthusiasm for revolutionary ideals. More than thirty years later he could write of the outbreak of the Revolution:

> Anaxagoras had first said that *nous* rules the world; not until this moment, however, did man come to know that thought should rule spiritual actuality. This was a magnificent sunrise. All thinking beings celebrated this epoch. A sublime feeling ruled in this time, a spiritual enthusiasm filled the world with awe, as if the actual reconciliation of the divine with the world had just taken place.[22]

According to Hegel, the recognition of the universality of freedom and reason lay at the heart of the French Revolution. The original insight of Anaxagoras that *nous* rules the world first appears in the public realm at this time, not, however, as a reality but as a public imperative—reason *should* rule; all men *should* be free. The nature of an imperative is futural; it directs one not to contemplation but to action; it establishes a task and in this case a public task involving the transformation of man, his institutions, and his world. It is not imperative that philosophers become kings or that kings become philosophers but rather that philosophy, i.e., spirit, be set to rule over nature and that nature be recognized as essentially spiritual, that the same reason rule in nature as in spirit. This vision, while compelling, was illusory; the French Revolution ended not in the unification of heaven and earth but, according to Hegel, in the "coldest, most insipid death, without any more meaning than the hewing of a head of cabbage or a drink of water," in the abyss of terror and war. Thus while Hegel was initially enthusiastic about the Revolution and continued throughout his life to recognize and propound the basic justice of its original principles, he also clearly recognized the defects of these principles and abhorred and denounced the disastrous course of the Revolution itself.[23]

Revolutions in the affairs of men and nations, according to Hegel, are preceded and prepared by invisible, secret revolutions in spirit itself.[24] The ground of the French Revolution was prepared in this sense by the revolution in thought wrought by Rousseau who recognized that the essence of man is freedom. This freedom with which Rousseau is concerned, however, is not the caprice of natural passions but rather the freedom of self-consciousness, i.e., the unity of thinking not with the natural world but with itself and consequently the capacity to remove itself from and oppose itself to nature. The freedom of self-consciousness, as the French understand it, is thus, according to Hegel, *free will*, i.e., the will of the self-conscious subject to relate himself to objective nature, the will to transform nature and subordinate it to the forms of human understanding. This freedom is thus not the caprice of the passions, not the freedom of personal self-interest, but the freedom to act rationally, i.e., according to and in harmony with the general will, the freedom thus to act according to the rules of a community.[25] In his particularity, man is natural, suffering from numerous wants, passions, and desires; in his generality, i.e., as a species or a community, man participates in the rational and hence becomes truly free. According to Hegel, for Rousseau, "the freedom of nature, the foundation of freedom is not actual [freedom]; for first the state is the actualization of freedom."[26] The state can only be the realization of this freedom, however, if it is itself founded upon rational principles. The inability to establish such a rational state in France through reform was directly responsible for the Revolution.

The *ancien régime* that the Revolution toppled was, according to Hegel, a desolate aggregate of privileges and legal systems contrary to all thought and reason. The original basis of the regime in the distinction of the noble and the base dissolved when the nobles no longer found it necessary to risk their lives in pursuit of honor. Their nobility consequently came to reside merely in their pride which was itself founded solely upon their position vis-à-vis the lower classes. The maintenance of this nobility and pride thus depended upon the maintenance of these now merely arbitrary distinctions. The regime thus came to rest upon a severe oppression of the general population justified by the doctrine of divine right supported and propagated by a corrupt clergy. This led to a fundamental corruption and perversion of customs and spirit, to a regime in which there was no place for freedom and humanity but only for tyranny, degradation, and exploitation. The pervasiveness of this moral and ethical decadence in both the church and state effectively closed off the possibility of reform from within.[27]

Reform was also crucially undermined in Hegel's view by the polarization of *hommes à principes* and *hommes d'état*, of *philosophes* who attempted to determine the true principles of just and rational government in the abstract without any experience of the necessities of power, and statesmen, ministers, and men of action who were responsible for the day-to-day business of government but who had little or no knowledge of the proper principles upon which government should be based. The idealistic dreams of the former and the stubbornness and stupidity of the latter made a mutual education or reconciliation and thus any effective reform impossible. Injustice and irrationality once recognized, however, could not be tolerated; if the realm of perfect justice and reason could not be established gradually, then it must be established immediately; if not peaceably, then forcibly; if there was no possibility of reform, then the only remedy that remained was revolution.[28]

The Revolution began, according to Hegel, with abstractions and, instead of recognizing the necessity of a reconciliation of the abstract and the actual, sought to transform the actual to conform to the abstract. For *hommes à principes* the *Rights of Man and the Citizen* established a sufficient constitution for the new regime; no concern for the establishment of an administration seemed necessary to them. Hegel argues further that administration was in fact contrary to the doctrine of liberty and equality in their view, for it established a framework of command and obedience. They believed that the world should be administered not by men set above their fellows but purely according to the laws of thought. These laws of thought were in their view to be determined by the general will. This general will, however, was not concretely general and rational but rather the universalized abstract will of the individual, not the will of a complex and intricately related whole but the prejudiced and implacable will of an atomized and arbitrary mass. It was this will that became absolute.

> So men practically applied themselves to actuality. As much as freedom in itself is concrete, so it was applied indeed as undeveloped in its abstraction to actuality, and making abstractions valid in actuality means destroying actuality.[29]

Freedom thus appeared in the political realm in and as the negation and hence annihilation of the actual, i.e., of human nature and natural necessity. Therewith, freedom enthroned itself as the sole legitimate end of all human endeavor, as the sole criterion of all justice and injustice, of all rationality and irrationality, and in its unrestrained exclusivity became tyrannical—it became absolute, sweeping away the world that had resisted it. As unitary and absolute, however, it was illimitable—there was no check, no power that could resist its excesses; it countenanced no object outside of itself, nothing that might have opposed it, and consequently it could not arrive at a positive accomplishment of anything. This freedom is only contradiction or negation; "there remains for it only *negative activity*; it is only the *fury* of disappearance."[30]

The legitimate assertion of human freedom against the absolutism and corruption of the *ancien régime* was in its execution illimitable and engendered in its restricted generality not a realm of fraternity and justice, not a humanely rational ethical community, but madness, terror, and war. The tyrannical power which Robespierre exercised grew in Hegel's view out of this demand for absolute freedom, especially the demand that everyone act virtuously, i.e., that everyone harken to the dictates of the general will, and the concomitant belief that those who were even *suspected* of acting "viciously," i.e., of acting in their own particular interest, should be *forced* to be free. "Virtue" as Robespierre understood it, however, was utterly abstract and thus lacked any real content. He thus represented the fanaticism of the abstract and of the empty; his sole work was death and destruction.

The answer that *Robespierre* gave to everything—here one
had thought this, done that, wanted this or said that—was: *la
mort*! Its uniformity is highly boring but it fits everything. You
want the coat: here you can have it; also the vest: here; you strike
one cheek: here is the other cheek too; you want the small
finger: cut it off. I can kill everything, abstract from everything.
Such obstinacy is indomitable and can in itself overcome everything. But the highest thing that could be overcome, that would
be precisely this freedom, this death itself.[31]

All private interests are merely particular, deriving not from reason but
from the desires and thus from nature. Virtue, however, especially among
those in power should be rational and general. The government, though, is
always particular, a group less than the whole, and thus a faction that is
opposed to the general will. Since by this logic only the general will is truly
free and rational, the faction must be destroyed. "The fanaticism of freedom,
put into the hands of the people, became terrible."[32] The attempt to institutionalize the general will results in the tyranny of all over each and the
attempt to establish an ethical community on the basis of the absolute
freedom of the general will establishes only the terror and chaos of universal death: becoming absolute, freedom becomes terrible.

The ethical community that the Revolution sought to engender was thus
swallowed up in the Chronian chaos of the utter negativity of freedom. As
much as Hegel may have admired the principles and intentions of the
French Revolution, he could not help but be horrified by its conclusion.
Unless and until the positive principles of the Revolution could be reconciled with the necessities of nature and in particular human nature, they
would remain only a negative and destructive force. Freedom must become
concrete. It cannot be based upon either the purely individual or the purely
general will because neither of these exists, but must instead be founded
upon the rational will, i.e., the will of the ethical community as it appears in
and through the mediating institutions of the modern diversified state.[33] The
modern world is the world of freedom in Hegel's view but, if that freedom is
to be made safe, it must be made rational and that means concrete. The
rational state presupposes the reconciliation of freedom with nature, and
that means for Hegel the reconciliation of the French Revolution with
bourgeoise society.

The basic principle of bourgeois society, according to Hegel, is self-
interested man, i.e., man as determined by his natural desires, not, to be
sure, man himself in a natural condition of isolation as he was described by
Rousseau, but man as a particular individual in relationship to other such
individuals, i.e., man in society.[34] This society, according to Hegel, differs
from the duality of family and polis, which characterized the ancient world,
and is in fact a purely modern phenomenon, forming a unity of sorts, but a
unity that is fundamentally only a commonality, a mere collection or

togetherness. This commonality, however, is far from unstable and indeed is bound together by the ties of necessity, i.e., of economic necessity, that arise out of the increasing specialization and division of labor. The self-seeking and self-serving purpose in each man's strivings is thus necessarily intertwined with the similar strivings of all other men and therefore must be regulated. This regulation is achieved, however, not through the constitution of rational government but through the institution of merely individual and particular positive rights and an agency to adjudicate disputes and enforce compliance through the application of penalties and sanctions. In this manner the traditional basis of human community in the family or polis is destroyed and supplanted by the "natural" bond of interrelated passions or needs. Justice thus becomes a mere tool to regulate the competitive pursuit of individual self-interest and pleasure. Right as such and hence a true ethical community are thereby lost. This, according to Hegel, was essentially the state of English society.

In the *Philosophy of History* Hegel remarks: "England's constitution is put together out of purely particular rights and special privileges: the government is essentially administrative, i.e., perceiving the interest of all special societal orders and classes."[35] English government in Hegel's view merely regulates preexisting societal groupings, which arise in consequence of the accidental similarity of interest and natural desires. The English state is thus essentially identical with that described by Hobbes, who recognized "that the nature and organism of the state should be established on the foundation of human nature, human inclination, etc."[36] In this respect he is typical of "English philosophy [which] is also only the grasping of the natural in thoughts; forces, laws of nature are fundamental determinations."[37] He and for that matter Locke thus remain within the Baconian premise, that the truth is to be found in the natural passions and perceptions of man, i.e., in experience. As the basis of English liberalism, however, this produces only the atomization of individuation. Rousseau's state was to be grounded in freedom, that of Hobbes in natural necessity, Rousseau's in the *general* will, that of Hobbes in *particular* self-interest. The English system is thus more concrete than the French for it is more decentralized, but this decentralization has its drawbacks: "The general interest is in this way concrete, and the particular is therein known and willed. [But] These institutions of particular interest allow no general system at all."[38]

The English political system in Hegel's opinion is not based on general will or centered in a predominate community spirit but resides in the individual self-interest of rational, i.e., calculating, animals. Government does not establish the national character but merely coordinates the various special interest groups. Thus, there is in fact no general or national interest but only a collection of concrete particular interests deriving from natural desires—consequently there is no state in the strict sense of the term. Indeed, membership in the state even becomes something optional. Thus, contrary to the prevailing view, "there are nowhere fewer institutions of real freedom than in England."[39] The English understand their freedom, according to Hegel, as the freedom of individuals and corporations, and government seems necessary to them only to insure the sanctity of contracts and defense and even here, i.e., in the military, positions upon which the very existence of the state depends can be purchased. This guarantees in Hegel's view the rule of natural necessity in the from of capricious individual desires and passions. Only the embodied general will can be truly rational and free, and it is precisely this will that is sacrificed to individual self-interest. English bourgeois society is thus not free but enslaved to natural desire. English liberalism, and indeed any liberalism that does not go beyond civil society, is thus in Hegel's opinion bankrupt because it is not and cannot ever be truly liberal, i.e., truly free.

The predominance of the individual ruled by natural desire also fosters a general corruption and degeneration of customs and morals, since the worth of everything is judged only in terms of its exchange value. The practice of buying and selling votes is particularly offensive and most clearly demonstrates the lack of any real freedom in England. Thereby property, not humanity, rules and the republican principle is subverted—the government represents and speaks not for the general good of the people but for the collective good of property.[40]

This is also the source of the great strength of the English government. In comparison with France this emphasis upon the particular and the practical assures a government of men trained from youth in the practical problems of state business. In no other state is national economy more important and in no other state is it more effectively managed, in large part because profit depends upon the ability to determine and fulfill the needs of others.[41] Men thus are naturally brought to consider the *particular* needs and desires of their fellowmen and are successful to the extent that they understand them and how to satisfy them. The wealth this system engenders, however, is inimical to rational law and tends rather to undermine than to support the common good. In the first place, if left to itself civil society produces a small number of wealthy citizens and a large pauperized rabble, not necessarily as the result of any exploitation—as Marx would have it—but because specialization and the division of labor magnify preexisting natural differences between men and because some start life with more capital and hence a greater likelihood of success than others due to accidents of birth. The resultant poverty is not merely politically destabilizing but also fundamentally dehumanizing, since in Hegel's view man's humanity arises not out of his natural individuality but out of the character of the ethical community of which he is a member. Nor are the rich immune—not only does their humanity suffer from the same disintegration and atomization and from an even greater narrowness and specialization than the poor, but insofar as they are also most capable of satisfying their needs they are also least likely to find satisfaction, since it is in the interest of everyone else to discover new needs for them and to subdivide and multiply the needs they already have. Hegel thus concludes that in peacetime bourgeois life is the bog (*Versumpfung*) of humanity and that it is only through war that bourgeois man is elevated above his own self-interest to concern himself with the state, and even in such cases his patriotism is bound up with his economic and personal well-being. Thus unless reconciled with the true principles of a free and rational government, this society can never constitute a true ethical community and consequently its members cannot achieve true freedom and humanity but remain trapped in the loneliness of their individuality and the slavery of natural desire.[42]

The political problem Hegel saw in England and France was the diremption or alienation of freedom and natural necessity. The abstract freedom of human self-consciousness as it is manifested in the general will had to be reconciled with the concrete necessity of natural desire as it appears in individual self-interest. The solution to Hegel's problem thus lies in the reconciliation of the principles of the French Revolution and the concrete reality of English bourgeois society. "In their national constitution the French began with abstractions, general thoughts which are negative versus actuality,—the English antithetically with concrete actuality for the shapeless building of their constitution; also their writers have not elevated themselves to general and fundamental propositions."[43] France and England, according to Hegel, are antithetical in their basic national character. The French accept as fundamental the concept of abstract freedom, which is nothing more than the negation of the actual, of the natural; the English, on the other hand, hold natural man in his concrete actuality of needs and desires to be fundamentally real, thus excluding the very possibility of freedom. A rational and good political system presupposes the reconciliation of these two positions. Such a reconciliation assumes the political transformation of the regimes themselves on the basis of principles that are themselves the result of a theoretical resolution of their contradiction. Hegel believed he discerned the beginning of such a political transformation in France with the establishment of the Directory and the *Code Napoleon*. Hegel highly esteemed Napoleon, though not so much as a general or conqueror but as a law-giver.[44] His good wishes for the success of Napoleon and the French thus probably arose out of his admiration not for the Revolution but for the combination of reason and measure in Napoleon's political institutions, although he was not uncritical of Napoleon's efforts, noting that his attempt to give a modern constitution to Spain failed because it was not in keeping with their national character and level of development.[45] Such constitutional monarchies, however imperfect, offered in Hegel's view at least a partial reconciliation of the principles of the Revolution and the self-interest of bourgeois society and at a very minimum restrained the most blatant abuses of each. Thus, Hegel believes:

It is, however, visible that through the ten year struggle and the misery of a great part of Europe enough at least in concept has been learned in order to become more intractable in opposition to the blind cries of freedom. In this bloody game the cloud of freedom, in whose attempted embrace the peoples have fallen into the abyss of misery, is dispersed, and certain forms and concepts have entered into the popular sphere. The freedom cry will have no effect; anarchy has separated itself from freedom, and that a stable government is necessary to freedom has deeply rooted itself, just as deeply, however, that the people must take part in the laws and the most important affairs of a state.[46]

In France itself, however, such reforms remained insufficient because the centralization of power begun by the Revolution, secured by the Terror, and institutionalized by Napoleon through his police system prevented the actual participation of the various social groups in the government.[47] If the rational state was to be established in France, this last remnant of Robespierre's "general will" had to be abolished. Such "decentralization," however, remained impossible in Hegel's view so long as there was no spiritual bond to replace the merely external political bond that held the nation together.

Hegel believed he discerned a similar although in itself insufficient transformation in England with Peel's reform of the criminal law and the introduction of the Reform Bill. Due in large measure to the recognition of irrationality of a regime based upon the particular interests of various individuals and groups, pressure had arisen in favor of a parliamentary reform to institute a greater symmetry in place of the chaotic and distorted system of representation with a view to what Hegel saw as a reconciliation of natural desire and free rational government.[48] It is of course true that Hegel believed the Reform Bill was inadequate to rectify the abysmal conditions of English society. Nonetheless, it would be incorrect to assume that he did not see an expansion of the franchise and an elimination of the most flagrant abuses as first steps toward such a rectification. However, such reforms necessarily remained insufficient in Hegel's view because there was no spiritual basis in England for a rational, more centralized state. While France and England each represented crucial elements of modern political life, neither could really serve as a model for the rational state. Such a state must necessarily combine elements of each, but without a fundamental spiritual transformation such a combination would be impossible. All reform must, therefore, ultimately remain insufficient without a true solution to the spiritual problem of this contradiction. Hegel had already indicated this as early as 1796 in reference to his own native Württemberg:

> So long as all the rest remains in the old condition, so long as the people do not know their rights, so long as no general spirit is

present, so long as the strength of the bureaucrats is not limited general elections would only serve to bring about the complete downfall of our constitution.[49]

Hegel saw his task as the establishment of the foundation for a solution to this problem.

Both the French Revolution and the bourgeois society that arose in England with the industrial revolution were made possible by previous spiritual revolutions in France and England. Since philosophy was responsible for these ills, it thus could in Hegel's view also effect their cures: as Rousseau prepared the way for the French Revolution, as Hobbes and Locke prepared the ground for bourgeois society, so Hegel believed he could prepare the ground for the reconciliation of the two respective principles first in Germany and then in Europe as a whole.

The Collapse of Spiritual Unity in Germany

That this reconciliation should occur first in Germany was in Hegel's view not accidental. He felt such a spiritual reconciliation was more necessary in Germany than in England or France, first, because the Germans were more spiritual and, second, because they lacked even the imperfect political institutions present in France and England and hence could rely only upon spirit as the source of unity. According to Hegel, in both their practical lives and philosophic speculations the English were rooted in the empirical particularity of experience, the French similarly in abstract generality, while "Germany began with the concrete idea, with concrete emotional (*gemütsvollen*) and spiritual inwardness."[50] Philosophy and religion were thus inherently more important to Germany than to England or France and indeed were the primary basis of national affiliation.

This spiritual unity had long been embodied in the Holy Roman Empire. This institution had constituted Germany, but in Hegel's view it had not been a state with powers and real political authority, i.e., a political actor, but an empire, i.e., a concept, a moral being with no motion in itself. The failure of the Germans to form themselves into a real state Hegel attributes to their misunderstanding of the true nature of freedom, a misunderstanding commensurate with their own characteristic inwardness. Freedom for them was not general but particular, based not upon a system of rational laws and rights but upon custom and positive property and political rights. Moreover, the particularism this conception of freedom engendered was enormously magnified by the rise of bourgeois society with its own atomizing force. This spiritual inwardness and the consequent lack of any real sense of rational responsibility and obligation effectively undermined the possibility of rational political institutions. This same inwardness, however, also increased the binding force of religion to such an extent that religion, supported by philosophy and art, replaced law and political institutions as the basis of communal life.[51]

For this reason the Reformation threatened the very existence of Germany. The spiritual unity that religion maintained was shattered, and the nation divided and set at war with itself. Rather than separating itself from the state, religion carried its divisions into the state with disastrous results. At the end of the Thirty Years War, with much of Germany in ruins and without a real victor, these divisions were recognized and institutionalized by the Treaty of Westphalia. However, this treaty served only to institutionalize the tension and antagonism that the religious schism had created, and indeed augmented even purely political differences, as in the case of the Seven Years War.[52]

Although it undermined German unity, the Reformation and in particular the Protestant principle also created the ground for the reconciliation of freedom and natural necessity and hence for the establishment of the rational state. The Protestant principle, according to Hegel, is the principle of free spirituality. Luther's insight that the truth of spirit does not have to be mediated by a privileged class but is open to all men was decisive. All men thus can know and understand what is fundamentally true, hence what is fundamentally right, and consequently what they ought to do. Human beings can act morally on the basis of their own conscience and without direction from their superiors. The Protestant principle thus gives rise to a new modern sense of freedom. This is not the old German freedom as positive right, nor the English freedom of capricious desire, nor the French freedom of the general will but freedom as self-determination: "This is the essential content of the Reformation: man is determined through himself to be free."[53] This freedom is thus individualistic insofar as it is open to every man to determine himself, but it is not capricious and does not liberate the desires because it is the freedom to act morally, i.e., in harmony with the divine and therefore concretely rational will as it manifests itself publicly in the Christian community and privately in conscience.

This principle in Hegel's view found its actualization not in England or France but in Germany because of the inwardness of German sentiment. In France access to the spiritual remained limited to the clergy, and the general population could only indirectly come to understand the fundamental truths. Hence, they were in principle incapable of knowing what they ultimately should do and depended upon the clergy for instruction in their moral duty. Consequently, the Revolutionary demand for freedom necessarily turned against the church in France and into the caprice of unfettered, utterly abstract subjectivity. In Protestant Germany the demand for freedom did not have to turn against religion because religion itself was a doctrine of freedom. Political freedom in Germany thus could be achieved in accordance with basic and general principles of morality and order. England, like Germany, was a Protestant country. Religion, however, was less important for the English and in any case, because the monarchical principle had no validity, there were no restraints upon the decentralizing influence of the nobility, who through their control of benefices were able to choose their pastors to suit their principles.[54] While Reformation is thus necessary as a prerequisite of the rational state, the principle it engenders is insufficient without the support of an enlightened monarch. Hegel's chief example is Frederick II.

The greatness of Frederick II in Hegel's mind lay not in his military genius but in his success in secularizing and institutionalizing this Protestant principle in the laws and thus establishing the framework for the reconciliation of the particular and general wills, i.e., for harmonizing individual self-interest and the needs of state. He found in the Protestant principle the grounds for the supremacy of the state over all other social groups as the spokesman and guarantor of every man's rights. The state consequently replaced religion as the ultimate authority in matters of justice and right. Hence, Frederick II was able to separate church and state and overturn the provisions of the Treaty of Westphalia in granting religious toleration, whereas Joseph II's similar attempt in Catholic Austria was defeated when the particular interests insisted upon retaining their traditional rights and privileges and refused to recognize the legitimacy of the natural or universal rights of man.[55]

The Protestant principle thus cannot merely be imposed from above by an enlightened monarch but must also flow up out of the sentiments of the people. Hence, it must already be present in the state at least in a vague sense before any political transformation is attempted and must then be systematically articulated and propagated so that the general public is informed by it. Without such a transformation of the basic disposition and sentiments of the people, in Hegel's view the state will lack the resolve necessary to maintain itself in times of crisis. This was the lesson Hegel learned from the collapse of Germany in the face of the French Revolution and Napoleon. In this confrontation the German states (*Stände*) failed to unite in the common defense, which made it clear that they had not really grasped and embodied the truth of the Reformation, i.e., that true freedom could exist only in and as a part of an ethical community of free men.[56] On one hand, they feared what appeared to them as the absolutism of a Frederick II or Joseph II because they had not comprehended the principles the monarchs espoused, largely because however liberal these rulers intentions their methods were absolutist. More important, however, the German states conceived of their freedom as the right to do what they pleased, to support or not support the nation as they saw fit, and even justified their lack of support on the basis of Robespierre's right of insurrection. This led to anarchy. The states' fear of despotic inroads upon their positive rights thus produced a situation in which just such a despotism seemed to be the only way to preserve national integrity. The Germans found themselves torn between their freedom and their self-interest and were unable to reconcile them with one another. Unable or unwilling to choose either the way of the English or that of the French they were paralyzed, defeated, and dismembered. In Hegel's view Germany had become nothing more than a *Gedankenstaat*, a state in thought, and the Germans little more than the Quakers of Europe. This political ineptitude, however, could not in Hegel's view be remedied by political means alone because it rested upon a deeper misunderstanding about the relationship of freedom and natural necessity. The solution lay not in the mere political imposition of the Protestant principle but in its systematic theoretical explication. Only when it had been clearly and thoroughly articulated could it truly inform the general public with the sentiments necessary to the rational state. A new way of thinking, a philosophic revolution, was necessary, and it was Kant in Hegel's view who set this revolution in motion.[57]

Transcendental idealism is an outgrowth in Hegel's view of English and French philosophy. "Hume and Rousseau," he asserts, "are the two points of departure for German philosophy."[58] Kant thus remains within the horizon established by Bacon and Locke, on one hand, and Descartes, Rousseau, and the French Enlightenment, on the other, and his thought is an attempt to resolve the contradiction between these two traditions and reconcile them with one another. This contradiction that characterizes modern European thought, however, is in principle nothing other than the contradiction of freedom and natural necessity that finds its foremost expression in the Third Antinomy and its provisional solution in transcendental idealism. For Hegel the Third Antinomy thus embodies the conflict that appears in the French Revolution and English bourgeois society. The practical political problems they represent appear in their clear juxtaposition in German spiritual life. While perhaps less politically disastrous than the tyranny of freedom in the Revolution and less debilitating than the rule of natural desire in bourgeois society, the contradiction of nature and freedom that appears in the Third Antinomy is, however, even more destructive of human spirituality. The failure of transcendental idealism to account for the relationship of the two sides of the contradiction opens up not merely the possibility but the actuality of utter alienation.

According to Hegel, transcendental idealism thus brings about the downfall of metaphysics, which as the bulwark of religion had provided the ground for the reconciliation of the antithesis of spiritual freedom and natural necessity. This collapse produces what Hegel calls "The strange play . . . *to see a cultured people* without metaphysics."[59] The same conflicting forces that had erupted so disastrously in France and obliterated so completely the ethical community in England lay in the very heart of human spirituality, and there was no longer even a metaphysical or theological ground for their reconciliation. Thus the prospect of the disintegration of human spirituality, even more than what for many of Hegel's contemporaries must have been the more fearful prospect of the triumph and tyranny of either unrestrained freedom or unconstrained naturalism, in short the prospect an all-embracing nihilism and the social and moral disintegration this entailed for Germany, revealed the need of philosophy to Hegel and called out for a new metaphysics to establish a new ground for the relationship of freedom and natural necessity, and thus for history. The source of Kant's failure in Hegel's estimation lay in his negative methodology. In the limitation of understanding to the finite Kant seems to renounce all pretensions to knowledge of the infinite or divine. But in Hegel's view this is only the renunciation of *positive* knowledge of the absolute. Since the absolute or whole transcends even an infinite totality of finite determinations, understanding, which is itself limited to the finite, attempts to grasp the whole negatively, i.e., through antithesis. Hegel saw this striving for a negative understanding of the absolute as the impetus behind transcendental idealism. Hegel thus characterizes transcendental idealism as an "apophatic" or negative theology that tries to demonstrate the existence of the divine or absolute by showing the incompleteness or contradiction of all attempts to grasp the absolute in terms of worldly or finite categories. This negative attempt to grasp the infinite, however, is insufficient without the unquestioned belief in God's immediate presence. If the existence of the absolute is already cast into doubt, such an attempt can only serve to further undermine man's faith in the unity of the whole. In such a state philsophy, which aims at positive knowledge of the absolute, becomes necessary. The contradiction in the antinomy between the objective realm of phenomenal or natural necessity and the subjective realm of noumenal or logical freedom through which Kant seeks to understand the absolute thus further undermines spiritual unity and opens up the possibility of utter political and spiritual alienation. In this aporia and with a view to its solution in the positive knowledge of the absolute Hegel's philosophizing begins.

From Antinomy to Dialectic

Hegelian philosophy is fundamentally dialectical. The meaning and character of this dialectical essence, however, arises out of Hegel's reception and transformation of Kant's antinomy doctrine. While his discussion of the antinomies and especially the Third Antinomy is thus, in one sense, a straightforward explanation of their importance for Kantian philosophy, in a second and philosophically more important sense it is a fundamental radicalization of the antinomy doctrine that provides the basis for Hegel's own system of philosophy. In both his lectures in Nürnberg and in the *Logic* he accurately restates Kant's presentation of the Third Antinomy and clearly recognizes that the Thesis argues in support of a causality through freedom *and* or *in addition to* a causality through nature.[60] In explaining the Thesis, however, and in his restatement of it in his *History of Philosophy*, he clearly and erroneously asserts that the Thesis argues in support of the *exclusive* causality of freedom.[61] This inconsistency is so manifest that it is hard to believe that Hegel's misconstruction is not intentional.

This transformation radicalizes the antinomy in a manner that would have been completely unacceptable to Kant: nature and natural causality were in his view incontestable. Hegel, however, apparently sharpens the antinomy in order to more distinctly display the conflict of nature and freedom as two at least seemingly self-subsistent alternatives. Moreover, he thereby apparently either overlooks or neglects the subsidiary question of the sufficiency of the explanation of the whole in terms of natural laws. Kant himself seems never to have considered the possibility that freedom alone might determine the whole and in fact argues that, if such were the case, freedom would then only be nominally different than natural necessity. Hegel's account of the French Revolution, as we have seen, seems to indicate that in contradistinction to Kant he took seriously the possibility of an exclusive causality through freedom: he saw the omnipotence of freedom in the tyranny of reason and the Terror.[62] His transformation of the antinomy thus seems to aim at expressing the true antinomy, the true danger to the human spirit as he saw it.

Kant solves the antinomy, according to Hegel, by making it absolute as the limit or horizon of all possible experience and knowledge.[63] This negative articulation of the absolute is likewise the denial of the possibility of positive knowledge of the true unity and ground of knowledge and being. Kant's philosophy thus ends not in knowledge but in belief, i.e., in a beyond knowledge can never attain. Transcendental idealism, according to Hegel, thus never reaches the highest things and especially never discovers the true ground.[64]

Kant solves the antinomy in Hegel's view only through the absolute separation of two utterly different but concomitant and, in Kant's view, possibly harmonious realms, a separation which, as Hegel points out, Kant positively asserts in his critique of speculative theology. Kant thus transforms what hitherto were always recognized as *things* into phenomenal *appearances* of the truly real noumenal *things-in-themselves*. Kant thereby is able to argue that not things-in-themselves but only appearances are contradictory and that this contradiction is produced by the limitation of human capacities, i.e., by the categorical forms of consciousness. Hegel, however, considers this explanation insufficient because, according to Kant himself, the application of the categories is *necessary*, for there is no determination except through the categories. Reason is thus bound by necessity to apply the categories or not to think and hence not to be; consequently the contradictions that arise through the categories are themselves necessary.

"So this antinomy remains in our inner life; as previously God had to assume all contradictions into himself, so now it is self-consciousness."[65] In

Hegel's opinion the solution to the antinomy according to transcendental idealism is secured only through the apotheosis of self-consciousness. In assuming the aspect of the transcendent and inscrutable God, self-consciousness is able to preserve the consistency of the things-in-themselves by subsuming their contradictions within its own substance. This, Hegel continues, is "too much tenderness toward things; it would be too bad, if they contradicted themselves. That spirit (the highest), however, is contradiction, that is not supposed to be bad." In order to secure and maintain the rationality of reality, according to Hegel, Kant sacrificed the unity of self-consciousness or spirit, which is itself the ground of rationality. The rationality of both phenomenal nature and noumenal freedom is dependent upon the unity of self-consciousness or spirit. Thus, if self-consciousness or spirit is itself contradictory, the order of nature and morality is *essentially* ungrounded and hence irrational. Thus as Hegel concludes, "The contradictory destroys itself; so spirit is ruin, madness in itself." While Kant found security and a sort of contentment in the contemplation of the lawful motions of the heavens above and the equally lawful moral realm within, Hegel like Pascal was aghast at those infinite dark spaces between, at the utter alienation in that spirit, in that self-consciousness through which both realms had their existence.

Hegel's critique here is well-founded but not entirely fair to Kant who was not merely interested in securing the consistency of the empirical realm for natural science but also the consistency of the noumenal realm for morality. The spiritual and the natural, as he understood them, are distinct, and the antinomy arises not in one or the other—and hence not within spirit—but at their interface within self-consciousness. The recognition of two different capacities of reason, however, is not necessarily the recognition of their mutual contradiction. They may simply be mutually exclusive. In such a case the unity of self-consciousness and reason is indeed mysterious but not necessarily impossible. The ground of this distinction, however, lies in the Leibnizian and Kantian distinction of two principles of rationality—the principle of sufficient reason, and the principle of noncontradiction. Hegel's radicalization of the antinomy undermines this distinction: it is not the question of the sufficiency of natural causality and the possible necessity of a free causality to secure this sufficiency but the juxtaposition of an exclusive causality according to freedom and an exclusive causality according to natural necessity that lies at the heart of the antinomy. Freedom in Hegel's view, as became clear in the French Revolution, is not confined to the noumenal realm nor is natural necessity merely something within the phenomena; they thus cannot be harmonized by a restriction to separate domains. They interact everywhere and always. The fact of their contradiction, according to Hegel, must be taken seriously and Kant's failure to do so is a sign of philosophic weakness.

Kant's attempt to avoid such a radicalization by the positive assertion in the *Critique of Practical Reason* of a moral realm in which freedom has an absolute and self-evident existence, independent of the natural realm, concealed but did not overcome the contradiction. "This contradiction, which cannot be overcome by this system and which destroys it, becomes really inconsequential, in that this absolute emptiness [i.e., absolute spontaneity and autonomy] is supposed to give itself a content as practical reason and extend itself in the form of duties."[66] Thus, according to Hegel, the principle of the absolute freedom of self-consciousness or spirit, which Rousseau recognized as essential, and its disastrous political consequences, i.e., the French Revolution, are trivialized and falsified in the theoretical restriction of freedom to the moral sphere. If freedom is active and hence truly causal, then it also must be capable of transforming and destroying the natural. Kant's belief that freedom was in fact identical with morality was in Hegel's view refuted by the French Revolution. This assertion of freedom struck nature with such vehemence that any attempt to characterize it as 'morality' must necessarily have merited universal disapprobation were it not for the fact that it was precisely the moral purity of its chief actors that produced its excesses. Morality and hence freedom become meaningless in such a context—the concept of universal human rights undermines the ethical community that gave them substance. Without the substance of the community, without an ethos, morality becomes merely formal and, at least potentially, terrible.

Kant himself apparently recognized the necessity of some sort of reconciliation of the realm of freedom and the realm of natural necessity. In addition to the obvious ontological difficulties that such a dualism engenders, it also fundamentally subverts the possibility of human happiness: without a reconciliation of the phenomenal and the noumenal man must ever be torn by the natural impulses of his desires and the liberating impetus of rationality. As self-consciousness, man is the conflict and reconciliation of freedom and nature. Insofar as he is merely conscious, man is subject to natural desire. Insofar as he is self-conscious, man sees only his own freedom in rationality, in the identity of self-reflection. Man is thus the battleground on which freedom and natural necessity meet. Only within human being is their conflict manifest, and it is only within self-consciousness that the potentiality for their unity arises.

This reconciliation takes several forms for Kant—religion, teleological judgment, art, and history. The last is of particular importance to us.[67] As particular, i.e., as an individual, man is generally motivated by desire. His own freedom and the good of others is almost always more distant than the immediacy of his passions. As general, i.e., as a species, however, man is predominantly rational: it is not the particular interest but the general interest that is determinative, if only as the establishment of just laws for the regulation of particular interests. Thus, while the individual in the exercise of his freedom may reject the imperative of rationality, the species tends toward its institutionalization in a rational world political order. Thus, while the individual may never be able to overcome this dualism, as a species he is continually progressing toward a true reconciliation and unity.

This argument, however, does not satisfy Hegel. He argues that "practical reason, which takes refuge in it [infinite progress] and is supposed to constitute itself in freedom as absolute, acknowledges even through this infinity of progress its finity and inability to make itself valid as absolute."[68] Practical reason should but never can be absolute; it can approach infinitely near to the absolute but can never attain it. Thus for Hegel transcendental idealism never gets beyond the level of an 'ought' and thus never achieves a true reconciliation of freedom and natural necessity. It thus fails to establish a ground for history.

Although Kant was responsible for opening up the problem of the antinomy, even he, according to Hegel, did not recognize its true proportions. Reason for Kant is architectonic and as such strives to form a coherent and symmetrical system. Rather than deriving the antinomies from an examination of what is, Kant merely adapts them to the completed schema of the categories. Kant thus recognizes only four antinomies. This may preserve the symmetry of the Kantian system but, according to Hegel, it also leads Kant into a fundamental error, for he thus does not see "that the antinomy is not only found in the four special objects taken from cosmology but much more in all objects of all species, in all representations, concepts and ideas."[69] The more profound insight into the nature of reason, the insight fundamental to all speculative idealism and to Hegel's philosophy in particular, sees that *every* concept is a synthesis of antitheses, which could be put in the form of an antinomy. Hegel thus concludes, "To know this and to recognize the objects in this characteristic belongs to that which is essential in philosophic observation; this characteristic constitutes that which furthermore determines itself as the dialectical moment of the logical." This is the origin of Hegelian dialectic out of the Kantian antinomy.

Hegel did not simply adopt the Kantian antinomy doctrine but also transformed it.[70] Kant in Hegel's view may well have identified the most important antinomies, but he did not grasp or express their true form nor did he comprehend their true extent, nor, finally, did he recognize or establish a real solution. It is this deficiency that Hegel attempts to remedy. The Kantian antinomy doctrine, *mutatis mutandis*, becomes Hegelian dialectic.

Dialectic for Kant is fundamentally sophistical. Returning to what he claims is the ancient meaning of the term, he asserts that dialectic "was nothing other than the logic of illusion, a sophistical art."[71] Conjoining this with the medieval definition of the term, "as the alleged Organon," Kant concludes that dialectic is nothing other than a sophistry unrestrained by the realities of substance. The antinomy in Kant's opinion is the example par excellence of the dialectical conclusions of speculative reason, which oversteps the bounds of experience. Thus, Kant concludes that "speculative reason in its transcendental employment is *in itself* dialectical."[72]

Hegel's reception and transformation of Kant's antinomy doctrine is also the reception and transformation of his concept of dialectic. According to Hegel, Kant discovered but misunderstood the fundamental truth that all reason is dialectical. Kant's conclusion that reason is incapable of knowing the infinite is, according to Hegel, very strange, since by Kant's own account the infinite is the rational. Kant's solution is thus tantamount to the assertion that reason is incapable of knowing itself. Man in Hegel's view is not limited to categorical understanding but is also capable of reason that grasps the infinite. Herewith Hegel denies the conclusion that Kant draws from the antinomy without, to be sure, denying the antinomy itself. Man is not fundamentally finite and isolated in his self-reflective subjectivity but a conscious being who takes part in the general and ultimately infinite activity of reason and spirit. Man is not isolated from the absolute but bound up with it through reason. In contemplation of the antinomy, reason does not give up its speculative enterprise in a recognition of its own limitations but recognizes its ownmost self, recognizes that reason is fundamentally dialectical.

Reason, however, is not content to remain in the alienation of the antinomy but attempts to reconcile or synthesize the conflicting forces—not through the dissolution of the contradiction itself, for this just is the dialectical, but through the recognition and establishment of both the contradiction *and* its unity. This reconciliation is the recognition of the mutual interaction and interdependence of the apparently contradictory and mutually exclusive positions. According to Hegel, Kant recognized the necessity of the contradiction—this was indeed one of his greatest services to philosophy—but he did not recognize or articulate the equally necessary *relation* or *synthesis* of the opposing positions. Kant's insight into the nature of the antinomy and hence into human knowledge as such, however, was insufficient, for he "did not perceive that the contradiction just is the elevation of reason above the limitations of understanding and the dissolution of these limitations."[73] For Kant the antinomy demonstrates the supremacy of understanding and the illusion of speculative reason; for Hegel, on the other hand, the antinomy is precisely the demonstration of the insufficiency of understanding and the superiority of reason.

This is the beginning of Hegel's reversal or transformation of transcendental idealism: reason recognizes in the antinomy both contradiction and interaction. The *purer* form of the dialectic of causality, which Hegel develops, is an explanation of this interaction and interdependence. Cause is *formally* differentiated from effect as the original and active element, the free element from which motion arises. *Substantively*, however, the cause is not distinguished from the effect and in fact is and can only be a cause in becoming an effect, just as the effect is and can only be an effect because it was a cause. The cause becomes the effect and the effect thus becomes the cause (of the next effect). Moreover, this transformation of each into its opposite, i.e., of cause into effect and of effect into cause, is necessary, for each only has meaning in *relation* to the other, only is therefore in and through the other. Thus, the cause in Hegel's view is also necessary and the effect is also free. The true resolution of the antinomy thus lies in the recognition that the truth of the cause is in the effect and the truth of the effect in the cause. "This reciprocity means that neither of the two moments of causality [is] for itself absolute," neither freedom nor necessity is self-sufficient—each is established (*gesetzt*) in opposition to the other as an antithesis (*Entgegengesetzte*) and hence has no independent self-subsistent existence but resides only in the unity of their establishment (*Setzung*).[74]

This reversal, however, already involves a subtle but nonetheless decisive transformation of the antinomy itself. Kant understood the antinomy as a conflict between opposing laws (*Gesetze*) or propositions (*Sätze*); Hegel, in his reinterpretation of the antinomy, is no longer concerned with either laws or propositions but with contradictory concepts, objects, representations, and ideas.[75] Hegel thus appears to transform Kant's antinomy of nature and freedom into the merely logical question of the apparent contradiction and mutual exclusion of the phenomenal and the noumenal, i.e., of nature and spirit, but in fact this transformation is an attempt to isolate the essential element in the antinomy, the relationship and especially the interrelationship of the phenomenal and the noumenal and thus to establish a truly *phenomenological* ground upon which and out of which the twofold of nature and spirit can arise.[76] Kant attempts to demonstrate the necessity and contradiction of both freedom and natural necessity and the possibility of their compatibility; Hegel attempts to show that the *necessity of the contradiction is their actual reconciliation*: each exists only as the opposite of the other and each is only in becoming the other. This is the necessity that is the bond of their unity. For Kant the contradiction excludes and isolates, for Hegel it relates and reconciles. Hegel is not concerned with the empirical or phenomenal question of truth as sufficiency nor with the noumenal or logical question of truth as noncontradiction but with the *phenomenological* question of the true ground that arises in and as the antinomy itself.

This is the task that is posed for Hegel by the antinomy: to grasp not merely the interaction of spirit and nature but the ground of their wholeness and thus the whole as such. Kant denied the man had access to this sort of knowledge and believed that the antinomy was the proof of this. It is precisely this knowledge, however, which Hegel seeks: the highest kind of knowledge in his view is not transcendental but speculative; man is not confined to understanding the finite but can comprehend the infinite in and through reason.

This just is the reversal of transcendental into speculative idealism. In the "Introduction" to his *Logic* Hegel writes:

> This result [Kantian dialectic], *grasped in its positive side*, is
> nothing other than the inner *negativity* of the same, as its
> self-moving soul, the principle of all natural and spiritual life as
> such . . . The speculative consists in the dialectical, as it is here
> understood, and therewith in the comprehension of the antith-
> esis in its unity or the positive in the negative.[77]

The inner, true principle of all natural and spiritual life is the negativity of
contradiction. This is dialectic, which for Hegel is the motive principle in
the essence of all that is. However, if all concepts, objects, etc., are merely
and utterly contradictory, if the issue of contradiction itself is and engenders
only further contradiction, then the diremption in the heart of things
remains. Thus, it is not sufficient merely to grasp the contradiction and the
issue of its interaction; rather one must comprehend the antitheses in their
unity, one must go beyond the interaction of the thesis and antithesis to the
original unity out of which they arise, to their ground. This is the essence of
the speculative—to discern and comprehend the fundamental unity and
ground.

Hegel thus accepts Kant's insight into what is consciousness or spirit and
that this consciousness or spirit is fundamentally contradictory. He rejects,
however, Kant's transcendental solution. The solution in his view lies not in
absolute separation but in absolute reconciliation, not in the distinction of a
noumenal or logical realm *and* a phenomenal realm of consciousness but
in a single *phenomenology* of spirit. To grasp this absolute synthesis,
however, it is first necessary in his view to face resolutely the contradiction
itself: to overcome nihilism one must first accept it *as* nihilism. Out of this
"abyss of nothing, . . . the feeling: God is dead, . . . the highest totality in its
complete seriousness and out of its deepest ground, at once all-
encompassing and in the most joyful freedom of its form can and must
arise."[78]

The transformation of transcendental idealism thus rests upon a new
understanding of contradiction. Kant, according to Hegel, recognized the
necessity of *contradiction* but he had failed to discern the *necessity* of
contradiction and hence believed it necessary to dissolve contradiction to
maintain the rationality of natural and moral law. In so doing, however, he
also dissolved the necessity present in the contradiction. It is precisely this
necessity, however, that is the real reconciliation and overcoming of the
contradiction. The basis of the reconciliation of the contradiction and thus
of the reconciliation of the phenomenal realm of natural necessity and the
noumenal realm of freedom thus arises out of the nihilistic essence of the
contradiction itself. If the contradiction were merely *accidental*, it could not
be absolute. As *necessary*, however, the nihilistic essence of the contradiction overcomes itself in the recognition of its own necessity to form itself
into a system of absolute knowledge or science. The highest irrationality
thus encloses within it in Hegel's view the highest rationality. Hence,

philosophy in performing its perennial task of reconciling what has been separated here comes to its conclusion and can finally lay aside the name love of wisdom and become wisdom itself because it has achieved the highest reconciliation: it has demonstrated the rationality of irrationality in demonstrating that contradiction, that nihilism is the highest reason.

The essence of the transformation of transcendental idealism into speculative idealism is the reinterpretation of dialectic and the resurrection of the possibility of speculative knowledge. For both the truly real is self-consciousness or spirit; herein they are both idealism. Both likewise recognize that self-consciousness is antinomious. Kant, however, understands the antinomy as the manifest proof of the transcendental character of self-consciousness, i.e., that there is a limit or horizon to both knowledge and experience that is determined by the form or shape of self-consciousness itself. For Hegel, the antinomy is the foremost expression of the essentially dialectical character of self-consciousness and reason, and gives rise to the speculative, to the knowledge of the unity and ground of the contradiction. This is the fundamental impetus of Hegel's philosophizing, to reveal the ground and unity of the antinomious or dialectical, to establish a ground for the twofold of nature and spirit, to reconcile the political and spiritual diremption in a rational political order grounded in the perfect knowledge of man, his institutions, and his world, in the knowledge of the phenomenological ground of history.

3
The Ground of History as Phenomenology

The Search for Reconciliation in Hegel's Early Thought

The antinomy of freedom and natural necessity, as we have seen, was the immediate impetus for Hegel's philosophizing. Hegel recognized this antinomy and its disastrous consequences in the political and spiritual constellations of his own age, in the Terror of the French Revolution, the tyranny of natural desire in English bourgeois society, and the nihilism of German spiritual life. This antinomy, however, was in his view not merely a contemporary and ephemeral problem but a universal human dilemma. Indeed, according to Hegel, it is precisely this diremption that characterizes all human history and impels man to seek a reconciliation.

Hegel's early thought and work is dominated by a search for such a reconciliation. His early admiration for the Greeks led him to believe that a reconciliation of the antithetical elements of the antinomy might be achieved through a revitalization and reinstitution of classical political ideals. While studying at Tübingen and later as a private tutor in Bern, Hegel along with Hölderlin and other friends believed that such a reconciliation had once been attained in the freedom and virtue of the Greek polis and that it consequently might be achieved again. This belief was apparently fostered by the perception Hegel and his friends shared that Kantian moral philosophy and the French Revolution were bringing about a fundamental change in European social and political institutions conducive to such a reinstitution of classical ideals. Their enthusiasm apparently fostered a real hope among them that the ethical community (*Sittlichkeit*) of the polis might be resurrected through a combination of the doctrine of *liberté, égalité, et fraternité*, promulgated by the French radicals, and the universal or categorical imperative of Kant's moral doctrine. Together these two doctrines seemed to them to contain the kernel of ancient republicanism. The course of events and of their own thought, however, brought about the recognition that these doctrines were fundamentally insufficient. Confronted with the disastrous consequences of the ideals of the Revolution and the empty formality of the categorical imperative, their hopes for a reconciliation on these grounds waned. However, they did not entirely abandon their hope of a resurrection of ancient political ideals. The new ground that they sought to establish, however, was more explicitly an amalgamation of Platonism and Christianity.[1]

The antinomy and concomitant distinction of spirit and nature, of freedom and necessity, of subject and object allowed in their view only two equally undesirable alternatives—an objective tyranny of nature and natural necessity, or a subjective tyranny of spirit or reason and freedom. Each of these alternatives overcame the antinomy but only by extinguishing the other element. Each alternative thus seemed to deny, if not to destroy, an essential element in human life. Hence, Hegel and his friends attempted to show that these alternatives were in fact the result of a false dichotomy, that the distinction of subject and object, etc., had been and could be overcome in and through love. Within both objective natural science and subjectivistic or Romantic philosophy all relationships, in Hegel's view, are reduced to the subordination of objects to subjects or subjects to objects. This, however, entails the necessary destruction of all ethical or communal life, for the ethical community is based not upon the subject or the object but upon love, which manifests itself within and as the basis of the family, the tribe, and the polis. This love sees in others not a possible object of use or another moral being but a *Du*, a thou, and is thus always within and yet always outside of itself in communion with another. Hence, it is *both* subject and object. This conception of love apparently had two sources—the Platonic conception of *erōs*, and the Christian conception of Christ as a God-man.[2] In both cases, in Hegel's view love provided the basis for the relationship of man and the divine and hence for man and man in the community: both the Greek polis and the Christian congregation were based upon this love and overcame in their own ways the diremption of the antinomy. It was on this ground that Hegel and his friends hoped to reestablish an ethical community. Hölderlin held fast to this hope into madness, but Hegel soon recognized that such a resurrection and reinstitution was impossible, due largely to the consideration—apparently prompted by his reading and detailed study of a German translation of Sir James Steuart's *An Enquiry into the Principles of Political Economy*—that the scale and complexity of modern society and especially the functional differentiation of the economy necessarily precluded any return to ancient ethical life. Such an ethical community as the polis or for that matter the congregation and the love upon which they were based depended upon an *immediate* attachment of man to man, upon the possibility of all men knowing one another, but in the large modern state such immediacy is impossible. One cannot really love those whom one has never even seen. Hence, modern social and political circumstances seemed to Hegel to render any retrieval of the substance of ancient life, i.e., of the ethical community based upon love, impossible.

The reconciliation of spirit and nature through a revitalization of the ancient ethical community that Hegel sought to achieve in his early work thus foundered on the Terror of the French Revolution and the economic necessity of modern society. Hegel, however, did not abandon his aspirations but recognized instead that they had to be made compatible with the modern world. Thus while he came to understand that the immediate, beautiful, ethical community (*die schöne Sittlichkeit*) that characterized the polis could not be reestablished within the bounds of modern society, he hoped to establish the basis for a mediated community through the reconciliation of freedom and nature within science. It was to this task, which was to occupy him for the rest of his life, that Hegel turned in Jena.

The speculative idealism of Fichte and Schelling, with which Hegel came into immediate contact in Jena, was an attempt to overcome the duality of transcendental idealism and to establish a speculative ground for the reconciliation of its contradictions in science (*Wissenschaft*). While Hegel's thought is deeply indebted to both Fichte and Schelling, he was not convinced that either had established a true reconciliation of the natural and the spiritual or had really come to grips with the political and social problems this antinomy entailed. While it is generally true that all speculative idealism attempts to resolve the diremption of transcendental idealism by articulating what it takes to be the concrete and absolute character of identity, of what Kant called the transcendental unity of apperception, the manner in which this resolution is achieved is crucial for both political and spiritual life. It is in this respect that Hegel parts company with Fichte and Schelling. According to Hegel, Fichte remained within the horizons of modern subjectivism; nature for him was ultimately nothing more than the negation of the self-conscious, self-positing I, and thus fundamentally subservient to the subjective categories of understanding. Moreover, in his consideration of moral and political subjects Fichte seemed to Hegel to approach all-too-near the tyranny and Terror of the French Revolution, which recognized no *natural* constraints upon the regime of reason. Indeed, Hegel himself went to considerable lengths to point out what we today would characterize as the totalitarian tendencies of Fichte's moral and political philosophy.[3]

Schelling's philosophical speculations were much more congenial to Hegel. Hegel, Hölderlin, and Schelling had been close friends in their university days in Tübingen and with Hölderlin's collapse, which Hegel experienced in the closest proximity, the hopes of a fruitful philosophic intercourse with Schelling drew him to Jena. These hopes were hardly disappointed. Although Hegel's junior by some five years, Schelling was then the rising star on the German philosophic horizon and in fact threatened to eclipse its older and more established luminary, Fichte. Indeed the philosophic community was to a large extent torn by the debate among the two schools that centered around Fichte and Schelling. Arriving in Jena, Hegel found himself caught up in this often heated and generally partisan debate. His first published work for instance was entitled *The Difference of Fichte's and Schelling's System of Philosophy*. During his first years in Jena, he and Schelling coauthored the *Critical Journal of Philosophy* in such close cooperation that they did not even distinguish their separate contributions. The intercourse of their ideas proved enormously fruitful for them both; indeed, the concept of the absolute, which was decisive for both their systems apparently developed as a result of this interchange. Hegel, however, became increasingly disenchanted with Schelling's system. In his view, Schelling's attempt to establish the ground in the absolute was ultimately insufficient—he was unable to return from this ground to the concrete multiplicity of the actual but fell instead into the Spinozistic abyss of an undifferentiated, absolutized nature, into "the night in which all cows are black," and thus failed to reconcile the absolute subject with actual human and natural existence.

Hegel's philosophizing can perhaps best be understood as the attempt to establish what he found in neither previous nor contemporary philosophy, a ground for the reconciliation of the contradiction that he believed characterized the modern world. This attempt to establish or reveal such a ground as a fully developed system was the project of his *System of Science*. The first part of this system was entitled *Science of the Phenomenology of Spirit*.

Hegel's Science of the Phenomenology of Spirit

Written in Jena between 1804 and 1807, the *Phenomenology* was originally to have been the first part of Hegel's *System of Science*, and to have been followed by a second part including the *Science of Logic* and the two concrete sciences of philosophy, the *Philosophy of Nature* and the *Philosophy of Spirit*. In the "Preface" to the *Logic* (1812) Hegel remarked that, due to the expansion of the original conception of the *Logic*, it alone was to comprise the second part of the *System* to be followed by a third part consisting of the two concrete sciences. This project, however, was never completed although the *System* itself in an altered form was completed in Heidelberg in 1817 as the *Encyclopaedia of the Philosophical Sciences*. In this work phenomenology as such was not included as a distinct part of the system, although some of the same material appeared in the last section, "The Philosophy of Spirit." Finally, in his revision of the *Logic* in 1831, Hegel remarked that the forthcoming edition of the *Phenomenology* would no

longer be entitled the first part of the *System of Science*, thus ending rather
ambiguously the question of the place of the *Phenomenology* in Hegel's
thought as a whole.[4]

The importance of the *Phenomenology* for philosophy as such has been
no less ambiguous. During Hegel's lifetime it was not the *Phenomenology*
but the *System* which was considered of central importance, and after the
collapse of the Hegelian School in 1844 Hegel's work as a whole and the
Phenomenology in particular were so largely neglected that Windelband
remarked in 1878 that the race of men who could read and understand the
Phenomenology was dying out. The so-called Hegel renaissance of the late
nineteenth and twentieth centuries, however, began not with the dead
System but with Hegel's early works and in particular with the *Phenomenology*, and in our century the *Phenomenology* has attained such an elevated
station that one of Hegel's most thoughtful interpreters, Kojeve, could
characterize it as the "book of all books." Thus, whether the *Phenomenology* is the original and authentic expression of Hegel's thought and hence
the true beginning of his *System* or whether it is merely the preparation or
propaedeutic for true science, its importance both for Hegel's thought and
for our own is incontestable and any consideration of Hegel's thought thus
presupposes an understanding of the *Phenomenology*.[5]

The *Phenomenology* was originally conceived as a much shorter work,
more or less identical with the first three sections of the work in its final
form, i.e., "Consciousness," "Self-consciousness," and "Reason," with the
title *Science of the Experience of Consciousness*. The title was changed at
such a late date that due to a binding error some copies of the first edition
appeared under this original title.[6] The term *Bewußtsein*, generally translated as 'consciousness', denotes what is certainly the central concept of
both transcendental and speculative idealism, and indeed modern philosophy as such. A compound of the adjective *bewußt*, 'known', 'aware', from the
verb *wissen*, and of *sein*, 'to be', or *Sein*, 'being', it appeared originally as
bewußtsein, a translation of *conscium sibi esse* in the late sixteenth century.
The noun *Bewußtsein* with the sense 'consciousness', however, only
appears in the eighteenth century as Wolff's translation of Descartes' *conscientia*. It is the name for the essential relationship of being and knowing that
is articulated in Descartes' *cogito ergo sum*, not as the *res cogitans* of the *res
extensa* but that in which both subsist and out of which both arise. Consciousness thus cannot be simply identified with the subject but is rather the
twofold of subject and object, i.e., that in which spirit and nature appear to
and for one another.

In his *Science of the Experience of Consciousness*, Hegel considers
consciousness primarily as individual consciousness, which, to be sure,
participates in the general but which is and remains the consciousness of an
I, i.e., the relationship of being and knowing in and through the I. The
experience of consciousness is, on one hand, the actual historical develop-

ment of the individual I as the process of its coming to know itself and, on the other hand, the development of the twofold of being and knowing, i.e., of the various forms of historical consciousness and hence of the world and knowledge as they appear in and through consciousness. The science of the experience of consciousness is thus not itself beyond consciousness, i.e., not a meta-language or theory, but the completed knowledge, the fully developed relationship of being and knowing, which knows itself in and as consciousness.

At some point in the composition of this work Hegel apparently decided to expand the work into its present form and retitled it *Science of the Phenomenology of Spirit*. Whatever Hegel's ultimate reasons for this expansion of the work, it is clear that an account of the development of natural or individual consciousness to self-consciousness and completed reason, i.e., to the knowledge of self-identity and the identity of self and nature, was in Hegel's view insufficient as the first part of his *System of Science*. This point is fairly clear in the text itself.

Consciousness, as Hegel presents it, discovers at the culmination of its individual development that it is a moment of spirit (*Geist*), i.e., that it is not isolated in the individuality of its own self-reflection but is fundamentally united with the community. Individual consciousness comes to the realization that its being is not accidentally but essentially and necessarily social, that its very individuality is only in and as a particular moment of the political. The experience of consciousness is not complete in its experience of its own individual self and its relationship to nature. Hence, "the individual must also pass through the content of the phases of development of general spirit."[7] Consciousness recognizes that its own experience and knowledge of itself can only be completed in and through an examination of its own general social and political existence. The execution of the original intention thus seems to necessitate a transformation of the project itself. Only when the social and political development of general consciousness or spirit is comprehended can the task of the self-realization and self-reconciliation of consciousness, of the twofold of spirit and nature, be completed. This reconciliation of consciousness with itself in all its forms is the task and goal of the *Science of the Phenomenology of Spirit*.

The term 'phenomenology' is a modern construction combining 'phenomenon' and 'logos'. Grammatically a participle, 'phenomenon' derives from the Greek *phainō*, 'bring to light', 'appear', 'shine'. As a participle its meaning is twofold: (1) the appearance (*Erscheinung*) as mere appearance of illusion (*Schein*), i.e., that which seems to be but is in reality not, and (2) the appearing (*das Erscheinen*) as the coming to be or shining forth (*das Scheinen*) of what truly is. For Kant phenomena (*Erscheinungen*) are not mere illusions (*Scheine*), for there is always an object represented; nor are they, however, real things-in-themselves, for "outside of our thoughts [they have] no existence which is grounded in itself."[8] For transcendental idealism that which appears, the phenomenal, is utterly separate from the noumenal thing-in-itself. It is precisely this dualism, however, that Hegel seeks to overcome. The key to the transformation of transcendental into speculative idealism thus lies in the combination or reconciliation of the phenomenal and the noumenal in the concept of *phenomenology*. Phenomenology for Hegel's predecessors (Lambert, Kant, Fichte) is the science that distinguishes between appearances and illusion, the science that attempts to determine what is a true representaton of the real within consciousness and what is merely imagined by consciousness. Phenomenology for Hegel, as we shall see, is the *appearing* of the truly real as the shining forth of the logical or noumenal in the phenomenal or empirical as the phenomenological. Phenomenology thus does not separate appearance and reality but reconciles or synthesizes them and thus brings to light the ground and unity of their twofold. The doctrine of transcendental idealism, that there is only knowledge of appearances, is thus subsumed in and transformed by the recognition of the concrete rational reality of the appearances as the appearing of what is. What is for Hegel, however, is spirit, and phenomenology is thus always the phenomenology of spirit.

The concept of spirit (*Geist*) plays a decisive role in Hegel's thought, and his usage encompasses its various connotations from its original Greek and Latin sense of breath, wind, and soul (*pneuma, spiritus*) through the Christian conception of the Holy Spirit (*hagios pneuma*) to the modern sense of spirit as a thing that thinks (Descartes), the universal soul or genius of a nation (Montesquieu), and the general character of humanity (Condorcet). In his early work the word is little used, and its place and function are generally filled by what Hegel calls 'life'. It was perhaps his intercourse with Schelling that led to his adoption of the term. In his work before 1797 Schelling had already characterized spirit as a preliminary form of the absolute:

> . . . all the activities of spirit are thus aimed at presenting the infinite in the finite. The goal of these activities is self-consciousness, and the history of these activities is nothing other than the history of self-consciousness . . .
>
> The history of the human spirit will thus be nothing other than the history of the various circumstances, through which it [spirit] gradually comes to the intuition of itself, attains pure self-consciousness . . . The external world lays open before us, in order that we may find in it the history of one spirit. We will thus not come to rest in philosophy until we have accompanied spirit to the goal of all its striving, to self-consciousness.[9]

Spirit is thus fundamentally universal or absolute consciousness for both Schelling and Hegel. However, in contradistinction to Schelling, who understood this reconciliation as the discovery of the absolute self in nature—and indeed after 1797 replaced 'spirit' with 'nature'—Hegel understands spirit as the process of reconciliation of the individual and the community, of the natural and the conventional, and of the human and the divine. Spirit thus constitutes the concrete history of man, his institutions, and his world, and at the same time the ground and unity of each age and of the historical process itself. In its fully articulated form as the absolute it thereby embodies that which Hegel hitherto sought as the ethical community of the polis and the love that binds man to man. Consequently, it replaces consciousness as the name for the fundamentally real but retains the character of consciousness as the relationship of being and knowing. The phenomenology of spirit is thus the development of spirit to the realization of itself as absolute, i.e., as the reconciliation and ground of the psychological, social, political, and historical.

Spirit for Hegel is *what is*.[10] What is, however, is *as* it appears—it is phenomenological. Phenomenology names the way of the appearing of what is, of the various moments of spirit (consciousness, self-consciousness, reason, spirit, religion, and absolute knowledge), and is thus the determination of their relationship to one another. The *Science of the Phenomenology of Spirit* is the account of the way in which spirit comes to be and to know itself in and as the unity of these various forms. The original title and intention are thus subsumed within the *Phenomenology*. The experience of consciousness is completed in and as the phenomenology of spirit. The phenomenology of spirit, however, is always the experience of consciousness.[11] Both titles thus give us two separate and important insights into the project that Hegel undertakes in the *Phenomenology*, although these remain only insights and indeed raise more questions than they answer. To answer these questions definitively would require a thorough analysis of the *Phenomenology*. Such an analysis has eluded all the efforts of scholarship and philosophy and shall not be undertaken here. Instead we shall attempt to shed some light on specific aspects of this project through an analysis of what is perhaps the most important section of the work, the "Introduction."

The "Introduction"

The "Introduction" is the true beginning of the *Phenomenology*. The "Preface" which precedes the "Introduction" in all editions is often assumed to be the preface to the work itself, but it was written after the *Phenomenology* was completed and was almost certainly intended as the preface to the entire *System of Science*.[12] The "Introduction" itself was originally untitled, and the title appeared in the first edition only in the table of contents, apparently at the prompting of the publisher. In fact, Hegel maintains on many occasions that there can be no introduction or propaedeutic to his system. Science or absolute knowledge is complete and total; consequently there can be no knowledge outside of it. Any introduction that was not already the beginning of science, therefore, would assume knowledge exterior or superior to this absolute totality. Such an introduction would refute the claim to completeness of the system itself and is consequently impossible. Thus the "Introduction" to the *Phenomenology* is not something separate from the work itself but its true and necessary beginning.

This does not mean, however, that the "Introduction" is like the other sections of the *Phenomenology*. The beginning is always unique. It rises up out of what is and constitutes itself as other. It necessarily establishes that of which it is the beginning as different from that out of which it arises. It is not, however, a mere demarcation or limit but indeed the entirety of what is to be. The beginning is always the unarticulated whole, the acorn that contains the oak. The beginning of the *Phenomenology* is no exception. It is the seed out of which springs the body of the *Phenomenology*, which distinguishes the *Phenomenology* from that which precedes it and constitutes it as it is. This does not mean that it is likewise the historical beginning—indeed it arises for consciousness only at the last; rather it is precisely because it is last that it is always first. It is the final realization in Hegel's view of the true character of what is—not, however, as the fully worked out system of the *Phenomenology of Spirit* but as its fundamental idea. Hegel's project in the *Phenomenology* can thus perhaps be best ascertained by an examination of the "Introduction."

The "Introduction" consists of seventeen paragraphs which seem to form two symmetrical sections of eight paragraphs each and a concluding section of one paragraph. The first major section (paragraphs 1–8) is an account of *natural* consciousness or *being*-that-knows as the development of consciousness from knowledge to science. It is thus an account of the manner and *necessity* of this development. The second major section is an account of *self*-consciousness, i.e., the noumenal aspect of consciousness or *self*-knowing-being as the development of consciousness itself to complete and therefore absolute knowledge. It is thus an account of the method which consciousness employs in its own movement and hence of the *freedom* of self-moving and, therefore, self-causing consciousness. The final section (paragraph 17) indicates the reconciliation or synthesis of these two moments, of the natural and the spiritual, of phenomenal necessity and noumenal freedom.

The two major sections each consist of four parts of two paragraphs each with a one-to-one correspondence of both parts and paragraphs between the two sections. The "Introduction" might thus be schematized as follows:[13]

I. The development of natural consciousness (¶ 1–8)
    A. The critique of modern philosophy as theory of knowing
      (¶ 1–2)

Paragraph 1. The *Phenomenology* begins with a rejection of the conclusion of transcendental idealism that absolute knowledge or science is impossible and that man must thus be content to dwell on one hand in the empirical or phenomenal realm of positive but limited knowledge and on the other in a noumenal realm of faith closed to positive knowledge. In this respect, however, transcendental idealism is typical of modern philosophy as a whole, which in Hegel's view is merely a theory of knowing or cognition (*Erkenntnistheorie*) that is less interested in truth than certainty and that therefore turns to an examination of knowing rather than to an investigation of the world. It thus conceives of knowing or cognition only as a tool or medium through which we have contact with reality and seeks to determine what we can know through an examination of how we do know. That it discovers an abyss between knowledge and reality is in Hegel's view hardly surprising. Kant believes that this conclusion is inevitable, but for Hegel it is only the result of a fundamental misunderstanding of human knowing as a technology with which man as subject conquers objective nature. If knowledge is indeed power, as Bacon asserted and modernity has come to believe, then the result, according to Hegel, is a necessary alienation of man from nature that ultimately allows no reconciliation and which culminates in the isolation of man in his self-reflective subjectivity.

The *Phenomenology* thus begins with a rejection of the modern conception of epistemology and the conception of ontology and experience that underlies it.[14] This rejection is conjoined to the assertion of a new view of the fundamentally real. The absolute, i.e., the *ens realissimus*, is not lost in a beyond in Hegel's view but is always already "in and for itself by us." This being-present-by, as Heidegger has pointed out, is in Greek *parousia*.[15] The *Phenomenology* thus begins with the assumption that we are already in the parousia of the absolute, within the all-embracing ground, and the task of the work as a whole is thus the demonstration of this parousia, of the possibility and actuality of science, and so of the ground of the twofold of knowing and being, i.e., of consciousness, in the absolute.[16] This ground is therefore not to be found only in a beyond of faith but is always, although often unperceived, already by us in knowing and consequently only needs to be recognized in its truth as the ground. Such a recognition, however, can only arise after our misconceptions and prejudices have been dissolved. The demonstration of the parousia of the absolute undertaken in the *Phenomenology* is thus neither a deduction nor an induction but rather a refutation of all human prejudice or error that strives not to prove that the absolute is but to allow it a place in which it may appear as it already and always is.

Paragraph 2. The failure of modern philosophy to discover this ground Hegel attributes to its *presupposition* that the absolute can only exist in a beyond of faith eternally closed to positive knowledge. It supposes that knowledge at best can only produce an image of what truly is and consequently that the real never exists in the immediacy of parousia but always only in the mediacy of representation. The failure of modern philosophy in Hegel's view is thus not that it is too critical but that it is not self-critical enough. Modern philosophy claims to fear error but in fact is in his view motivated by fear of the truth.

Paragraph 3. Modern philosophy in Hegel's view would thus rather plunge man into a perpetual ignorance of the real than admit what is undeniable, i.e., that "the absolute alone is true and the true alone is absolute."[17] Modern philosophy and Kant in particular want to maintain that, in spite of man's inability to grasp the absolute, there is still a truthful knowledge of appearances. For Hegel this is an equivocation: there can be no truth of mere appearances, of the phenomenal or empirical, unless the absolute is present in and as the phenomena. All other knowledge, even the limited knowledge of natural or social science, is thus only relative or apparent knowledge.

Hegel's critique of modern philosophy here is fundamentally a critique of the Enlightenment. The Enlightenment in his view fought a necessary and successful battle against the superstition of religion. Its separation of faith and knowledge was crucial to the establishment of the modern conception of truth, which in turn served as the basis for natural and social science as well as secular humanism and liberalism. However, it paid a high price for its victory, for it found itself obliged to construct a "science" of the merely phenomenal that explicitly denied any ground in the ultimately real. The triumph of the Enlightenment over religion, over the "Kingdom of Darkness," was thus achieved only by admitting a new darkness, a perhaps even more dangerous darkness, which obscured the highest and most important things.

The assertion of the real, of the parousia of the absolute, is Hegel's response to this darkness. The identification of the true and the absolute provides the link between the real ground and the phenomena and thus provides the ground for his refutation of modern philosophy and transcendental idealism. The absolute is the true, i.e., the most fundamental reality, but the true is also the absolute, i.e., in the truth about everyday things the absolute is always already by us. In this sense Hegel seeks to overcome the distinction of the divine and the natural, of the noumenal and the phenomenal, to which the Enlightenment gave rise. He argues that there can be no reconciliation of these two realms and consequently no real natural or social science except on the basis of the recognition of this parousia.[18]

Why then does modern philosophy fear the truth that provides the basis for such a reconciliation? One might assume that this fear is the result of the real or perceived danger that religion and religious zeal or fanaticism pose to social and political peace. Hegel, however, discounts such an interpretation. The real danger to man lies not in the fanaticism of religion but in the fanaticism of revolutionary freedom and the tyranny of nature in bourgeois society. Modern philosophy fears the truth in Hegel's view not because the truth is dangerous but because the truth upsets the world of its satisfaction, i.e., the realm of subjectivism that finds everywhere and always only what it wants to find, the world in which all standards are established by the individual himself, the world governed by unfettered natural desire or the emptiness of the categorical imperative and public opinion. Modern philosophy fears the truth in Hegel's view because the truth means absolute knowledge and hence absolute standards that cannot be overturned by the caprice of passions and opinions. Modern philosophy is thus perhaps distraught by the lack of a real ground, but it fears an absolute science more than the abyss of diremption and alienation. Modern philosophy thus remains fundamentally subjectivistic and relativistic.

Paragraph 4. Hegel admits, however, that the claim to truth of absolute knowledge or science at first appears no greater than that of any other system of knowledge. The difficulty in demonstrating its superiority lies in the relativistic criterion of truth modern philosophy has promulgated. Modern philosophy asserts that the truth of a theory or system of knowledge can only be established by an appeal to being, which shows that the theory is the true image or representation of reality. The trouble with this correspondence or verification theory of truth, however, is that it is ultimately being itself that is in question. Hence, such a theory can provide no more than a mere assurance of truth. Being thus cannot serve as a standard: one assurance is as valid as another, and so truth has no standard outside of the theory itself.

Modern philosophy in Hegel's view consequently ends in relativism. If man has no knowledge of what truly is, as transcendental idealism concludes, then truth is always only a comparison of thought with that which thought produces, of the logical with the phenomenal moment of consciousness. Truth of this sort cannot transcend the bounds of an essentially capricious human imagination and hence ends in relativism. If there is only the duality of the phenomenal or empirical and the noumenal or logical, there can be no ultimate determination of what is true and thus no way to justify one system of knowledge vis-à-vis another. Hegel's solution to this problem is phenomenology.

Phenomenology, or what Hegel characterizes in the "Introduction" as the "presentation of appearing knowledge," is the criterion of truth that he raises up as an answer to modern philosophy's conception of truth as verification. The word 'appearing' (*erscheinenden*) is already used interchangeably by Kant with 'phenomenon'. What is presented (*dargestellt*) has already been collected or recollected. 'To gather or collect' in Greek is *legein*, from which 'logos' derives. The "presentation of appearing knowledge" is thus the phenomenology of knowlege, i.e., the collection as the re-collection and re-presentation of all the various forms or systems of knowledge.[19] Phenomenology is thus the criterion by which truth can be determined as the account of the progress of all merely apparent or relative knowledge to absolute knowledge. It is the demonstration of the insufficiency of every other form of knowledge and the demonstration that only in absolute knowledge and science is the truth that they all seek attained. Phenomenology is thus also the appearing of the absolute that establishes itself in its parousia through the recollection and presentation of its own genesis in and through the various forms of relative knowledge or natural consciousness. The *Phenomenology* thus presupposes the absolute in a manner reminiscent of Schelling but does not in his Spinozistic manner merely assume or assert it. Rather, as the "presentation of appearing knowledge," it is a deepening of Kantian or Fichtean subjectivism that demonstrates the link that binds all forms of consciousness and apparent knowledge to science and the absolute. Thus it does not seek merely the infinite but rather attempts to demonstrate the integral and necessary conjunction of the finite and the infinite in all forms of life and thought. Hegel, unlike Schelling, does not seek to demonstrate merely that the absolute *is* but first and foremost that the absolute is *by us*.[20]

Paragraph 5. Hegel thus begins not with the absolute as such but with natural consciousness. Natural consciousness is, on one hand, consciousness of nature or of the phenomenal and, on the other hand, consciousness itself as naturally appears, i.e., as soul.[21] As consciousness of nature it is determined by and thus subservient to the objective structure of the natural or phenomenal world and hence not free. Its end, the truth about the phenomenal, is something other than itself, and it is moved by its desire to attain this end. As the account of the consciousness of the natural or the phenomenal, phenomenology is an absolute epistemology or the epistemology of the absolute in all its manifold phenomenal forms. As an account of soul, phenomenology is fundamentally psychology, the account or logic of the unfolding of the natural capacities or possibilities of soul in and as history. From this perspective the *Phenomenology* appears to be an account of the various historical forms in which man has appeared.

Phenomenology thus seems to be an account of the various forms of human consciousness or knowing, a sort of intellectual history of humanity.[22] In this sense it is reminiscent of Rousseau's account of the development of man in the *Second Discourse* as the transformation of human being, from natural soul in harmony with the natural world into self-consciousness that is alienated from nature, other men, and ultimately even itself. History in this view is thus degeneration and leads man to despair; from the perspective of nature it is only the process of loss and alienation. Phenomenology, understood from the same perspective, thus also seems to be only a negative science, i.e., only the revelation of the insufficiency of all knowledge, the imperfection of all forms of life, of all morality, ethics, and politics, of all art, religion, and philosophy.

This impression arises, according to Hegel, only because the end of phenomenology, i.e., science, has not been grasped. From the perspective of completed knowledge it becomes clear that all the errors and misconceptions of human history are justified as integral and necessary moments of the dialectical development of humanity to perfection. While Hegel thus may adopt the premise and methodology of the *Second Discourse*, he does not accept its conclusions. In his view consciousness has already passed through all of its forms in the pursuit of this final truth, and there remains only the re-collection and re-presentation of them in their truth as the

Science of the Experience of Consciousness or, since soul is essentially spirit and Hegel's psychology essentially sociology, as the *Science of the Phenomenology of Spirit*.

Paragraph 6. This end, however, is not apparent to the historical or natural consciousness that undergoes this experience. Man historically always understands himself in terms of what and how he knows but does not understand that this knowledge is fundamental to his being as consciousness, nor that through this knowledge his being is bound up with the completed and hence perfected knowledge of the absolute. This development thus seems to him to be "the way of doubt or actually the way of despair." Natural consciousness does not know absolutely. However, insofar as it knows at all, it already contains the concept of absolute knowledge as the ideal. For the most part the discrepancy between the actual and the ideal remains concealed, and natural consciousness remains satisfied with certainty. It is certain of what it knows and is. Philosophy, however, which demands truth and not mere certainty, necessarily confronts this discrepancy and recognizes this so-called knowledge as mere prejudice and opinion. This recognition of the discrepancy between knowledge and science, according to Hegel, is doubt (*Zweifel*). *Zweifel* originally meant 'twofold sense'. Consciousness doubts in Hegel's view because it is always both in itself and beyond itself, sunken, on one hand, in its own knowledge and, on the other, already a moment of science. Doubt thus arises because consciousness is always already aware of what it has not yet attained, because consciousness is fundamentally dirempt (*entzweit*). This doubt or skepticism is not a mere Cartesian suspicion or mistrust of traditional authorities which accepts the judgment of common sense but the conscious insight into the insufficiency of *all* appearing knowledge, the despair (*Verzweiflung*) of the soul that knows it does not know. Phenomenology is thus the way of doubt and despair, the history of philosophy that finds its way to wisdom in aporia and antinomy.[23]

Hegel is primarily interested here in distinguishing true skepticism from Cartesian positivism. He had already considered the differences between ancient and modern skepticism in the *Critical Journal of Philosophy* and rejected the latter as unphilosophic. Ancient skepticism, as he indicates in "Self-consciousness," gives rise to the despair of the unhappy consciousness, to an unconquerable sense of sadness and loss. Nor is this unhappiness merely a psychological disturbance. The doubt and despair that skepticism suffers arises in consequence of concrete human experience, as a result of the loss of everything of value. Doubt and despair are in this sense the driving force of natural consciousness that propels it to science. They are the natural response to the loss of unity in life that gives rise to the need of philosophy and that leads to a new reconciliation.

Phenomenology is thus the painful education (*Bildung*) of natural consciousness to science. To natural consciousness, however, this end seems to be only an ideal, a beyond that can never be attained. It recognizes its immediate progress when it overcomes one form of alienation and despair, but it does not understand this development as a whole, i.e., as the way of soul to complete self-knowledge. It is, however, precisely because consciousness does *not* grasp this truth that "the series of forms which consciousness passes through is the history of the *education* of consciousness itself to science."[24] If this truth were already present at the beginning, there would be no alienation of consciousness and hence no need to overcome alienation. The pain that this alienation engenders and that consciousness overcomes is thus the immediate source of historical motion that propels consciousness toward reconciliation. The *Via Dolorosa* of doubt and despair is thus also the education of humanity as the process of reconciliation of spirit and nature, of the noumenal and phenomenal in and as the parousia of the absolute.

In this sense the *Phenomenology* is a vehicle not merely for the education of those already predisposed toward speculative science but for those who dwell in the blindness of partial or apparent knowledge. It is an account of the journey of the soul, like that described in the allegory of the cave in Plato's *Republic*, out of mere opinion into the sunlight of true knowledge. This way, to be sure, is not the pure vision of the eternal forms, i.e., not science itself, but the gradual recognition by natural consciousness of the limitations of its own particular self, of its own prejudices, and the consequent recognition of its essential unity in and with spirit as a moment of the community and the absolute.[25]

This way for Hegel is the way of aporia and dialectic, the path on which natural consciousness is continually confronted with the contradictions implicit in its prejudices and opinions and thus forced to abandon what it holds dear, its customs, its community, and its gods. However painful, this way is justified as the way to truth. The aim of the *Phenomenology* in this sense is both descriptive and pedagogical, an account of the way to wisdom which consciousness has both followed and can follow, which indeed the individual must follow to free himself of his natural prejudices and raise his thought from the capricious ratiocinations of individuality to the true rationality of the general movement of spirit. The *Phenomenology* is the re-collection and re-presentation of this way.

True knowledge for Hegel, as for Plato, thus arises in and through the re-collection (*anamnēsis*) of what is always and therefore already present. This recollection, however, depends upon experience which evokes the memory of what is already implicitly known. Thus, while science is eternal—"the presentation of God, as he is in his eternal essence before the creation of nature and a finite spirit"—it can only be known in and as it is recollected.[6] Science thus presupposes history as both the dialectical journey of the soul and as the collection of the concrete forms of human consciousness through which it passes. Science is not history, but history is a necessary presupposition of science, and the truth itself thus can only fully *be* insofar as history is not, i.e., insofar as history has come to its conclusion. If consciousness has not passed through all its possible forms, it cannot recollect them in their totality and thus cannot know absolutely.[27]

Paragraph 7. The question of course arises how a process of dissolution can be complete and sufficiently grounded or determined. At least natural consciousness sees this dissolution of its truth and world not as a rational historical development but as the presencing of nothing, the utter and continual annihilation of everything. For natural consciousness all change seems to be degeneration. According to Hegel, such skepticism or what is perhaps better called nihilism is lost in the negativity of the present, in the moment of its own loss, and objectifies its particular pain as universal and utter negation. Properly understood, however, this nothing that skepticism experiences is only the nothingness of that which passes away, and change is not the result of utter but of determinate negation, negation that is a bridge to and the source of a new form. Thus, while natural consciousness may despair of finding reason in history, this despair arises out of a misconception of the essence of history itself. Understood as a process of determinate negation, the necessity of the sequence of forms and the completeness of the series itself becomes apparent. This concept of determinate negation that Hegel introduces here is thus the crucial concept in his transformation of transcendental idealism.

At first glance, however, it would seem that Hegel is simply wrong, that the negation of something is just as likely to be nothing as something else. Even if negation does indeed produce another thing there is apparently no reason why it should be any one thing rather than another. However, as Hyppolite has pointed out, every historical situation is determinate and as such is always already a negation (*omnis affirmatio est negatio*).[28] Hence, all historical negation is the negation of negation. To negate or destroy a historical form is thus to destroy the negation, i.e., the contradiction or alienation that is present within that form and that characterizes or determines it. The new form that arises out of the negation is thus in Hegel's view the necessary consequence of the determinate character of the preceding historical form. Historical change in this sense is not the result of the application of external force but the consequence of the overcoming or reconciliation of internal contradiction. As noted in the last chapter, it is the *necessity* of the contradiction or negation that is the source of reconciliation, and it is thus this necessity that establishes the unity of the historical process itself. History is not the process of coming to be and passing away. In history, as Hegel understands it, nothing is ever lost, each moment or form of consciousness is preserved and gathered up into the wholeness of the absolute. Hence, "the *completeness* of the forms of unreal consciousness will follow from the necessity of the progression and its continuity." Hegel's solution to the antinomy thus forms the basis of his conception of determinate negation and hence of the necessity and completion of history itself. This necessity and completion, however, is nothing other than the phenomenological ground.

Paragraph 8. The end or goal of this process is as securely established in Hegel's view as the order of progression, since it must end when all contradiction is overcome and the subject and object reconciled in the parousia of the absolute. The end of the development of consciousness is implicit in consciousness itself. As determinate, consciousness is contradictory—it is subject *and* object. It is, however, also the negation of this contradiction, and thereby reconciles itself with itself. Consciousness has this dual character in Hegel's view because in contradistinction to the merely natural, consciousness is its own concept, i.e., it is *self-consciousness.* It thus always already transcends itself and contains and indeed is its own beyond. It is both in itself and outside or above itself. In this way it both alienates itself from itself and reconciles itself with itself.

Consciousness thus rises above nature and frees itself from nature's laws. What is merely alive, merely natural, can only be unified or reconciled with its opposite, i.e., with the whole from which it is sundered in its individuality, through death, for only death destroys the natural individuality of living things. Consciousness in Hegel's view, however, carries with it its own death, since it destroys its own separateness and reunifies itself with itself in and through this "death."[29]

It is this characteristic of consciousness to be always beyond itself that expels it from the world of its satisfaction and propels it toward a new reconciliation and unification with itself. This pursuit of reconciliation, according to Hegel, may thus appear to natural consciousness as the loss of its world, of its home, customs, government, and gods, and natural consciousness may attempt to preserve this world. Such resistance or what Marx was later to characterize as reaction, however, is in fact the fear of truth. The truth in this case is a sort of violence that consciousness exercises on itself, and consciousness naturally tries to avoid this violence and conserve its traditional world. Natural consciousness does not recognize the necessary development of knowledge and hence of consciousness itself toward the absolute. Progress seems to it to be only the cry of those who want to upset the natural scheme of things. Natural consciousness is thus fundamentally conservative and strives to maintain the world that is for it not as a transient moment of historical development but its permanent home. Consciousness, however, is unable to prevent this transformation— not because it is too weak but because it is too strong, because the enemy, the agent of change that consciousness struggles against, is its own true self.

As consciousness, self-consciousness is the perception and hence consumption of its natural object.[30] Self-*consciousness* is thus desire, but the satisfaction of desire depends not upon consciousness but upon the object. As *self*-consciousness, on the contrary, it is conscious and hence desirous only of itself. It is thus liberated from the tyranny of natural desire, from the natural object independent of itself. The freedom that arises from this reconciliation with itself, however, is purchased at the price of its former happiness, which depended upon the natural object, and hence evokes resistance and reaction. Consciousness, however, is essentially self-consciousness and thus overcomes this resistance, for the dissatisfaction of consciousness arises not merely as a result of the loss of external necessities but because these objects no longer fulfill the needs and desires of consciousness itself.

Summary: Paragraphs 1–8. The first section of the "Introduction" is an account of the development of natural consciousness as phenomenology. The section began with a consideration of modern philosophy's denial of the possibility of science. This denial was shown to rest upon the unquestioned assumption of the absolute separation of subject and object, of the phenomenal or empirical and the noumenal or logical. In the third and fourth paragraphs, Hegel argued that modern philosophy's subsequent notion of knowing as a tool makes truth impossible and ultimately leads to relativism. To this relativism of modern philosophy Hegel juxtaposed phenomenology, the presentation of appearing knowledge, which in the fifth and sixth paragraphs was portrayed as the necessary development of natural consciousness or soul. Finally, in the seventh and eighth paragraphs, Hegel presented a refutation of utter skepticism or nihilism and natural conservatism, which call into question the rationality of the historical development phenomenology describes.

This section of the "Introduction" is thus an account of the relationship of knowledge to its object as other. This is the essential characteristic of natural consciousness: it does not comprehend itself as its own object but instead understands its object as an external other. Hegel opposes the doctrine of natural consciousness and modern philosophy that knowing is fundamentally separate from its object, and argues instead that both subsist within and arise out of the parousia of the absolute. His proof is phenomenology, the conceptualized history of consciousness or spirit as the rational development of knowledge to science and hence as the mediation between all forms of natural consciousness and the absolute.[31]

This account, however, is insufficient. Consciousness is not merely natural consciousness but also self-consciousness; it is not merely the knowledge of the phenomenal or empirical but also of the logical or noumenal. The first section of the "Introduction" is an account of the knowledge and truth of modern philosophy and the knowledge and truth of phenomenology from the perspective of nature. The second section is a consideration of the same subjects from the perspective of self-consciousness and spirit.

Paragraph 9. The second section of the "Introduction" parallels the first. Whereas in the foregoing section Hegel considered the manner and necessity of the development of consciousness, he concerns himself in the second section with the "method of execution." This method of execution is not, as is often mistakenly assumed, the method of Hegel's inquiry but rather the method of consciousness itself in carrying out its development. The first section of the "Introduction" described this development, the second section is an account of its inner mechanism.

'Method', which derives from the Greek *meta*, 'with' or 'after', and *hodos*, 'way' or 'path', literally means 'with or after the way'. The way, as we saw in the first section, is phenomenology as the presentation of appearing knowledge, as the way of consciousness from knowledge to science. The method of phenomenology thus lies in consciousness itself as the way in which free and self-moving consciousness develops itself.[32] The way of consciousness, as Hegel argued in the first section, seems to be determined by nature. Grasped from within, this way appears not as a series of natural forms but as the *experience* of consciousness. Experience, however, is to be understood not as that which consciousness undergoes but as the way in which consciousness itself is, as its inner essence and truth that determines the course of its development. While history in one sense is thus only a great temporal stream in which individual human beings are caught up and hurled to and fro by contrary currents only to be shattered on the rock of death, it is in another sense the *free* movement of consciousness itself, of consciousness directing its own course, continually transcending and continually reconciling itself with itself.

This second section begins like the first with a discussion of modern philosophy's conception of knowing. Hegel previously argued that modern philosophy conceives of knowing as a tool (¶ 1); he here explains the way in which this tool is supposed to function. The tool of modern philosophy, according to Hegel, is the *standard* (*Maßstab*) with which it measures reality. Modern philosophy, which conceives of knowing as technology, understands the method of this technology as measurement or calculation. From the perspective of modern philosophy it thus seems that science cannot test the reality of knowing without first establishing a standard of its own.

This demand for an independent or self-subsistent standard poses a real difficulty for speculative science. Unlike modern philosophy that accepts the *cogito* or the *percipio* as the standard against which all knowledge must be measured, science, as Hegel understands it, attempts to transcend such a subjective or objective standard and to establish an absolute standard. Such a standard, however, can apparently only arise as the result of a standardless wandering through error, i.e., only at the end of the phenomenological development of consciousness. Thus, it seems that science must presuppose what it wants to prove in order to accomplish anything at all and hence can be nothing more than a labyrinthine tautology. Hegel discovers the solution to this dilemma in the structure of consciousness itself.

Paragraph 10. The demand modern philosophy makes for an objective standard is in Hegel's view the necessary consequence of its misunderstanding of consciousness and knowing. Just as it assumes that knowing is a tool or medium which stands between man and reality or the absolute (¶ 2), modern philosophy conceives of what is known as mere being-for-consciousness, which it distinguishes from what it takes to be truly real, i.e., being-in-itself. It thus seems to modern philosophy that we can have at best only a truthful knowledge of representations, as Kant argues, and must eschew any claim to speculative knowledge, since that would presuppose access to the unattainable being-in-itself. This apparent disjunction dissolves in Hegel's view when consciousness is properly understood.

Consciousness, according to Hegel, is what is. There neither is nor can be anything that is not consciousness. This is not, however, the empirical consciousness of a subject confronting an alien, external object. Rather, consciousness is the twofold of knowing and being. Consciousness (*Bewußtsein*) in Hegel's view distinguishes something from itself or projects itself outside itself as being (*Sein*) and then relates itself to its projected or objectified self through its knowledge (*Wissen*) of that thing as known (*gewußt*). Being-for-consciousness and being-in-itself are thus, according to Hegel, two moments of consciousness itself. As such, consciousness always contains its own standard, for the twofold of knowing and being it is the *comparison* of knowing and being and hence the measurement of each in terms of the other. Consciousness is thus always its *own* standard.

The *Phenomenology* as the presentation of appearing knowledge is the conceptualized history of humanity as the development of human consciousness through all its forms to science. Each of these forms of consciousness (*Bewußtsein*) in Hegel's view is a particular form of the relationship of knowing and being. According to Hegel, the *Phenomenology* does not measure the truth of these forms according to a preconceived standard but adopts the standard that each form of consciousness recognized and employed itself. It is thus not the objective account of the development of consciousness from the elevated perspective of pure science but the re-collection and re-presentation of the various forms of consciousness, of their truth and their contradictions, as they immediately present themselves to retrospection.

Every historical epoch in Hegel's view has some standard of its own to measure the truthfulness of its own knowledge or the propriety of its own actions. In Nietzsche's terms, each age has its own set of values which, according to Hegel, are determined by the particular relationship of being and knowing in that age, i.e., by the phenomenological or ontological structure of that age. The ontological structure, which provides each age with the standards of truth and propriety, is thus determined by the character or form of consciousness of the age. It is this ontological structure that Hegel attempts to retrieve and re-present. The standard that guides the *Phenomenology* at each stage is thus the standard of that stage itself. That these standards are faulty goes without saying. Indeed, it is indispensable to the fulfillment of Hegel's task that these standards be imperfect and ultimately self-contradictory, for it is precisely this self-contradictory or antinomious character of consciousness that is the source of historical motion and development. Consciousness always tests itself, its knowledge and its customs, and thus the very standards by which this test is carried out. In and through this testing it comes to the recognition of its own contradictions and the necessity for self-overcoming. The *Phenomenology* is thus not merely the account of the ontological structure of each age but also of the defects of these ontologies, of how these defects give rise to new ontologies, and of the dialectical or historical development of ontology as a whole.

Paragraph 11. Hegel's project is thus an investigation of the various historical forms of consciousness and knowledge in their multiplicity and their unity. Is such an investigation, however, possible? It would seem at least to modern philosophy that Hegel could never understand a historical epoch as it understood itself because in understanding it he would transform it, since it would be mediated through his consciousness or in modern terms since it could only be understood from his own point of view. What Hegel recognizes as the ontology and standard of an age could thus never be identical with that standard itself.

Such an objection arises in Hegel's view because modernity misunderstands what is. It conceives man as a subject confronted by an objective and fundamentally alien nature that must be subjugated to subjective categories and the imperative of the human will. The certainty and power that modern man attains in and through modern science and technology is, however, incomplete and ultimately unsatisfactory, because the orderly, calculable world he thus constructs is fundamentally artificial and destroys even the possibility of a natural ground or a reconciliation with nature. Thus what he does not achieve and cannot find is the truth, i.e., what is in itself, which the prerequisites of power and certainty relegate to a beyond of incomprehensibility.

Modern philosophy cannot find the truth because it denies the parousia of the absolute, i.e., that the absolute is by us. As Hegel argued earlier, the absolute alone is true and the true alone is absolute (¶ 3). True knowledge is absolute knowledge and the absolute is present in all truth. Absolute knowledge is not merely completed knowledge but the knowledge the absolute has of itself as all of its incomplete forms. As the perfect self-knowledge of consciousness in and as the absolute, absolute knowledge is not distinct from its object but knows in and through pure introspection. This introspection, however, is also pure retrospection, for in absolute knowledge consciousness recognizes itself as what is, and that means as what was, i.e., as the entirety of the various historical forms of knowledge and consciousness. It is thus possible for man to understand all the various historical epochs and modes of thought by understanding himself.

Absolute knowledge is thus in one sense the completion or perfection of the Socratic self-investigation, of the command: "Know thyself!" Hegel's completion of this imperative, however, is fundamentally conditioned by his reception of Rousseau—to know oneself is to know the separation of man from nature, the essential history of the free development of human being from mere sense-certainty to absolute knowledge and science. Introspection thus becomes retrospection and discovers or perhaps recovers the truth about its own genesis in and as history.

Paragraph 12. Science in Hegel's view thus transcends the distinction of "subjective" and "objective" that characterizes modern philosophy and consequently has no need of the "independent" standard modern philosophy demands, since consciousness always gives itself its own standard and is always a comparison with itself.[33] Hegel argued earlier that modern philosophy's correspondence theory of truth leads to relativism and presented phenomenology, i.e., the presentation of appearing knowledge, as an answer to this problem (¶ 4). This same question arises again here as the question of the standard of truth. What appeared from the perspective of natural consciousness as the presentation of appearing knowledge or phenomenology appears here as the self-examination of consciousness or spirit.

In absolute knowledge consciousness recognizes itself as the unity that embraces all the various forms of consciousness, spirit, and the absolute. This retrospection or historical recollection is thus not merely the "objective" account of the development of the twofold of knowing and being, i.e., of consciousness, as pure introspection. The *Phenomenology* as completed knowledge or science is the contemplation of knowledge not merely as it is *in itself*, i.e., as natural consciousness in all its historical forms, but as it is *in and for itself*, i.e., as the knowledge of these forms from the perspective of the *experience* of consciousness itself as it passes through them.

Paragraph 13. Since consciousness tests itself, any retrospective application of a standard is not only unnecessary but in Hegel's view would distort historical actuality. There thus remains for those who participate in the phenomenological investigation only the pure contemplation of appearing knowledge as the movement of consciousness.[34] The *Phenomenology* in this sense is thus the unity of pure retrospection, which surveys the "objective" development of human knowledge and history (¶ 5), and of pure introspection, which is the "subjective" recollection of this development from the perspective of the consciousness that lived through it. Phenomenology is thus always also the science of the experience of consciousness as introspective retrospection, as the contemplation by consciousness of its own genesis, of consciousness as it is both in and for itself.[35]

The source of this genesis of consciousness is consciousness itself as self-consciousness. In the amount of self-consciousness, consciousness rises above itself and observes the relationship of knowledge and object that has hitherto characterized it. This moment is in Hegel's view the comparison by consciousness of knowledge and its object. If these two do not correspond, then consciousness concludes that either its knowledge or the world is defective or false and must be transformed. Since both are bound together, however, the transformation of one is likewise the transformation of the other and consequently of the standard itself, i.e., the reality, which was used to test the truth of knowledge. By rising above itself consciousness (*Bewußtsein*) thus transforms both the knowledge (*Wissen*) and being (*Sein*), which were hitherto its essence. Insofar as consciousness is self-consciousness it is thus dialectical.

For Kant consciousness is thetic and sets or establishes laws. It determines what is true within knowledge and thus what is true *for* consciousness. It cannot, however, go beyond consciousness to the infinite or absolute without becoming entwined in antinomy. Kant thus concludes that positive knowledge is only possible within the phenomenal or empirical realm and can never grasp the noumenal or logical. Both of these realms, however, are manifestations of consciousness qua reason and are thus bound together in and as the transcendental unity of apperception. As we have seen, Hegel was not satisfied with this solution and attempted to demonstrate the reconciliation implicit in the antinomy itself as the necessity of the contradiction. This necessity in Hegel's view resides in consciousness itself: as the twofold of natural consciousness and self-consciousness, of truth and knowledge, of the phenomenal or empirical and the noumenal or logical, consciousness itself is dialectical. Consciousness thus is both the source of division or opposition and the movement toward and ground of reconciliation.

In this sense Hegel's conception of dialectical consciousness is his answer to the emptiness of the transcendental unity of apperception. It has often been remarked that speculative idealism might be described as an extended meditation upon this transcendental unity. It must be noted, however, that speculative idealism transforms this placid eternity into the ceaseless struggle and strife of a fundamentally thetic and that means dialectical spirit. Kant's eternity of rest becomes in the hands of Fichte, Schelling, and Hegel the eternal struggle of what is with itself.

The *Phenomenology* is the account of this thetic or dialectical motion as the continual interaction or altercation of the phenomenal or empirical and the noumenal or logical moments of consciousness. Consciousness or spirit as thetic, antithetic, antinomious, and dialectical is the source of the motion of history, and history is thus the self-movement of consciousness. Moreover, as self-reflective and synthetic, consciousness is the ground and unity of this motion, for this motion in Hegel's view is simply the movement of consciousness to self-consciousness and the recognition in science by consciousness that it is itself the ground of the reconciliation of the phenomenal or empirical and the noumenal or logical as the phenomenological ground of history.

Paragraph 14. This dialectical movement of self-consciousness is *experience.* Experience is thus the name for the fundamental motion of and within consciousness itself. In the moment of consciousness the object is in itself, i.e., in but not for consciousness; in the moment of self-consciousness the object is merely in itself *for* consciousness and hence no longer independent and self-subsistent. The original object and consequently the diremption of subject and object is thus negated in the moment of self-consciousness. The negation of this original object, of its independence, is, however, also the negation of self-consciousness itself, since consciousness no longer has a consciousness *and* an object in front of it but only a consciousness. This consciousness thus becomes its new object and self-consciousness becomes the mere consciousness of this new object. The synthesis of self-consciousness, which overcomes or reconciles the phenomenal and logical moments, thus dissolves, and consciousness thereby divides or alienates itself from itself. The reconciliation of consciousness and its object in self-consciousness is thus necessarily followed by the alienation or externalization of its own self, i.e., the self of self-consciousness, as the new object. In finding itself in the object and the object in itself consciousness loses itself. Every reconciliation thus engenders a new opposition.[36]

History from the perspective of self-consciousness is in Hegel's view this dialectical experience. The unity of each historical epoch arises through the reconciliation of antecedent contradictions and manifests itself as a naive, unself-conscious faith in this synthesis. When, however, the contradictions that have been overcome are forgotten, consciousness turns to an examination of its own naive faith in itself. This act of self-examination, however, is the division of this form of consciousness against itself and thus the source of the contradictions that this self-examination discovers. The harmony of the epoch dissolves into the strife of contradiction. Nor can this age regain its original faith in its own rectitude and truth, for it has recognized the contradiction that is at the heart of its own character. Conservatism in Hegel's view is thus futile, first because it seeks to conserve what has already passed away, and second because its very effort at conservation is entwined in the same consciousness that recognizes what is to be conserved as other, as an object opposed to consciousness. The way to reconciliation thus seems to lie only in the future, in the abandonment of the old ways in favor of the new.

Consciousness in this sense is fundamentally Faustian, continually seeking, continually finding, and continually losing the satisfaction that arises out of the reconciliation with its object. Consciousness is thus also fundamentally tragic. Hegel earlier described the way of consciousness as the way of doubt and despair (¶ 6). The source of both is located here in consciousness, which is itself doubt (*Zweifel*) and hence twofold. Consciousness continually strives to reconcile this diremption but is continually unable to achieve a lasting reconciliation because the activity that engenders reconciliation is also the source of alienation. Consciousness thus comes to despair.

It is this futility of all human striving that Hegel seeks to redeem through the re-collection and re-presentation of human history by demonstrating humanity's apotheosis in the parousia of the absolute at and as the end of the historical *Via Dolorosa* of doubt and despair.[37] The experience of consciousness is despair, but that despair has as its issue the perfection of humanity and the complete reconciliation of spirit and nature in science. Consciousness is thus itself the source of historical motion and determinate negation. This negation is always a self-negation, a negation of negation as the motion from consciousness to self-consciousness. Such a negating thus can only be completed when all diremption and alienation have been overcome. It may appear in the moment of dissolution that this negation is the appearance of the nihilistic essence of existence, but such a view fails to recognize the higher unity that this dissolution produces, in part because this new unity is not yet clearly articulated, in part because it is incomprehensible for the previous form of consciousness, and in part because it involves the destruction of the customary objects that brought satisfaction to natural consciousness. Dissatisfaction and restlessness are thus intrinsic to consciousness, since it is separated from its object throughout its development. It is in fact only in pure introspective retrospection, i.e., in absolute knowledge, that consciousness recognizes the truth of this experience as the experience it has of itself, as the unfolding and enfolding of the twofold of subject and object, of noumenon and phenomenon in and as phenomenology.

Paragraph 15. Historical consciousness does not recognize its new object as the negation of its previous object and believes, on the contrary, that it simply experiences or discovers a new truth that refutes and supersedes its previous truth. Hence, it does not recognize the necessity in the series of objects that arise out of negation. This underlying identity, however, is not merely the capricious addition of retrospective reason, according to Hegel, but the consequence of a "*turning around of consciousness itself,*" of the alienation or externalization of the self of self-consciousness as object and the return of self-consciousness to consciousness.

The recognition and delineation of historical change as the method of self-moving and therefore self-causing consciousness or spirit thus is available only in absolute knowledge and that means only to a skeptical introspective retrospection that has also become speculative and that as science recognizes and establishes the true ground in and as the parousia of the absolute. Hegel earlier argued that the skeptical way of natural consciousness leads to a thorough skepticism or nihilism that grasps change as utter rather than determinate negation (¶ 7). Referring explicitly to his previous discussion, he indicates here the source of that misconception: historical consciousness recognizes only the content, which indeed is utterly transformed, but in contradistinction to science does not recognize the formal continuity and unity of change. This is the active element in an otherwise passive and contemplative science. In its observation of the dialectical movement of consciousness, science refrains from acting and merely observes self-testing, self-transforming consciousness. However, it is science alone that sees this underlying *speculative* unity and ground in the historical development. Its seeing is thus an establishing of this ground and hence its true *activity*.[38]

Science establishes this speculative unity and ground for the dialectical movement of history in and as the twofold of consciousness. The being (*Sein*) of consciousness (*Bewußtsein*) is always as being-known or being-that-knows (*Bewußst-sein*). Knowing is the self-testing of consciousness, i.e., skeptical introspection. This skeptical introspection, which previously appeared as the irreconcilable dialectic of consciousness and world, appears here as the continual reconciliation of consciousness with itself. The new object that arises out of the dialectical process contains the previous object as its necessary presupposition. It *is* that object as it was in itself for consciousness in the moment of self-consciousness. The dialectical process thus is the self-gathering or self-collecting of consciousness or spirit as the reconciliation of the phenomenal or empirical and the noumenal or logical. This self-gathering is thus the establishment of the phenomenological ground of history. The truth of this development, however, is only visible when this self-collecting has been completed, i.e., when skeptical introspection becomes speculative retrospection, and thus the re-collection and re-presentation of history as the manifestation of this ground, as the necessary development of consciousness to science.

Paragraph 16. History in this sense is the necessary way to science as the self-movement of consciousness or spirit. Moreover, through this necessity, according to Hegel, this way to science is already science as the science of the experience of consciousness. From the perspective of natural consciousness, phenomenology as the way of appearing knowledge is not yet "the free science which moves itself in its peculiar forms" (¶ 5). Viewed from the perspective of self-consciousness, however, consciousness appears as free and self-moving and therefore as science. This is not, however, the pure science (*Wissenschaft*) that has liberated itself from its otherness, i.e., from being (*Sein*), and that thus considers only the logical forms, but is defined in terms of its content, i.e., in terms of its being, as the science of the experience of consciousness (*Bewußst-sein*).

The scientificality of this way of consciousness resides in the necessity that characterizes its free development. This necessity is the necessity

inherent to the contradiction, i.e., the determinate negation that consciousness exercises upon itself. Consciousness as self-consciousness *is* this negation and is thus the source of the necessity of this negation. In action
consciousness negates. Its freedom thus consists in its capacity to negate its
object. This negation, however, is not annihilation but the negation and thus
the reconciliation of the twofold of being and knowing, i.e., of consciousness, with itself. As such it is already a moment of the absolute and hence
already absolute knowledge or science.

Hegel earlier argued that it was futile to resist the dialectical movement
toward science (¶8). Here he indicates the ground of that futility. The way to
science is not merely a natural process that consciousness can more or less
successfully resist but the necessary way of consciousness itself, which in
the freedom of self-determination strives for complete self-knowledge and
reconciliation. History is not merely something external that may or may
not be struggled against but the movement of humanity itself to perfection.
As such it is in Hegel's view necessary and irresistible.

Summary: Paragraphs 9–16. The second section of the "Introduction" is
thus an account of the development of self-consciousness as experience.
The first section was an account of the nature of knowledge, truth, change,
and rationality from the perspective of natural consciousness. First and
foremost, however, it was a refutation of modern philosophy, which
pointed toward the alternative of phenomenology. This second section is a
consideration of knowledge, truth, change, and rationality from the perspective of self-consciousness, and is as a whole the presentation of Hegel's
alternative to the erroneous conceptions of modern philosophy. The two
sections thus represent the two moments of consciousness or spirit that
appear in and as the Third Antinomy and transcendental idealism. They are,
however, also the implicit ground for the reconciliation of this diremption.

Paragraph 17. The end or goal of the *Phenomenology* as a whole cannot
merely consist in the delineation of the phenomenal development of
natural consciousness and the noumenal development of self-consciousness but must necessarily reside in the demonstration of the unity and
ground of both in and as absolute knowledge. This ground, however, can
only arise in Hegel's view as a result of the completion and presentation of
the entire system of the truth of reason and spirit. This is absolute knowledge or science in which natural consciousness finally overcomes the last
vestiges of otherness and in which self-consciousness recognizes itself as its
own all-pervasive object.

Absolute knowledge in this sense is the reconciliation of the phenomenology of spirit and the experience of consciousness. Phenomenology always seems to be concerned only with appearances or phenomena
and the experience of consciousness always only with the essence or
noumenon. The end of both, however, is their reconciliation. The science of
appearances becomes the appearing of science, and the experience of

consciousness becomes the consciousness of experience. Skeptical introspection and speculative retrospection are united in and as the pure seeing
or contemplation of absolute knowledge.

This pure seeing is nothing other than the parousia of the absolute as the
immediate presence of the ground and unity of the twofold of phenomenology or consciousness as science. Phenomenology is always the representation of appearing knowledge. Consciousness (*Bewußtsein*) is the twofold of
knowledge (*Wissen*) and being (*Sein*). Science (*Wissenschaft*) is, on one
hand, the completed form of consciousness (*Bewußtsein*) that has freed
itself from its object, from being (*Sein*) as other and thus recognized itself as
its own self-being. It is, on the other hand, the completing of appearing
knowledge as the recognition of the true and eternal knowledge of the
necessity of appearances. Both phenomenology and consciousness become
science in and as the recognition of the parousia of the absolute. Science is
thus skeptical speculative introspective retrospection and therefore not
merely the recognition of the momentary presence of the absolute but of its
eternal, albeit concealed, presence as the phenomenological ground of
history.[39] Science is absolute knowledge, not merely as perfect or complete
knowledge but as knowledge of the absolute, as knowledge of the ground of
the twofold of the phenomenal or empirical and the noumenal or logical, of
spirit and nature, and therefore of history. It is thus the self-gathering of the
absolute as the re-collection and re-presentation of its own unfolding and
enfolding as the twofold of phenomenology or consciousness.[40] This re-
collection and re-presentation is the *Science of the Phenomenology of Spirit*.

4
The Philosophy of History and the Question of Its Ground

he *Phenomenology*, as we have seen, is the re-collection and re-presentation of history as the parousia of the absolute, as the presencing of the unfolding-enfolding twofold of nature and spirit. This re-presentation is not merely the *historia rerum gestarum* of the *res gestae*, i.e., not merely the recollection and preservation of the apparently accidental events of history, nor is it simply the logical or conceptual organization of the parousia of the absolute as the science of appearing knowledge. The former, which is the concern of the science of history strictly understood, is concerned solely with the phenomenal or empirical realm of practical actuality, i.e., with what actually took place, and thus can attain at best only empirical truth. The latter, which strictly speaking is not history at all but psychology or historical epistemology, is concerned only with the logical realm of theoretical activity, i.e., with the development of knowledge, and thus is capable of only logical truth. The *Phenomenology* is rather "both together, conceptualized history," the conceptualized or phenomenological history of humanity.[1] This does not mean that the *Phenomenology* is merely history and logic but rather the *togetherness*, the speculative synthesis of the phenomenal or empirical and the noumenal or logical as the phenomenological, i.e., as the phenomenological ground of history out of which both the *res gestae* and the *historia rerum gestarum* arise and in which they subsist. The *Phenomenology* thus is Hegel's attempt to establish a ground for history.

The *Phenomenology* is consequently the presupposition of the philosophy of history. Hegel argues in the *Philosophy of History* that there are three types of historical observation: original history, reflective history, and philosophical history. The first is merely the contemporary account or chronology of events, the second the retrospective reflection upon these events, and the third the recognition of the rational order of or in these events. Philosophical history thus is distinguished from the other forms of historical knowledge that are concerned merely with the observation and delimitation of events by the attempt to discern and explicate the rationality, generally conceived to reside only in the eternal truths of logic and mathematics or in the cyclical motion of nature, in the apparently capricious sequence of historical events. "The single thought which philosophy brings with it is the simple thought of reason, that reason rules the world, that therefore world-history also has taken place rationally."[2] This is the presupposition of a philosophy of history that speculative philosophy must justify. Such a justification is necessary because the traditional and natural presupposition is that history in contradistinction to nature is inherently irrational, since it is dependent upon unpredictable and essentially capricious human actions or fortune. The philosophy of history as the account of the rationality of history thus necessarily presupposes the speculative demonstration of the phenomenological ground or rationality of historical events.

The *Phenomenology* proper is the detailed execution of the tripartite program established in the "Introduction," as the development of natural consciousness, spirit, and their reconciliation, religion, to absolute knowledge and unity. The development of natural consciousness is the subject of the first section of the *Phenomenology*, i.e., the chapters "Consciousness," "Self-consciousness," and "Reason." The development of spirit is considered in the chapter "Spirit" and the development of their reconciliation in the chapter "Religion." These three paths of development are considered separately and successively in the *Phenomenology*, but it is clear that Hegel understood them as simultaneous and interdependent moments of a unified whole, for, as becomes evident in Hegel's discussion of absolute knowledge, it is only the whole of which these three are moments that truly develops. Whether the *Phenomenology* successfully coordinates or demonstrates the correspondencies between these three moments is questionable, but that Hegel attempted such a demonstration is relatively obvious. At the beginning of the second section of the work in chapter 6, "Spirit," Hegel argues that all of the preceding forms of consciousness, i.e., sense-certainty, perception, understanding, self-consciousness, and reason, are merely moments of spirit and that they have only been abstracted from it for purposes of examination. At the beginning of the third section of the work in chapter 7, "Religion," Hegel attempts to show that the historical development of religion parallels the development of individual consciousness in the first section of the work. The development of individual consciousness in the first section is thus, despite its character as an abstraction, a historical progression. Indeed, it seems to be an abstraction not of the logical or psychological from the historical and concrete but an abstraction of the historical development of individual consciousness from that of general consciousness or spirit. This then establishes at least in principle the parallel and coordinate development of individual consciousness (chapters 1–5), general consciousness or spirit (chapter 6), and religion (chapter 7). Chapter 8, "Absolute Knowledge," is the account of the reconciliation and unity of these three moments in the parousia of the absolute.[3] The *Phenomenology* is thus the attempt to demonstrate the unfolding-enfolding phenomenological ground of history as the interaction and reconciliation of nature, spirit, and the absolute.

The *Philosophy of History*, on the other hand, is the consideration of historical development, not with a view to the demonstration of the interaction and reconciliation of the phenomenal and the logical as the presencing of the phenomenological ground but rather the account of the rational development of the absolute itself in its concrete actuality as history. Whereas the *Phenomenology* is a consideration of the apparently independent movement of the three moments of the whole toward reconciliation in and as the absolute knowledge or science, the *Philosophy of History* is the consideration of this same movement from the perspective of science as the unified movement of the political whole. The three fundamental moments that comprise the *Phenomenology*, i.e., natural consciousness, spirit, and religion, do not, however, disappear in this account but remain intact as the formal and hence implicit elements of historical actuality.

Natural consciousness is, on one hand, consciousness of nature and, on the other hand, consciousness as it naturally appears, i.e., as soul. As consciousness of nature, it is pure I.[4] Pure I, according to Hegel, is non-reflective, pure consciousness (*Bewußtsein*) as the unmediated relation of knowledge (*Wissen*) and being (*Sein*). As nonreflective, consciousness is not cognizant of its own existence and hence of its own part in its apprehension of being, i.e., it does not distinguish itself from its perceptions and hence does not characterize its perceptions as *mine*. It is and only is what it perceives. Hence, the diremption of knowing and being that otherwise is the characteristic condition of consciousness is not present for the pure consciousness of nature.

As soul, natural consciousness is reflective I, i.e., individual self-consciousness. According to Hegel, this is the negative moment of pure I as the negation of the subsistence and independence of the objective. Soul as self-conscious individuality recognizes and knows only itself—objective being is understood only in and as a moment of the self, only as *mine*. Natural consciousness as soul is thus distraught and hence impelled by the apparent independence and self-subsistence of objects, by its apparent *separation* from the objective moment of itself, toward reconciliation. Soul, according to Hegel, is therefore *desire*, the process of taking-into and making-part-of oneself, for it is only by consuming and subsuming its object that soul can alleviate the pain engendered by this estrangement from itself and attain satisfaction, i.e., reconciliation with itself.[5]

This natural consciousness, i.e., the knowing and desiring individual, in

Hegel's view is the motivating force in history. Needs, desires, and passions, which are essentially natural, are the immediate source of all human and therefore all historical motion. In a real sense the individual human being *is* these natural forces. According to Hegel, "these natural forces lie immediately nearer to man than the artificial and protracted training in order and measure, in law and morality." Man by nature is individual, "for the individual is such that *is* there, not man as such, for he does not exist, but rather a particular one," and is motivated not by general rational concerns but by his particular appetites.[6]

If, however, the individual alone is the source of all historical motion and is himself determined in his knowledge by the natural realm of objects and in his action by the impulses of natural desires, how can history, which is the totality of such actions, be rational or grounded in any sense of the term? This problem, which led the Greeks to deny the rationality of history, is a real obstacle for all conceptions of rational historical progress. Hegel does not adopt the obvious recourse of denying the causality of the passions; indeed, he asserts the *exclusive* causality of the passions. However, while the passions motivate, according to Hegel, they do not direct. Desire, to be sure, is always for a specific object and in that sense self-directing. Desires themselves, however, can be regulated and directed by education and the specification and limitation of possible objects of desire. It is in this general sense that tasks are set or objects determined by the customs of a specific people. The possibility for the satisfaction of desire and thus the direction of the motion that results from desire is something general, originating not in natural passion or desire but in rational conventions of a particular social whole. This direction of the passions is what Hegel calls "the cunning of reason."

The individual passions, which are the source of historical motion, are themselves organized into a rational whole by the direction of reason. Reason is by its very nature general; it is not a particular characteristic of one individual but of human being per se. Each individual, however, is also rational and thus participates in reason. He has, to be sure, his own particular needs, passions, and desires, which motivate him, but the specific objects toward which these desires are directed and the means of attaining them are determined not by the individual but by the society in which the individual is reared and resides. All men in all ages may desire the good, as Aristotle argued, but the specific character of the good, the sources of pleasure, the activities that are honored, the sorts of wisdom men pursue are determined by convention and thus vary from age to age. The variety of convention, however, is not an indication of its irrational basis. On the contrary, convention in Hegel's view is the province of reason—it is the structure of reason's rule, which encompasses without extinguishing the natural individual. Moreover, insofar as the individual pursues the objects these conventions establish for his desires, he serves the purposes of reason in its general movement toward science, for it is precisely the pursuit of these conventional objects that is the source of the transformation of these conventions themselves. The pursuit of honor and glory among the Greeks, for example, was in Hegel's view the bulwark for the defense of the polis and the reconciliation of individual desire with the public good. The continual pursuit of martial glory, however, ultimately undermined the polis itself for it drew the Greek cities ineluctably into an ever more destructive conflict with one another. The result was the annihilation of their independent communities and their subordination to a universal empire.

The transformation of convention, thus, is not merely a gradual and undifferentiated process. Although by and large incremental, the process periodically reaches a point at which a quantitative difference becomes a qualitative difference. In this moment the individual who acts stands on the shoulders of those who came before him and is able to scale the wall they all sought to climb and thus is privileged to lead humanity into a new world. The object of this individual's own particular desire coincides with the general objective movement of spirit itself, with "what is necessary and what is timely." It is in this sense that he is a world-historical individual. Such individuals are not theoretical but practical and political men, and their actions are motivated not by altruism but by self-interest. Their genius is not creative but cognitive—they recognize and desire what is politically necessary and bring this to the awareness of others. They thus are irresistible because the truth and necessity of their goal, of their particular desire, is apparent to every other man as the inner truth of his own heart. These men, for example, Alexander, Caesar, and Napoleon, are consumed by their single passion, and in attaining their goal they are left only to discontent or death. After bringing about some fundamental transformation in the world they either like Alexander, having fulfilled their every wish, find only the ennui of purposelessness and a diminution into early death, or like Napoleon exile from a world that they in a sense have created.[7] The natural individual is the source of historical motion, but the path and direction of this motion is determined not by the individual, and not even by the world-historical individual, but by spirit itself.

Spirit, according to Hegel, is general consciousness. As general it transcends nature and all natural laws, for natural causality presupposes a particular object. Spirit, moreover, is not merely consciousness of nature, i.e., not merely in itself (*an sich*), nor is it merely self-consciousness, i.e., merely for itself, but rather "essence that is in and for itself" and therefore free from the necessities of nature. It neither perceives nor is perceived by anything other than itself; it is neither for another nor is there any other for it. According to Hegel, "the essence of spirit is freedom . . . Spirit is being-by-itself. This just is freedom."[8] As that which is in *and* for itself, spirit is likewise by itself, i.e., self-subsistent and independent of the connections of natural causality. It thus is the free self-moving absolute that has not yet come to a reconciliation with natural individuality. As pure spirit it is by itself and not yet by us, i.e., it is not yet present in and as the parousia of the absolute but is rather separated from the individual as the objective structure of society, the social conventions and institutions, which transcend the individual and within which the individual always finds himself. For the individual this generally seems to be an alien other in which he as an individual has no part and yet which demands much of him and with which he has to come to terms. In this sense "spirit is the *ethical life* of a people, insofar as it is the *immediate truth*; the individual that is a world."[9]

Spirit, as Hegel understands it, is the ethical or social world, the *ēthos* or *Sittlichkeit* within which all individuals subsist. These conventions and institutions, however, have an existence and a development independent of the individual. Moreover, this development is not the result of the action of individuals but follows in Hegel's view a rational and irreversible path of its own toward a specific destination. This development is not the result of natural forces and thus not subject to natural necessity but is rather the movement of spirit or general consciousness itself toward absolute knowledge and science. This movement is essentially dialectical and proceeds according to the inner necessity of spirit itself to come to complete self-consciousness of itself in and as the absolute. This inner necessity we have already examined. The reconciliation of natural consciousness and general consciousness, of the individual and society, however, was only indicated in our discussion of the "Introduction" to the *Phenomenology* and neither thoroughly examined nor sufficiently explained. It is, however, precisely this reconciliation that forms the real ground and the concrete actuality of the twofold of nature and spirit, and therefore of history.

This reconciliation of natural consciousness and spirit, of natural causality and freedom, of the individual and society is the state. "This essentiality is itself the unification of the subjective and the rational will: it is the ethical whole—*the state*, which is the actuality in which the individual has and enjoys his freedom, but in which it is the knowing, believing, and willing of the generality."[10] True freedom for the individual is only possible insofar as his actions are in accordance with the general movement of spirit itself. The "freedom" of capricious natural desires is only license and in truth the subjection to natural causality. Real freedom is thus only possible in and through the ethical life of the political community which unites the natural desires of the individual with the rational objects established by society for those desires: it is only the state that can guarantee a reconciliation of these two through laws and education.

Human beings in Hegel's view can be truly free only when they live within convention, within the prevailing *ēthos*, and yet they tend naturally to obey only their desires and to seek only their own satisfaction. The state imposes a necessity supported by force and ultimately by the power of life and death that constrains the individuals to act in accordance with prevailing conventions. The freedom that men enjoy within the state is thus not the freedom that arises from a mutual limitation of their natural freedom but the concord of individual and society, of the subjective will of the individual and the objective general will of the society. "The subjective will, passion, is the motivating, the actualizing; the idea is the inner; the state is the present-at-hand, actual ethical life. For it is the unity of the general, essential will and the subjective, and that is the ethical community." The state in Hegel's view is neither a collectivity of individuals nor a people (*Volk*) as a whole, but the concrete actuality and ground out of which both arise and within which both subsist. Both the subjective will, i.e., natural consciousness as both consciousness of nature and natural desiring soul, and the objective or general will, as the inner idea or rational form, constitute the twofold that in its synthesis is the state: "For the true is the unity of the general and the subjective will; and the general is in the state in the laws, in general and rational determinations." What is fundamentally true and real is neither the individual nor the society but the state, which establishes and maintains laws as the expression of its rationality. Moreover, as we saw earlier, the absolute alone is true or the true alone is absolute. The state is not merely the corporeal and therefore ephemeral reconciliation of the individual and society but a moment of the absolute itself, of the ultimately real phenomenological ground. It is in this sense that Hegel concludes, "The state is the divine idea, as it is present-at-hand on earth."[11]

Thus, in Hegel's view the state is fundamentally bound up with and determined by what he calls *Religion*. This is not the apothesis or deification of the state, as many of Hegel's detractors have argued, but rather the recognition of the necessary interaction of the divine and the political, which characterized life in antiquity and which in Hegel's view continued to characterize life, if in a less obvious manner, up to his own day. The city for Hegel is always the city of the gods or of God and is modeled not upon ephemeral earthly things but upon the eternal divine forms. The character of the prevailing view of the divine manifested in religion or culture determines the fundamental character of the state. "As the religion thus is constituted, so the state and its constitution; it [the state] has actually come forth out of religion."[12] Religion as Hegel understands it here is not religion in the narrow sense, i.e., not merely the devotional service and adoration of the gods or God, but the entire cultural life of a people. Thus, religion includes all the arts and philosophy. Indeed, in his *Encyclopaedia* Hegel describes absolute spirit as art, revealed religion, and philosophy. With this conception Hegel seeks to transcend the Enlightenment distinction of a realm of culture separate from and in many ways opposed to religion. It is not, however, a reactionary attempt to restore the traditional contiguity of pre-Revolutionary and pre-Enlightenment European civilization, as many have argued, but rather a return to what Hegel believed to be the true political conception of antiquity. Here Hegel owes much more to Rousseau than to the Restoration. Traditional European civilization recognized, to be sure, the fundamental unity of culture and religion, but this unity itself was predicted upon the separation of the church (and culture) from the state. It is this fundamental separation *and* the Enlightenment separation of culture and religion that Hegel seeks to overcome through a revitalization of the ancient political-cultural unity.

Religion in Hegel's view is the understanding the state has of itself as the absolute, the image of itself that it paints upon the heavens to make itself visible and hence comprehensible to itself. The absolute, conceived as the beautiful, the divine, and the true, however, is not yet comprehensible in its truth as the state but remains concealed in the duality of the state and the absolute. Athens for the Athenians, for example, had a double meaning—on one hand, the totality of institutions, i.e., the state, and, on the other, the goddess, Athena, who, according to Hegel, personified the spirit of the people, externalized in and as the divine. Indeed

> religion is the place where a people gives itself the definition of that which it holds to be true . . . . From this side the religion stands in the closest connection with the principle of the state. Freedom can only be there where the individual is known as positively in the divine essence.[13]

The individual can be free if and only if his action is within the rational structure of the state as it is articulated in the prevailing religion or culture, for it is only thereby that the individual acts in accordance with the general will and spirit of the people and hence rationally.

Hegel's early search for reconciliation, for a revitalization of classical ideals, thus finds its solution in the foundation of the state in art, revealed religion, and philosophy, i.e., in culture understood in the widest sense. The attempt to resurrect the immediate political unity of spirit and nature in the modern world is in Hegel's view impossible and leads in fact not to a reconciliation of this diremption but to the Terror of the French Revolution. It is not the substance but the spirit of antiquity that must be recaptured. The recognition of the impossibility of an *immediate* synthesis and reconciliation does not prove the impossibility of all synthesis but indicates the necessity of a different sort of synthesis and reconciliation, the necessity of mediation.

Such a *mediated* reconciliation, a reconciliation grounded neither in the amalgamation of the ideals of the French Revolution and Kantian moral philosophy nor in the Platonic and Christian conception of love but in the all-embracing synthesis of speculative idealism or, in short, in science (*Wissenschaft*), is the solution that Hegel develops in the *Phenomenology* and the *Philosophy of History* to the problems of his youth, to the antinomy of the French Revolution and English bourgeois society and the insuffi- ciency of transcendental idealism. This reconciliation, however, is discovered not in an examination of existing institutions nor in a consideration of nature but in and as the investigation of the historical appearance of the state. The absolute that hitherto appeared over against man appears for Hegel in and as the political history of humanity. From this perspective the antinomy of spirit and nature that was predicated upon the distinction of the individual and society and of the state and the absolute dissolves.

> In that the state, the fatherland, constitutes a community of life, in that the subjective will of man subjects itself to the laws, the contradiction of freedom and necessity disappears. Necessary is the rational as the substantial, and we are free in that we recog- nize it as law and follow it as the substance of our own essence: the objective and the subjective will are then reconciled and one and the same unclouded whole.[14]

Hegel's historical understanding of the state as the ground of the twofold of nature and spirit, of the individual and society, is a transformation of the conception of freedom and necessity with which we have hitherto been concerned. Necessity as it appears in Kant's antinomy is *natural* necessity, the necessity imposed by a universal natural causality. Freedom in the antinomy is not specifically the freedom to act rationally, according to determinate laws, but freedom from the laws of nature. Kant, as we saw, attempted to harmonize these two in transcendental idealism, relegating natural necessity to the phenomenal realm and freedom to the noumenal realm. In Hegel's view, however, this solution is insufficient because it does not explain the ground of the twofold of the phenomenal and the nou- menal, in part perhaps because Kant did not properly grasp the nature of the political constellations of his age and hence did not recognize the true significance of the French Revolution and English bourgeois society, and thus the true nature of the antinomy as a fundamentally political problem. He consequently did not recognize the necessity of a synthesis of the phenomenal and the noumenal, i.e., of a reconciliation of the realms of natural science and morality within the political and cultural realm. Indeed, he believed such a reconciliation impossible. From the perspective of absolute knowledge the necessity in question is not the necessity of nature but the necessity of reason as it is embodied in political and cultural institutions and the freedom not the empty freedom of the individual to act morally, but the freedom of the individual to act within and as a moment of an all-encompassing political and cultural whole.

As we have seen, history for Hegel is essentially the process of the reconciliation of individual natural consciousness and general conscious- ness or spirit in and as culture and the state. History in Hegel's view is thus fundamentally the political development of humanity. The *Phenomenology* is the account of the independent historical development of these three moments, of natural consciousness or the individual, spirit or society, and culture or religion. The development of these three moments constitutes the essence of political development and consequently of history itself. Natural consciousness, according to Hegel, comes to recognize itself as both consciousness of nature *and* as soul, i.e., as reason and therefore as spirit. Spirit on the other hand comes to the realization of its own particularity in and as morality, and religion or religious consciousness comes to the realization of the immanence of the absolute in the synthesis of individual and society within the parousia of the absolute as science. This phenomenological process, however, is an abstraction of these three moments from their concrete historical actuality in and as the state. This abstraction, however, is appropriate, since it is precisely the alienation and apparent irreconcilability of these moments that characterizes humanity's historical existence. The fundamental unity of these three moments only becomes evident at the end of history to speculative retrospection in and as the recognition of the hitherto concealed parousia of the absolute. The demonstration of this parousia is thus the presupposition of and preparation for science and thus for a true philosophy of history. This is the goal of the *Phenomenology*. On the basis of the *Phenomenology*, however, it is then possible to reconstruct the actual history of humanity in its fundamental truth as the history of the absolute itself. The concrete embodiment of the absolute, however, is the state, and the true history of humanity is thus fundamentally political history.

According to Hegel, there are four major stages or phases of historical development: (1) the Oriental world, (2) the Greek world, (3) the Roman world, and (4) the Germanic or European world. The historical process itself is the movement of the twofold of nature and spirit from an unmediated unity or togetherness based upon nature through disunity and contradiction to the reconciliation based upon a mediated unity of spirit. The four worlds Hegel delineates are the four crucial phases of this development. Spirit at first is sunken in nature, and "every development of the same is the reflection of spirit into itself, against the natural immediacy."[15] In turning away from this immediacy, spirit alienates itself from nature. This alienation, however, is in fact the turning of spirit into itself, out of the unreflected and hence unmediated unity with nature as the unreconciled other and into self-consciousness and therefore freedom. The fundamental motion of spirit is thus a self-liberation, the continual pursuit of freedom. However, this freedom when it first appears is only partial and therefore incomplete because nature is still present as *other* and has not yet been grasped and subordinated as the substantive moment of spirit itself. It is this fact that in Hegel's view characterizes the ancient world, i.e., the Oriental, Greek, and Roman worlds. Complete freedom presupposes a reconciliation of spirit with nature and a return to unity—not, however, to the mere togetherness of undifferentiated natural immediacy but to a fundamental and comprehensively differentiated spiritual unity. The pursuit of such a reconciliation and the establishment of such a unity in Hegel's view is the chief and decisive characteristic of the modern Germanic or European world. History as a whole is thus in Hegel's view the process of alienation and reconciliation, the unfolding and enfolding of the twofold of nature and spirit from the immediacy of nature and natural necessity to the mediacy of spirit and freedom.[16]

This reconciliation of spirit and nature finds its final and ultimate expression in the highest moment of cultural life, in philosophy as science (*Wissenschaft*), and thus in Hegel's speculative idealism.

> The *present standpoint* of philosophy is that the idea is apprehended in its necessity, the sides of its diremption, nature and spirit, each as the representation of the totality of the idea and not only as identical in itself, but bringing forth out of itself this *one* identity and this is thereby recognized as necessary. The *final* goal and interest of philosophy is to reconcile thought, the concept, with actuality.[17]

The end or goal of philosophy is the establishment of the final reconciliation of nature and spirit. This does not mean the recognition and explanation of the identity of spirit and nature as two separate realms à la Kant but rather the production of the ground or unity of the twofold of nature and spirit itself and the derivation of spirit and nature from this unity as a twofold. In contradistinction to the identity of nature and spirit that characterized the Oriental world, which was merely a phenomenal or empirical identity, merely in itself, the identity that speculative idealism establishes, according to Hegel, is fundamentally phenomenological. Philosophy is thus needed to establish the phenomenological ground of the twofold of nature and spirit, i.e., of history, as the parousia of the absolute, and it is the fulfillment of the task established by this need that Hegel undertakes in the *Phenomenology* and the *Philosophy of History*. History as a whole, understood from the unity of its ground in the twofold of the parousia of the absolute, is the progress of spirit out of nature, the recognition of its independence in Christianity and its triumphant return to and conquest of the natural world. It is thus the unfolding of the merely empirical unity of nature and spirit or the natural spirituality of the Oriental world into the harmony of nature and spirit of the Greek world and the utter alienation of spirit and nature in the Roman world. The Germanic or European world then is the process of reconciliation or the enfolding of nature and spirit into the unity of the twofold, on the basis of the real ground. This progress is likewise the progress of freedom from the despotism of the Oriental world, which recognizes that only *one* is free, through the democracy and aristocracy of classical antiquity, which recognize that *some* are free, to the monarchy of the modern world and the recognition that *all* are free. Thereby the natural individual is tamed and reconciled to the laws of spirit or the society, and the society is transformed from a realm of capricious and absolute determinations and laws into a rational state, which countenances free individuality.

The development of freedom and civilization thus reveals itself as the unfolding-enfolding twofold of the absolute. It is the goal of science to reveal the absolute as the ever-present essence of this twofold, as the source of its dialectical motion and its speculative unity, the demonstration " . . . that eternal life is this, to eternally produce and eternally reconcile the contradiction.—To know contradiction in unity and unity in contradiction, this is *absolute knowledge*; and science is this, to know this unity through itself in its entire development."[18] Philosophy, according to Hegel, is necessary to articulate and secure this ground. To finally understand this ground, we therefore must turn not to an examination of the *Phenomenology* or the *Philosophy of History* but to an investigation of the articulation of the essence of absolute knowledge itself in Hegel's *Science of Logic*.

Absolute Knowledge, Science, and the Ground

Does Hegel then finally succeed in establishing a ground for history? To answer this question we must determine on the most rudimentary logical and ontological level whether Hegel's notion is both consistent *and* complete. This involves three questions: (1) the logical question of consistency or noncontradiction, (2) the empirical or phenomenal question of completeness or sufficient reason, and (3) the ontological or phenomenological question of the compatibility of consistency and completeness. The logical question is the question of history as a process, the phenomenal question the question of history as a whole, and the phenomenological question the question of history as a complete process. History, however, is in Hegel's view always and only the development of consciousness or spirit to perfect self-knowledge. The question of the ground of history thus becomes the question of the ground of spirit or consciousness itself. Consciousness for Hegel, however, is fundamentally dialectical or antinomious and therefore self-contradictory. How then can Hegel maintain that his theory establishes a true ground when he himself admits, or seems to admit, that consciousness, which is the basis of history, is itself contradictory?

This objection misses the true subtlety and profundity of Hegel's thought. Consciousness is indeed contradictory in Hegel's view, but it is precisely the *necessity* of this contradiction that is the truth and underlying unity of consciousness and therefore of history itself. The two contradictory moments are both *necessary* moments, i.e., each can only be and hence be defined in terms of the other. They each subsist only within the synthesis or unity of this encompassing necessity. Hegel's speculative idealism consequently does not deny or avoid contradiction but rather subsumes it within the speculative synthesis. Each synthesis, however, by Hegel's own admission, engenders a new contradiction. In raising itself above itself into self-consciousness, consciousness recognizes and establishes the speculative unity of what it hitherto had recognized as the duality of self and object. It thus enfolds itself. Consciousness, however, subsequently becomes conscious of its own consciousness and thus unfolds itself again into the contradiction of self and object. Consciousness consequently is and remains always both dialectical and speculative, a concatenation of contradiction and unity. The consistency requirement of the ground thus seems at best to be only poorly met. What sense does it make to argue that all contradictions are subsumed within the speculative synthesis if the ground of that synthesis, i.e., consciousness, is itself a process of unification and contradiction? Has Hegel really gone beyond the Kantian insight of the antinomious character of consciousness in any but the most superficial way? Has he not indeed succeeded only in extending the sphere of contradiction, which Kant so carefully confined, to encompass all life and thought without thereby really demonstrating an underlying unity that would make such universal contradiction comprehensible?

The question of the consistency of consciousness and thus the ground, however, is not the question of the consistency of any particular moment of the process, but of the process as a whole. The logical requirement of consistency is thus fundamentally bound up with the phenomenal requirement of completeness. Indeed, in Hegel's thought both the logical and the phenomenal are united in such a way that each depends upon the final and highest or most comprehensive synthesis of consciousness in and as absolute knowledge.

If consciousness is the dialectical process of historical development, which while uniting every contradiction also dissolves every synthesis, how can it ever be a whole? To use the language of the Third Antinomy, how can a chain of dialectical causality ever be complete or sufficiently grounded and at the same time noncontradictory? Even if each moment in some sense becomes complete and hence a whole, how can that satisfy the principle of sufficient reason, if every whole is itself imperfect and incomplete? Hegel's answer to this question is straightforward: history is teleological, it has both a beginning and an end, and the beginning and end are identical; the process itself is circular. With this notion of a circular teleology Hegel attempts to overcome the problem posed by the Third Antinomy and thus to establish a true phenomenological ground for history.[19]

Hegel argues that

> . . . the progression is a retrogression into the ground, to the original and truthful, upon which that with which the beginning is made depends and by which it is brought forth.—Thus, consciousness on its way out of the immediacy with which it begins is led back to absolute knowledge as its innermost *truth*.

This conclusion, the ground, is then also that out of which the
first goes forth, that at first appeared as immediacy . . . What is
essential for science is not so much that a pure immediacy be the
beginning but that the whole is a circular motion in itself, in
which the first also becomes the last and the last also the first . . .
    . . . the line of scientific locomotion thereby forms itself *into a
circle.*[20]

The problem that Kant recognized, i.e., that the ground of history required
that the causal series be both finite or complete and infinite or noncontradictory finds its solution in the dialectical circularity of historical development. History, however, is not *merely* circular but also, as we have seen,
teleological, the progress of consciousness and mankind to perfect self-
knowledge in the parousia of the absolute. These two apparently incompatible conceptions are reconciled in Hegel's thought in the identity of the first
and the last, of the pure mediacy of the absolute and the pure immediacy of
sense-certainty.

In absolute knowledge (*absolutem Wissen*) consciousness (*Bewußtsein*)
comes to know (*wissen*) itself as absolute. Consciousness thus becomes
pure knowledge and loses its dual character as knowing and being. Indeed,
it is in this sense that it is absolute, i.e., in that it is absolved or freed from
being as its object. In fact it is only in this sense that it is complete or perfect,
since it thereby overcomes the inner separation of knowing and being. It
knows only itself and is only the knowing of this knowing. This knowing
furthermore knows itself to be absolute, i.e., to be completed and hence
perfect as the embodiment of everything that is or can be. Consciousness in
absolute knowledge thus becomes pure and universal mediacy. This mediacy, however, is in Hegel's view nothing other than the pure immediacy
with which the entire process began, the pure immediacy of being. Pure
form is pure content, knowing is being.

In this perfect self-knowledge, consciousness returns to the original
immediacy of being.

In its going into itself it [spirit] is sunken in the night of its
self-consciousness; its existence which has disappeared, however, is preserved in it [this night]; and this existence which has
been overcome—the previous one which, however, has been
newly born out of knowledge—is the new existence, a new
world and form of spirit. In it spirit has to naively begin again
with its immediacy and raise itself up again, as if all of the
preceding were lost for it and it had learned nothing from the
experience of earlier spirits.[21]

The reconciliation and ground established in the parousia of the absolute
thus itself collapses in the night of self-consciousness, i.e., in the moment
that absolute knowledge becomes conscious of itself as absolute knowledge

and thus loses its synthetic unity and returns to the original diremption of pure being and knowing. The reconciliation and synthesis of all the preceding moments and therefore of history itself is, however, retained in and through spirit's going-into-itself (*Insichgehen*) and recollection (*Erinnerung*) of the multitude of past forms within this immediacy. The ground in this sense lies in the speculative retrospection of absolute spirit, i.e., in the recollection of the past moments in and through the phenomenology of spirit. The ground itself thus is the highest moment of the circular process in which spirit constitutes itself as a whole.

This moment and hence the ground, however, appear to be transient, to dissolve from the fullness of absolute knowledge into the emptiness of mere sense-certainty. If the ground itself passes away, how can Hegel argue that history is sufficiently grounded? Here one must distinguish between the ground itself and knowledge of this ground. The parousia of the absolute is the *kairos* in which consciousness grasps the truth about the ground, i.e., that the absolute has always been the ground of history. That this insight, i.e., that absolute knowledge, dissolves is equally necessary. This dissolution is indeed the proof of the absolute as the absolution of consciousness itself. Indeed, if the process ended with absolute knowledge as the completion of the circle and the final end, then the sufficiency requirement would not be satisfied, since the question would necessarily arise about the cause of the whole of which we were no longer a part. Absolute knowledge is the knowledge of the absolute, i.e., the knowledge that the absolute is the ever-present all-encompassing ground. If indeed absolute knowledge were the end, then the absolute itself would also be completed and past. The absolute must thus absolve itself from itself, i.e., it must give itself as perfect knowing over into unknowing being and thus free itself from itself. This just is the characteristic of consciousness that makes it absolute, that it continually absolves itself. Is there, however, a ground for consciousness and absolute knowledge if it is a continual self-overcoming or self-absolving? Can the parousia of the absolute as absolute knowledge serve as the ground? Does it fulfill the logical requirement of consistency necessary to a ground? The question about the comprehensibility of the ground of history thus becomes the question of the comprehensibility of absolute knowledge and the absolute itself. The answer to this question resides in the system of absolute knowledge itself, i.e., in Hegel's *Science of Logic*.

The articulation of the explicit character of absolute knowlege, i.e., of the constitution of the historical process from the perspective of the ground and the fundamental character of that ground itself is the project Hegel undertakes in the *Logic*. His *Logic* thus differs from the *Phenomenology* in that it is the articulation of the development of knowledge (*Wissen*), which has been absolved from being (*Sein*), and not of the appearance of knowledge in conjunction with being in and as the experience of consciousness (*Bewußtsein*). The *Logic* is the explanation of absolute knowledge (*Wissen*) as a conceptual or logical whole and is thus the *Science (Wissenschaft) of Logic*. This is possible because the task of the *Phenomenology* already has been completed. The *Logic* thus does not have to recount the development of consciousness from the perspective of developing consciousness itself but has the entirety of this development before it as it is delivered by speculative retrospective introspection and can thus grasp what is in its absolute truth. It is the logic of the development of consciousness or history as a whole, i.e., from the perspective of the ground. Consciousness (and hence history), however, is not simple but twofold and thus, as we have seen, fundamentally dialectical. The *Logic* itself is the articulation of this speculative and dialectical logic of consciousness, the demonstration of the synthetic unity of all contradictions and therefore of consciousness itself, and of the genesis of all contradictions out of this all-encompassing synthesis. Whether and to what extent Hegel is successful in generating all contradictions out of the universal synthesis of the twofold of consciousness itself shall remain unexamined here, and we shall focus instead upon the character and principle of this fundamental synthesis itself.

The *Logic* begins with the consideration of this all-embracing speculative synthesis, i.e., with the assertion that being and nothing are the same. Being is indeterminate immediacy and has no distinction within itself or with anything outside itself. It is pure emptiness. Nothing, on the other hand, is complete emptiness, contentlessness, undifferentiatedness itself. Being is and can be defined only by its opposition to nothing and nothing only by its opposition to being. Each *is* only as the opposite of the other and beyond this opposition has no defining characteristics. They are only because they contradict one another, only because they are logically and that means dialectically united. This logical or dialectical relationship subsists between them because they are nothing other than pure intuition itself, i.e., absolute knowledge that in the night of self-consciousness has absolved itself from itself, that has overcome itself and become conscious of itself as the universality of the absolute. In this manner consciousness (*Bewußtsein*) as absolute knowledge (*Wissen*) becomes pure and empty being (*Sein*) or nothing. Both absolute knowledge and being thus represent the unity of consciousness with itself seen from its two sides, as the unity of knowing and the unity of being. What from the perspective of the *Phenomenology* appeared as the unity of subject and object, particular and universal within the parousia of the absolute in absolute knowledge, appears in the beginning of the *Logic* as the unity of being and nothing. The highest psychological or epistemological or historical moment becomes the most rudimentary and fundamental logical moment.[22]

This speculative unity of being and nothing is thus, in Hegel's view, the most fundamental and most thorough of unities, for the phrase "either being or nothing" apparently exhausts all possibilities. Nonetheless, neither being nor nothing exists as such. "Their truth is thus this *motion* of the immediate disappearing of the one in the other: *becoming*." Pure being and pure nothing do not exist in the world but are only the constituent elements of and abstractions from what is ultimately real, becoming. "*Becoming* is this immanent synthesis of being and nothing"; and "it is the dialectically immanent nature of being and nothing themselves, that they show their unity, becoming, as their truth."[23] The postulated unity of consciousness as either the unity of knowing in absolute knowledge or the unity of being and nothing in logic is itself an abstraction from the moment of parousia, an abstraction because this moment contains *both* pure knowing and pure being. This does not, however, mean that the moment of parousia is itself dirempt: both pure knowing and pure being are present as abstractions from the twofold of consciousness because in this moment the two sides of consciousness are identical and the twofold collapses into a unifold. This unifold is the identity of pure mediacy and pure immediacy in and as the parousia of the absolute. This parousia as we now see, however, is the pure process of knowing and hence the pure process of being. It is thus, however, becoming.

The contradiction of being and nothing thus does not entirely disappear but is rather subsumed and retained within becoming. It is indeed their conceptual unity within becoming that constitutes the ground,

> ... the concept of the unity of being and nothing—or, in more reflected form, the unity of being-differentiated and being-undifferentiated—of the identity of identity and non-identity. This concept could be seen as the finest, purest, i.e., most abstract definition of the absolute.[24]

This unity of being and nothing in becoming is the most general and hence most abstract definition of the absolute and hence of the ground. All other determinations and developments, as Hegel points out, are thus only a fuller articulation of this definition. Becoming, the ultimately real, is thus essentially the unity of being and nothing. This characterization or definition of the ground, however, hardly goes beyond that already articulated in the *Phenomenology* as the unity of pure mediacy and pure immediacy in the completion of history. The historical process appears here, abstracted from concrete consciousness, in its truth as becoming, but it is still not clear whether and how history or becoming constitutes a rational or comprehensible ground. It seems that Hegel's solution to the contradiction of being and nothing rests upon the very twofold of consciousness for which a solution was sought in the *Phenomenology*. It is thus not to becoming that thought must turn but to the ground of the unity of being and nothing within becoming, which Hegel characterizes as the identity of identity and non-identity. The absolute is not becoming itself but the principle of unity or synthesis that unifies becoming. Hegel calls this principle absolute negativity.

At the beginning of the second of the three parts of the *Logic*, the "Logic of Essence," Hegel establishes the essence of becoming and hence of history in absolute negativity. He argues that

> . . . the immediate or being is only this likeness itself of negation with itself, the negated negation, absolute negativity. This likeness with itself or immediacy is thus not a first, from which is begun and which goes over into its negation, nor is it an existing substratum, that moves itself through reflection; but rather the immediacy is only this motion itself.
>
> Becoming in essence, its reflected motion, is thus the *motion from nothing to nothing and thereby back to itself*. The transit or becoming overcomes itself in its transit; the other, that becomes in this transit, is not the non-being of a being, but the nothing of a nothing, and this being the negation of a nothing, constitutes being.—Being is only as the motion of nothing to nothing, so it is essence; and this does not *have* its motion *in itself*, but rather is it as absolute appearance itself, pure negativity, which has nothing outside of itself, that negates it, but which negates itself through its negative itself, that only is in this negating.[25]

Becoming is in essence absolute negativity. Absolute negativity is, on one hand, negativity that is absolute, i.e., the complete and utter rule of nothing as negation, and, on the other hand, the negativity of the absolute itself as the absolving of all finite forms. Negativity in this sense names the absolute itself as the absolving, as the infinite. The absolute is this negativity, and it is only thus that the negativity can itself be absolute. As absolute, this negativity is, moreover, the essence and ground of the dialectical process itself and the source of *both* contradiction and unity. The original negation is the source of contradiction and historical motion in that it dissolves the speculative unity. The second negation, the negation of the negation, is the establishment or reestablishment of what is: the negated nothing of becoming is thus being. History in this sense absolves itself from itself and establishes its own ground in and as the absolute.

However, this absolute, the ultimate ground upon which all else rests, is thus nothing. This nothing is not, however, the nothing of something, i.e., not no-thing, but rather negativity, the nothing that *reflects* back upon and negates itself, thus constituting the pure process. Reflective nothing is negativity, and as such it has the same absolving character as consciousness: in constantly negating itself, negativity does not obliterate its present but subsumes it within itself as that which it has absolved itself from and hence overcome. The process of consciousness and negativity is thus the same, a rising above, a separation from and encompassing within, an absolving and hence an overcoming. It seems indeed to be Hegel's purpose here not to demonstrate the existence of nothing but rather to describe the fundamental character of consciousness as the absolute. If consciousness, however, is what is and is itself fundamentally nothing that reflects upon itself, can Hegel's speculative idealism be anything other than systematized nihilism? Can the nothing, even as negativity, serve as the ground of history?

In his consideration of transcendental idealism Hegel recognized that consciousness is what fundamentally is and that consciousness is itself contradictory. As contradictory, however, it does not refute itself but rather is a dialectical process and therefore historical. This process, however, is consciousness's coming to itself, coming to know itself as the absolute. The absolute, however, is the recognition of the identity of identity and non-identity, i.e., of the unity of consciousness with itself as the self-absolving. This unity, however, is itself the unity of absolute negativity and hence nothing. This nothing is not the nothingness of everything but rather the negativity of absolution that characterizes the process of knowing itself.[26] Negativity is thus *how* consciousness is, and as this *how* it is the unity of the dialectical process. If, however, consciousness is *what* fundamentally *is* and yet *is* in the truest sense only as a process and therefore only on the basis of the *how* of that process itself and that *how* is itself nothing as negativity, can anything be said to be and to be sufficiently grounded and a whole? Can the fundamental principle, the *how*, of a process serve as the ground of that process itself? Even if this is possible, can that principle serve as a ground, if it is itself self-contradicting, self-negating, self-absolving, and fundamentally nothing? If the parousia of the absolute is the recognition in absolute knowledge of absolute negativity, can we still speak of the ground of history? Even if history as this absolute negativity forms a circular whole, does this whole itself make any sense *as* a whole? Is the principle that determines its motion and wholeness itself comprehensible? Or must we perhaps conclude that, at a very minimum, Hegel's speculative ground remains fundamentally dark, a mystery that must either be accepted or rejected but that cannot be proved or disproved? Must we, despite the real magnificence and profundity of the Hegelian system, conclude that it rests upon an aporia still deeper and still more mysterious than the aporia of transcendental idealism it sought to solve? Does Hegel overcome the nihilism that appeared in the antinomy and establish a true ground for history, or is the ground that he establishes at best incomprehensible? Does Hegel truly determine *what* history *is*, or does he only more securely establish the identification of history and nihilism?

Critique and Conclusions

We have tried to show in the preceding discussion how Hegel attempted to resolve the question of the ground of history. We have now to determine his success. Does Hegel then manage to establish a ground for history that is both compatible with actuality and logically satisfying, or does he only present us with a new and more dangerous mystery that leads us even deeper into the nihilism he himself attempted to overcome?

This question seems obvious to us, but many critics do not confront it largely because they do not believe that it captures the essence of Hegel's thought. Hegel in their view is not interested in the ground of history but either only in the ground or only in history. These two alternatives have in fact characterized the interpretation of his thought almost since the moment of his death. The Left Hegelians and the so-called neo-Hegelians of the Hegel renaissance have favored a "historical" interpretation, while the Right Hegelians and others have preferred a "theological" or "metaphysical" reading. Thus men such as David Friedrich Strauss and Fachenheim understand the essence of Hegel's thought to lie in his notion of the unity of God and man, while others such as Feuerbach and Lukàcs see this merely as a deviation from his original and fundamental concern with dialectical historical development. His metaphysics in their view is thus a betrayal of his revolutionary beginnings in the service of the European Restoration and the ascendent bourgeois society. Like Kojève they thus conclude that the "historical" Hegel is the authentic Hegel. The "metaphysical" school on the contrary sees such a "historical" interpretation, especially of the earlier, "theological" Hegel as mistaken and motivated more by ideological fervor than the love of truth.[27]

Both of these interpretations are one-sided and fundamentally obscure Hegel's "synthetic" intention. While Hegel may indeed have been concerned with establishing a speculative metaphysics to fill the void left by the collapse of Christianity, this does not prove that history was irrelevant for him. From his earliest days in the *Gymnasium* he demonstrated an abiding enthusiasm for history that is evident in many of his works, not the least of which is his *Philosophy of History*. The presence of this historical element, however, does not indicate that Hegel was uninterested in speculative metaphysics or rational theology. Philosophical reflection, as he argues in the "Preface" to the *Phenomenology*, is in fact superior to history as a form of knowing. Hegel thus does not mean to exclude either history or metaphysics but strives instead to demonstrate that history is the unfolding of the absolute and that the absolute is the end and completion of history. Hegel thus aims at establishing a ground for history that will bring metaphysics down to earth without destroying its speculative essence and lift history above the realm of mere contingency without obliterating its actuality. The question, then, is not whether Hegel was actually concerned with the question of the ground of history but whether he successfully answered it.

The question of the ground of history arose for Hegel out of his dissatisfaction with Kant's solution to the antinomy of freedom and natural necessity. In his view transcendental idealism is insufficient because it only resolves the contradiction by subjectivizing it, i.e., by transposing it from the actual world into consciousness itself. Hegel's own solution, however, is liable to this same objection, and many of his critics have characterized his thought as just another form of subjectivistic idealism that never comes to terms with the actual world but only generates it a priori out of pure thought. The solution that Hegel establishes to the antinomy in his notion of the absolute is thus, according to Marx, for example, only a reconciliation in thought that may please the philosopher but that never overcomes the actual alienation that characterizes man's political and natural existence.[28]

This objection, however, rests on the misidentification of Hegel's notion of consciousness and subjectivity. His critics, beginning generally from the standpoint of empiricism, attribute to Hegel a similar understanding of consciousness as a human capacity, something within the subject that allows him to perceive and hence know the objective world. As detailed in Chapter 2, however, consciousness (*Bewußtsein*) for Hegel is always the twofold of knowing (*Wissen*) and being (*Sein*), of the subjective and the objective, of the noumenal or logical and the phenomenal. Hegel thus understands the world not in terms of pure thought but on the basis of experience or phenomenology as the twofold of thought and actuality. Hegel, in an even more forceful manner than Kant, thus rejects both the "objectivism" of empiricism and the "subjectivism" of rationalism. Just as there can be no subject without an object, so there can be no object without a subject. Both arise out of consciousness as experience or phenomenology. Hegel's thought in this sense is, therefore, not subjectivistic.

There is a deeper sense, however, in which Hegel's thought might be accused of subjectivism. Hegel, it is argued, may not deduce the objective world from pure thought but more fundamentally derives both subjectivity and objectivity from what is an essentially subjectivized absolute. According to this argument, Hegel's speculative idealism like that of Schelling is fundamentally Spinozism, a pantheism or, as Erdmann called it, a panlogism, that conceives both the *res extensa* and the *res cogitans* as extensions of divine essence or modes of divine substance. Hegel's thought in this light is understood as a secularization of the Christian conception of God and his creation or as an unconscious projection of human subjectivity into an abstract but still theological absolute.[29]

While this objection does point to a salient feature of Hegel's thought, it does not give sufficient credit to countervailing aspects that prevent it from degenerating into mere Spinozism. In one sense it is clearly true that Hegel's thought is an absolute subjectivism. The same, however, might be said of Newton who recognizes space and time as forms of divine substance. Moreover, unlike both Spinoza and Schelling, Hegel does not derive actuality from the concept of the absolute but, as shown in Chapter 3, tries to reconstruct actuality on the basis of the experience of consciousness. He may thus end up in the absolute but only after passing through all the realms of ordinary human experience. He thus does not produce a "night in which all cows are black" but a realm of mediation that connects all human possibilities from the most mundane to the most exalted. In this sense his thought seems more Aristotelian than Spinozistic.

Even if we grant that Hegel's thought has an experiential component, however, we cannot completely remove this objection. Another obstacle, Hegel's teleological conception of nature, stands in our way. Hegel's nature has little in common with the natural world as it is conceived by natural science, and the ascendency of this science leaves us with little choice but to reject Hegel's view. It seems to be both anthropomorphic and antiquated, a product of Romanticism, that describes not the visible nature world but a divine or rational essence imagined to reside in that world. In point of fact, even many of Hegel's most avid supporters have found it necessary to reject his philosophy of nature, and the Hegel renaissance of the late nineteenth and early twentieth centuries was predicated upon such a rejection. If, however, Hegel's nature has no connection to actuality, it would seem that his purported reconciliation of freedom and nature is merely imaginary. If this is the case, then his notion of history and the ground of history must also be inadequate. Some have attempted to circumvent this problem and retrieve Hegel's philosophy of history by simply rejecting his philosophy of nature. This, however, not only distorts the systematic character of his thought but ultimately even undermines his philosophy of history, which depends upon a reconciliation of man and nature and thus upon a teleological nature that tends toward such a reconciliation. It seems impossible to either accept or reject Hegel's notion of nature without rejecting his philosophy as a whole.[30]

This problem, however, is not insoluble. Although we may be forced to reject Hegel's philosophy of nature, it does not necessarily follow that we must reject his philosophy of history or the ground of history that he discovers in the reconciliation of freedom and natural necessity. In fact the source of the unacceptability of Hegel's philosophy of nature as a whole may well be the source of its success in explaining the confrontation of freedom and nature in man. Modern natural science begins from the motions of physical bodies and determines the causal laws that govern these motions. These laws are then used to explain human motion. Hegel on the contrary begins with man and delineates the laws that govern his motions, applying these in turn to physical nature. While he thus may come to erroneous conclusions about the physical world, it does not follow therefore that his conclusions about human nature are equally erroneous. It has been a firmly established belief that there is an unbroken natural continuum that encompasses both physical and human nature, but even modern natural science is beginning to doubt that it can adequately describe biological processes with merely causal explanations and is at least in part returning to teleology. This is not to suggest that Hegel's teleological conception of nature as a whole is correct but only that such a conception of human nature is not necessarily wrong. If this is indeed the case, then his conception of human nature may be separable from his notion of nature as a whole and thus defensible on its own grounds as an understanding of man.

On the most immediate level, Hegel's conception of human nature is not so different than that of Hobbes. Human motion is determined by passion or desire. The metaphysics that underlies this motion, however, is widely different. In contradistinction to Hobbes, Hegel does not believe that the objects of these desires are fundamentally natural. This is not to deny that the desires have a natural origin. He argues instead that despite their origin they are fundamentally formed and directed by spirit, i.e., by freedom as it is embodied in customs and laws. These laws determine what is good, and this notion of the good serves to guide and regularize the desires. Thus, while we naturally desire to eat, custom determines what, how, when, where, with whom, and in many instances even why we eat. Freedom, however, cannot simply ignore nature in its determination of the good. Man's physical nature is in fact counterposed to his freedom and plays a role in determining the character of this good. In the most radical case, i.e., suicide, freedom in Hegel's view demonstrates its superiority to nature and all desire, but this demonstration is also self-negating. In all other cases freedom must come to terms with the natural structure of desire and discovers in the end that the only complete notion of the good is that which is in harmony with man's desires. Thus, just as freedom informs natural desire, so human nature sets limits upon and directs freedom. It is in this sense that history for Hegel is the process of reconciliation of freedom and nature. Thus, the rejection of Hegel's philsophy of nature does not inevitably entail a rejection of his notion of history and its ground. Such a conclusion of course rests upon a distinction of physical and human nature that is foreign to Hegel.

The objection that Hegel is guilty of distortion is much more plausible when leveled against his philosophy of history. Such an objection has often been raised. Dilthey among others argues that Hegel distorts history in order to harmonize it with the rest of his system.[31] The reliance upon untrustworthy sources, the disregard for historical evidence, and the commission of numerous errors are certainly clear to anyone with even a passing knowledge of history. It is thus probably true that Hegel's account distorts historical actuality. To blame Hegel for this, however, is to misunderstand his fundamental intention. Hegel, as we noted at the beginning of this chapter, is not concerned with historical actuality but rather with the demonstration of *reason* in history, with what he calls conceptualized history. Conceptualized history is the account of the development (*Bildung*) of human consciousness and thus of reason to its completion in absolute knowledge and science.[32] To this end Hegel turns not to the "objective" understanding of the past established by modern historiography but to the understanding each age had of itself. Historiography in his view does not come to the truth about history because this truth does not reside in the mere facts of an age but in its spirit, and this spirit is revealed only in the consciousness and self-consciousness of the age itself, in its art, religion, philosophy, and historiography. This is the meaning of Hegel's otherwise puzzling assertion that an age does not have a history unless it has a historiography, i.e., unless it is conscious of itself and thus constitutes itself as a whole. That each age partially misunderstands itself is intrinsic to its own historical and dialectical existence. Hegel's "errors" are thus more often than not the errors or contradictions of the age itself, which more clearly reveal the spirit of the age than all the facts unearthed by modern scholarship. To demand an "objective" account of an age is thus in Hegel's view to misconstrue its historical character and to demand such of Hegel is to misunderstand his entire project.

There remains, however, at least the suspicion that many of Hegel's apparent errors are decisive for the demonstration of the dialectical rationality of the historical process. If reason truly is in history, then one might expect that the *res gestae* and therefore the *historia rerum gestarum* would properly reflect this rationality. While such an objection has great force, it is not altogether sufficient. Hegel makes no claim that every event is determined by or part of the dialectical development of history. The *res gestae* may correspond by and large to the rational laws of development, but the force of accidental causality may nonetheless produce numerous deformations in the historical process. In Hegel's view, however, such accidents are historically meaningless, since they cannot ultimately deflect the dialectical development. One has to wonder, however, whether accident does not play a much greater role in history than Hegel believes. It is hard to believe, for example, that the early deaths of Alexander, Caesar, or Napoleon would not have had a decisive impact upon the course of historical development. Löwith rightly sees this recognition and dismissal of chance as the product of an underlying eschatological and therefore Christian element in Hegel's thought that leads him to reject the ancient notions of chance and fate as the ruling forces in human affairs. That he underrates the importance of these forces seems incontestable.[33]

In direct contrast to the complaint that Hegel distorts historical actuality in favor of a systematic metaphysics or philosophy is the objection that he in fact undermines all philosophy and replaces it with history, that far from eschewing or corrupting history he enthrones it. He is thus seen as the foremost proponent of historicism. This objection has been substantially met in Chapters 2 and 3. That Hegel resisted historicism and attempted to establish a ground for history is undeniable. The notion that he was a thorough historicist must thus be rejected. The more subtle form of this objection, however, is not so easily met. Hegel, it is argued, may not himself have been a historicist, but by opening up philosophy to history he nonetheless created the possibility for the replacement of philosophy by history and thus for historicism. The force of this criticism, particularly in light of the development of history and historicism among the Left Hegelians and neo-Hegelians, is quite strong. The conjunction of history and philosophy did not, however, begin with Hegel, and in fact Hegel himself struggled to prevent philosophy from degenerating into mere history. As we saw in Chapter 1, the idea of history had already become a revolutionary force in Europe in the period immediately preceding Hegel. Hegel recognized quite correctly that it thus could not simply be cast aside but at best only tempered and controlled. This he attempted to do. The assertion that he should have rejected history as such in favor of ancient naturalism and its corresponding political philosophy overlooks what was clear to Hegel, that any return to antiquity flew in the face of modern society and could end only in a fanaticism of freedom or practical reason. While one may disagree with this assessment, it is hardly fair to blame him in the end for historicism.

We may ask, however, whether Hegel succeeded in grounding history, i.e., whether he does in fact demonstrate that reason is in history or that history has a ground. In the first instance this is the question of the adequacy of his principle of historical or dialectical motion, i.e., the principle of determinate negation. As noted in Chapter 2, this principle arises out of Hegel's transformation of Kant's antinomy doctrine. Kant believed that the antinomy could be resolved only through the recognition of an utter separation of the phenomenal and the noumenal realms. Hegel, on the contrary, argued that the *necessity* of the contradiction was the basis for reconciliation. Determinate negation is the assertion of this necessity and is thus always the negation of the contradiction, i.e., of the previous negation. The consequence of determinate negation is thus not utter annihilation but a new form that arises out of the previous negation. The principle of determinate negation that governs historical motion is thus crucially dependent upon the *necessity* of all contradictions, for it is only out of this necessity that the speculative ground of unity arises. One may well wonder, however, whether all the contradictions that Hegel adduces are necessary and, indeed, what the ground of such a necessity could be. Why, for example, is the contradiction of being and nothing necessary? Why not being and appearance? Or being and knowing? What characterizes the *necessity* of this contradiction? Does it arise out of our conventional use of language? Is it merely historical? These problems are real and palpable. Moreover, as shown in Chapter 2, Hegel does not recognize some limited number of contradictions but asserts that they are "in all objects of all species, in all representations, concepts and ideas." Thus, every object and concept must not only have one and only one necessary opposite but it must itself be the reconciliation of another contradiction. Whether and to what extent Hegel is able to justify this rather tremendous claim is by no means clear and would involve a detailed examination of his *Logic* that cannot be undertaken here.[34] One has to doubt, however, that such an examination would or even could justify such a claim.

The basis for determinate negation, according to Hegel, is consciousness, and the necessity of all contradictions arises out of their existence in and for consciousness. Every object and every concept in his view is the result of the conjunction of knowing and being, of a subject conjoined to or aware of an object. There is thus in *every* case an implicit diremption that arises out of the separation of subject and object. This diremption is the basis of the contradiction. Each side of the contradiction, however, is dependent upon the other for its meaning and existence. This mutual dependence is the source of the necessity of the contradiction, and the recognition of this dependence is the determinate negation of the original diremption or contradiction. Determinate negation is thus nothing other than the moment of self-consciousness in which consciousness rises above itself and recognizes that subject and object are fundamentally one. What becomes clear in this light is that Hegel's notion of contradiction is less stringent than that of traditional logic, since it is in fact only the formalization of diremption. This does not, however, mean that it is inferior to the traditional notion. The necessity of each contradiction may not be logically justifiable in the traditional sense but may arise nonetheless out of human experience, out of the unfolding of consciousness itself. It is thus not history or logic that is fundamental in Hegel's view but consciousness, which generates and resolves all contradictions through its dialectical experience.

The necessity of historical motion, however, does not depend merely upon the necessity of each individual contradiction but upon the series of contradictions that constitutes dialectical causality as a whole. This whole, however, depends upon a necessary end or ground to the series itself. Chapters 2 and 3 show that this necessity also arises out of consciousness for Hegel. Consciousness is not merely the motive principle of historical motion but as absolute knowledge also its end or goal. Concretely, however, this necessity is more difficult to define. Is history merely the history of absolute spirit, of art, religion, and philosophy that culminates in absolute knowledge and science? This can hardly be the case. History is not merely the development of human thought but also of actuality. These two are inseparable. The end of historical development in science must have its concrete embodiment. This concrete end is in Hegel's view the rational state. Insofar as this state is the culmination of historical development, it is also the concrete solution to the problems that have driven history forward. It is thus the resolution of all previous contradictions and provides us with a concrete analogue to absolute knowledge. As such, we can evaluate the success of Hegel's attempt to overcome diremption and establish a true ground for history through an examination of this state.

Hegel's notion of the rational state has long been an object of controversy. Many have argued in fact that it is only a projection of Hegel's latent but nonetheless irrational and ultimately even fascistic nationalism. The characterization of Hegel as a *German* nationalist, however, is clearly wrong, the result of a misappropriation and misrepresentation of Hegel's thought after 1870. Although his early unpublished work reveals on occasion some national sentiments, Hegel saw the future Germany in his published works not as a united nation but as an aggregate of self-contained territorial states whose political unity rested not upon an instinctual patriotism or dedication to the people (*Volk*) but upon the sanctity of rational institutions. The characterization of Hegel as a *Prussian* nationalist, while initially more plausible, is equally unfounded. It is true that Hegel was employed by the Prussian state, but this does not mean that he was its uncritical defender. Prussia, as Hegel understood it, was a generally enlightened but far from perfect state. Indeed, while it is often argued that Hegel deifies the Prussian state in his *Philosophy of Right*, a comparison with actual Prussian institutions reveals that his notion of the rational state is decidedly more liberal than even the generally liberal Prussia of Hegel's time, let alone the more conservative Prussia of the years following 1848.[35]

This characterization of Hegel as a nationalist is often, however, only a superficial reflection of a more profound disagreement with his notion of spirit. His belief that man's humanity lies not in his individuality but in his connection to the people or community contradicts one of the most deeply held beliefs of modern liberalism. Liberals often see in this notion of spirit an insidious denial of individual rights that opens up the door for collectivist fanaticism. Such an objection, however, is simply wrong. Hegel's notion of spirit is directly opposed to the expressivist or Romantic notions of Herder, the Historical School, and Fascism. Moreover, he also clearly recognizes the dangers of such notions, as his critique of Fries in the "Preface" to the *Philosophy of Right* indicates. He is equally aware of the necessity of institutions for restraining the tyrannical will of the majority in the interest of individual rights. The dangers of a general will that was not also a rational will had been made all too apparent to him by the French Revolution. Hegel, however, also saw the dangers of individualism in the degradation and atomization fostered by the economic life of liberal society. His notion of spirit aims at avoiding both untamed collectivism and atomistic individualism. He does not mean to deny the empirical reality of the individual human being, but he does not believe that it is the source of man's humanity. As an individual, man is characterized by his natural desires and only becomes human through the rational organization of these desires by the laws and customs of the community. On this level Hegel's notion of spirit differs little from that of Montesquieu. The difficulty arises in its connection to the absolute, which seems to inject a religious or mystical element into community life that excessively elevates the collectivity above the individual and grants it a claim to absolute obedience, while removing all grounds for individual resistance. Such an interpretation, however, misconstrues Hegel's notion of the absolute. The absolute that manifests itself is not some dark god but reason, a dialectical reason that by its very nature eschews the contradictory extremes in pursuit of synthesis. This reason manifests itself in rights and institutions aimed at guaranteeing a rational liberty in the context of a spiritual community. Far from transforming the state into an omnipotent being, Hegel thus strives to give it a rational foundation and limitation.

The question of course is whether the rational state is in fact rational, i.e., whether it successfully resolves the basic contradictions that characterize political life. This question cannot be unambiguously answered. Hegel's political solution to the contradiction of freedom and natural necessity is achieved through the separation of bourgeois society, which embodies the so-called subjective freedom of the individual's natural desires, and the state, which is the concrete expression of the objective freedom of rational laws.[36] This has led many critics to conclude that Hegel either fails to understand the interpenetration of economics and politics or prescribes an artificial separation that leads, according to the Left, to the predominance of the bourgeoisie in the state or, in the opinion of the Right, to an unjustifiable intrusion of the state into the economic realm. Such complaints, however, do not do justice to Hegel, since he himself clearly recognizes the necessity for the mediation of these two realms and consequently argues, for example, that corporations must be represented in the legislature and that the state must intervene in the economic realm to ameliorate the inhumanities that arise out of unfettered economic activity. Indeed, the very basis for his separation of the two realms seems to be his awareness of the dangers they pose for one another. He also recognizes, however, that a total separation is neither desirable nor possible.

Is not such a mechanical or institutional solution to the contradiction of freedom and natural necessity, however, the admission of the failure to find a true ground for their reconciliation? Such a suspicion is hard to avoid and is further augmented by Hegel's failure to consider or explain the role of competition, class or factional conflict, and technological innovation in the rational state, all of which call into question the harmony of freedom and nature that Hegel claims to have established. We thus seem to be driven to the conclusion that Hegel's solution to the fundamental contradiction of political life is deficient, that he fails to provide an actual or concrete solution and flees instead like Kant into an ideal realm of mere thought in order to establish an apparent but fundamentally imaginary reconciliation. Such a conclusion, however, rests upon a distinction of thought and actuality that is foreign to Hegel.

In Hegel's view all entities that rise above mere empirical particularity are fundamentally spiritual. The so-called concrete institutions of communal life, the family, the corporation, the legislature, the monarch, the army, and all other components of the state and society are *concretely* only aggregations of individual human beings. Their reality thus resides not in their "concreteness" but in their embodiment of a universal concept. The family, for example, is not an empirical entity that one can touch or see. One *sees* only individual human beings. The family is an embodied concept, an "idea" in Hegel's terminology. The being and meaning of ethical and political entities thus derive from the conjunction of the phenomenal and logical that constitutes their phenomenological or spiritual actuality. The objection that Hegel's solution is merely spiritual is thus insufficient. Hegel's spiritual solution is the solution to a spiritual problem.

One of course might well reply that this is only a nominal solution that leaves unanswered the question of the relationship between two realms of spirit. Such an objection, however, is considerably weaker than the assertion that Hegel's solution is merely ideal since it grants that the distinction between the "real" and the "ideal" is merely a distinction in thought. It is thus vulnerable to the Hegelian demonstration of the dialectical conjunction of these two realms and is reduced to an attack either upon Hegel's logic as a whole or upon the specific dialectical transition between the two realms.

Such an objection also runs into the practical obstacle of the human historical experience, which Hegel uses to support his argument. As we saw earlier in this chapter, Hegel attempts to show that this conjunction of politics and religion is neither unique nor revolutionary, that in fact all states arise out of and are maintained by a religion. Indeed, Hegel sees the rational state as the conclusion and perfection of this conjunction of religion and politics. Just as all past states have understood themselves politically in and through their religions, so in Hegel's view men in the rational state will grasp the unity of their political life through absolute knowledge and science. This is not, however, a merely ideological synthesis of actual antagonisms. As the recognition of the real *necessity* of these antagonisms or contradictions, it is the basis of their underlying *unity*. The contradiction that seems to exist within the rational state between natural necessity and freedom as the contradiction of bourgeois society and the state is, to be sure, both real and necessary, but it is precisely this necessity that both overcomes and preserves the contradiction. The contradiction thus remains, but remains only as a constituent moment of a higher and more comprehensive unity. In itself it has become meaningless.

The crucial and decisive question about Hegel's thought is not whether he adequately and accurately demonstrates the unfolding of consciousness or reason as the absolute in historical and political actuality but whether the absolute as the final synthesis of freedom and nature, of the subjective and the objective, of the noumenal and the phenomenal is itself rational and comprehensible. Hegel's system stands or falls with his notion of consciousness as the absolute. Reality for Hegel is consciousness and the rationality of the ground thus depends upon the rationality of consciousness. This rationality, however, depends upon the completion of the experience of consciousness in absolute knowledge and science. Absolute knowledge, however, rests upon absolute negativity, upon the negation of negation or the identity of identity and nonidentity. This, however, seems to be little more than a logical or ontological restatement of the basic fact of self-consciousness. The highest ground thus seems to be a rather mysterious tautology that consequently serves as the first principle or premise of Hegel's thought.

Is this premise, however, correct? Hegel claims that reason or consciousness can penetrate and understand all reality, that it can know absolutely, because this reality is nothing other than consciousness itself. The end of absolute knowledge, however, is the recognition that absolute knowledge itself rests upon the mysterious factuality of consciousness. Reason may be able to penetrate all reality, but it seems that its final discovery is only the brute fact of its own existence. If consciousness is the fundamental reality of course, then no further investigation or explanation is possible. Even if this is the case, however, we might still be dissatisfied. Hegel claims to begin with the most immediate and simple experience or form of consciousness, sense-certainty, but even this proves to be complex and contradictory. Nowhere in his thought do we find a simple moment that is immediately accessible in its own right.[37] All knowledge except for absolute knowledge is partial, a mixture of ignorance and opinion, and absolute knowledge itself rests upon the mysterious notion of absolute negativity. We are thus called upon to accept a ground that can neither be demonstrated nor observed. Here, however, the distinction of reason and faith dissolves. This dissolution, however, points to what is perhaps the real truth, that consciousness is *not* fundamental, and hence that reason does *not* permeate all reality but rests upon an underlying darkness that is the true source of human motion and life.

The 150 years since Hegel's death have witnessed the ascendency of this darkness that has broken with astounding vehemence into political life and increasingly captured the interest of thought. We today look back upon Hegel with both nostalgia and disdain: we wish for such an optimistic rationalism but see it at the same time as naive. Who today after Nietzsche and Freud, after Hitler and Stalin, after Verdun and Dachau can still believe in the triumph of reason? How can we avoid the conclusion that not reason but unreason rules in history? The brutal facts of the post-Hegelian age thus seem to necessitate a rejection of Hegel.

Yet even in our extremity we cannot overlook the possibility that Hegel may have run ahead of us, that he may have understood us more fully than we can understand ourselves. At the end of the *Phenomenology* he explains that, when consciousness has overcome all diremption and constituted itself as absolute knowledge, it is enveloped in "the night of self-consciousness," the night in which everything is lost, in which reason which has coursed through all reality is cast again upon an unknown sea. Spirit must begin again from the beginning, and there remains only the recollection of its previous development, which in its entirety as science forms what

Hegel terms the Golgotha of spirit. Ordinarily, it is assumed that this new journey to which Hegel here refers is nothing other than the journey of thought through the categories of the *Logic* and the rest of the practical sciences. This, however, captures only one side of Hegel's conclusion. The brightness of this recollection is bound to a darker and more ominous possibility that reflects the fateful character of Hegel's project as a whole. In fact on one level Hegel here admits that his answer to the question of the ground is ultimately ephemeral, that the parousia of the absolute passes away, and that man is again separated from the truth. This does not mean, however, that the world is fundamentally irrational—it means only that the human condition is a continual striving for perfection, a continual attempt to rise above error and opinion to true knowledge. This striving is not, however, an infinite progress toward the good that never in point of fact comes to its goal but a circular process that continually finds and continually loses its perfection. In this light Hegel's project takes on a new meaning and his rationalism dissolves into a melancholy recognition of the inevitability of fate.

Hegel, however, does not abandon himself to the wind and the waves. Like Faust he builds his dikes against a dark sea to open up a free land for a free people. He recognizes, however, what is never clear to Faust, i.e., that the dikes will not hold and that it is only the recollection of the ideal they represent, the ideal of reason, that can offer us guidance and consolation in a world dominated by ignorance and opinion. Hegel's project that aimed at a demonstration of the universality of reason thus seems to end ironically and in a sense tragically with the melancholy recognition of the necessity of error, and consequently holds up the truth not so much to proclaim the advent of the millennium in the manner of the Enlightenment but to provide a distant ray of hope to guide us on our long voyage through the dark night of nihilism.

5
History as Being

What is for Hegel is the absolute as the dialectical twofold of spirit and nature that appears in and as the history of consciousness. This dialectical motion is phenomenology and experience. The absolute is thus always the motion toward self-apprehension and only is in the fullest sense when it has come to complete self-knowledge, i.e., when consciousness recognizes itself as absolute. The absolute thus only truly is when it is by us in its parousia, i.e., when we recognize the absolute as the ever-present but hitherto unperceived reconciliation of spirit and nature. The absolute thus constitutes the ground of history in two senses: as the unity of consciousness throughout the course of its historical development and as the all-encompassing recognition of itself *as* the ground in absolute knowledge.

Whether the absolute, as Hegel understands it, is ultimately comprehensible, however, remains questionable. Its fundamental premise, as we have seen, seems to rest upon contradiction. In his *Logic* Hegel attempted to show that a consistent account of the world could be generated from an initial premise that is both contradictory and noncontradictory, but the nature of this premise is dark and elusive. It seems that it can at best only be characterized in an enigmatic fashion as the identity of identity and non-identity, or of being and nothing, or as the negation of negation. Thereby Hegel perhaps indicates that the absolute is the unity of determinate being and pure process within the manifold of the concept, but the ground itself remains dark. Indeed, this ground—*what* in the truest sense *is*—apparently can only be insofar as it annihilates itself, i.e., as the annihilation of annihilation.

Whether this is meaningful or comprehensible, however, is at least in one sense irrelevant, since it is fairly clear that such a ground, however it appears or is conceived, cannot in the strict sense still be conceived as *what is*, i.e., as something or as what-being. Hegel, to be sure, seeks to rectify this insufficiency with his assertion that the process of negation is circular and, therefore, complete. This solution is in its simplicity an answer to the problem Kant raises in the Third Antinomy, since it establishes both freedom and natural necessity, both the consistency and completeness of history that Kant demanded. Even if this process itself is consistent and complete, however, it is by no means clear that this is equally true of the principle that underlies and determines it, or that the succession itself can in the strict sense be said to be. Consequently, we must wonder perhaps if Hegel does indeed solve the problem of the ground of history that Kant opened up, or whether he does not attempt to conceal this abyss in the mystification of the absolute.

Hegel's philosophy begins with political and spiritual nihilism and ends with the annihilation of annihilation. Speculative idealism recognizes that God is dead but attempts to show that the death of God is the ground for the reconciliation of heaven and earth, of the divine and human, of the immortal and the mortal. God is dead, but God rises from the dead. The parousia of the absolute for Hegel is the truly understood Parousia of Christ and thus not merely the promise but the actualization of eternal life in and as spirit.[1] We must, however, ask whether Hegel's system in its entirety is not based upon a logical illusion or does not presuppose a particular sort of belief or faith, i.e., Christianity, which bridges this mystery but which the system itself cannot explain, whether for all of its magnificence and profundity it does not finally fail to resolve the antinomy and instead only adopts it as its first and hence unquestioned principle.

The failure to establish a generally satisfactory reconciliation of the two sides of the antinomy and especially to articulate a position capable of encompassing the movements of thought predicated upon this disjunction, i.e., natural science and Romanticism, was at least in part responsible for the collapse of Hegelianism and the rise of neo-Kantianism after 1844. It cannot be denied that the retirement in 1838 of Hegel's friend and supporter von Altenstein, who had guided the development of classicism in Prussia as Minister of Culture, and the succession of Fredrick William IV to the throne of Prussia in 1840 had a decisive impact upon the transformation of German intellectual life, but this does not seem to offer a sufficient explanation for either the rapidity or the magnitude of this transformation. The new king was attached to that same Romantic nationalism that Hegel had criticized in the "Preface" to the *Philosophy of Right* in the person of Fries and was consequently antipathetic to Hegel and his more cosmopolitan thought. This change in the political realm did indeed lead to a revision in education and cultural policy, highlighted by the appointment of the Romantic Schelling, Hegel's one-time friend but later rival, to fill his chair in Berlin and root-out Hegelianism, but it is unlikely that a system of philosophy that enjoyed such widespread stature and pervasive influence could have been so suddenly and so decisively cast aside, so generally and so swiftly forgotten, had it been truly comprehended and met the needs of the times. It seems more likely that the support of the Monarchy and the Ministry of Culture only delayed the collapse of a philosophic system that could not survive without the continuing support of its author because it did not succeed in establishing a comprehensible ground for contemporary spiritual and scientific developments. We thus seem to be driven to the conclusion that Hegel's solution to the problem opened up by the antinomy was either insufficient altogether or at best sufficient only within the idiosyncratic political and spiritual horizon of his own times.

Hegel attempted to establish a ground in the absolute for the reconciliation of nature and freedom and thus to resolve the contradictions that had manifested themselves in the French Revolution, English bourgeois society, and German spiritual life. In this attempt he was at least temporarily successful. The collapse of Hegelianism, however, opened up anew these dangerous possibilities for human life. Indeed, it would not be so farfetched to assert that the history of philosophic thought since Hegel has in many respects been an attempt to come to terms with these possibilities and the history of political affairs an indication of the manifest failure to do so.

The signs of this collapse, however, were already apparent in the split within the Hegel School itself during the 1830s between the "Old" or "Right" and the "Young" or "Left" Hegelians. The Right Hegelians attempted at first to preserve the Hegelian synthesis, fastening upon his systematic reconciliation of man and God, which had raised the ire of traditional Christianity, and on his liberal political prescriptions, which they hoped to see embodied in a reformed Germany. After the failure of 1848, however, they turned increasingly toward Romantic nationalism and a rapprochement with traditional Christianity and the Bismarckian state. This turn was in part the result of a perceived spiritual affinity but was driven as well by the inner dynamics of their debate with the Young Hegelians.

The Young Hegelians, on their part, were not interested in the preservation of the Hegelian system but in its actualization. Indeed, they believed that the conservative systemic element in Hegel's thought was fundamentally at odds with its radical dialectical methodology. Hegel's claim that "the rational is actual and the actual is rational" seemed to them only a quietistic buttress of the traditional order. They thus turned increasingly toward a dialectical investigation of the empirical actuality of nature and history that Hegel in their view had improperly neglected. They did not, however, simply abandon rationality in favor of actuality but rather posited the rational as the goal of the actual. They thus returned to the Enlightenment notion of progress and historical accelerationism that in Hegel's view had produced the French Revolution. In contradistinction to the Right Hegelians who saw the nation or *Volk* as the real historical actor, the Young Hegelians and especially Marx and Engels argued that the masses were the source of historical change and that history was consequently not the development of the absolute through the various forms of national spirit or consciousness but an ever-sharpening class conflict engendered by the dialectical development of the means of production.

The Young Hegelians and ultimately even the Right Hegelians thus came to abandon Hegel's systematic resolution of the antinomy. They were consequently able to free themselves from the mystery of Hegel's absolute synthesis while preserving his dialectical methodology, but only by sacrificing his all-embracing ground and the political and spiritual reconciliation that it entailed. Thus, while the Right Hegelians were able to come to terms with Romanticism and the Young Hegelians with natural science, they failed to provide a real solution for the fundamental political and spiritual contradictions.

At first glance, neo-Kantianism seems even less likely to provide such a solution, and its success is thus somewhat surprising. On closer examination, however, the reasons for this success become relatively clear. From the perspective of Romanticism, on one hand, and natural science, on the other, the Hegelian synthesis of the truths of science and the truths of morality within the absolute seemed ridiculous and artificial. That the fervor of nationalistic feeling should be subordinated to rational laws or that the exactitude of the experimental method should be beclouded with metaphysical speculations seemed to those of the time and still to many today foolish or indeed obnoxious. Neo-Kantianism, however, accepted the separation of facts and values. It was thus compatible with both natural science and Romanticism and seemed to provide the ground for their mutual coexistence and indeed, in its notion of a progressive realization of the truth, for their mutual reconciliation. The ground for this reconciliation, however, was never demonstrated and thus remained fundamentally obscure, which consequently served only to conceal the real contradiction at the heart of modern life and thought. The superficiality of this "rostrum" philosophy and its failure to come to grips with the question of facts and values, did not, however, long remain concealed. The recognition of this failure though did not lead man back to a systematic metaphysics on the Hegelian model but opened up instead the terrifying abyss of nihilism.

Hegel had attempted to resurrect and preserve the metaphysical unity that Christianity had established through his speculative synthesis of the absolute. While many traditional Christians believed that this was little more than a concealed atheism or panlogism that in Spinozistic fashion denied the transcendent God, Hegel saw that the basis for traditional Christianity had been decisively undermined by the Enlightenment and that consequently only a Christianity that could come to terms with reason henceforth would be viable. It was such a reconciliation of reason and revelation, of the finite and the infinite, that he sought to achieve. The collapse of the Hegelian system, however, obliterated the ground for such a rational Christianity and led, on the one hand, to the increasing predominance of pragmatic and positivistic reason in the form of natural science and technology and, on the other hand, to the growing recognition that "God is dead" and that God does not arise from the dead, as Hegel had maintained, but that "God remains dead."[2] The collapse of Hegelianism thus led to the implicit nihilism of a science and technology that despite their magnificent capacity to improve the conditions of human life are constitutionally unable to recognize or come to terms with the question of the ground, and to the explicit nihilism of a "poetic" thinking that grasps the question of the ground as a result of its experience of the meaningless flux of historical actuality but that lacks the concrete foundation in practical life necessary to resolve it. This nihilism, however, also gave rise to the profound attempts of Kierkegaard, Nietzsche, Dilthey, and Husserl to provide an adequate answer to it.

Kierkegaard, like the Young Hegelians in general, was dissatisfied with Hegel's systematic solution. He did not, however, follow their path toward a scientific examination of historical actuality but turned instead to the consideration of the unique and inexplicable reality of individual existence and its relationship to the divine. It was on this point that Hegel in his view had gone astray, for in reconciling reason and revelation he had undermined the basis for the real choice *between* reason and revelation that is central to an authentic Christianity and an authentic human existence. In establishing a merely intellectual connection in place of a passionate commitment of man to God, Hegel had thus destroyed the real basis for human life and thought. In view of this, Kierkegaard abandoned all systematic solutions to the question of the ground in favor of an all-grounding leap of faith. His solution, however, was not completely satisfying, for he was only able to overcome the contradiction at the heart of Hegel's absolute synthesis by driving a theological wedge between man's existence and the ground of that existence. He thus left man with a fundamental choice but without any ground for making such a choice.

In contrast to Kierkegaard, Nietzsche was unwilling to accept any solution that hearkened back to Christianity. God in his view was dead, and any appeal to the divine or absolute was consequently untenable. The world, as he saw it, was not the creation of an eternal God nor was it governed by a universal reason. It was rather the chaos of becoming, the will to power that continually constitutes and reconstitutes itself in an unending variety of forms. Thus, the rationality of historical development that Hegel believed he had secured in the absolute becomes in Nietzsche's thought the irrationality of a world and history that rest not upon a ground but upon an abyss. The ground, therefore, cannot transcend the world, and thought cannot fly off into absolutes to explain or overcome the contradictions of this world but must confront historical actuality itself. The result of this confrontation, however, is nothing other than the explicit recognition of historicism, relativism, and nihilism, i.e., the recognition that there is no ultimate goal or purpose and thus no inherent reason or meaning to existence.

Nietzsche, however, did not thereby simply abandon the notion of the ground but attempted to show that the ground was implicit in actuality itself. This is his doctrine of the eternal recurrence. While there is no eternal reason or being, according to Nietzsche, becoming constitutes itself into an eternally recurring circular whole. In this way he believed it was possible "to press onto becoming the form of being" and consequently to retrieve life from the utter meaninglessness that becoming seems to entail. The doctrine of the eternal recurrence, however, is merely posited and cannot be demonstrated on Nietzsche's own terms. It too, as Nietzsche at times seems to admit, depends upon a "leap of faith" in the form of the creative insight of a "divine" madness. Like Hegel's notion of the absolute and Kierkegaard's transcendent God, Nietzsche's conception of the eternal recurrence thus remains obscure.

While Nietzsche and Kierkegaard seek to resolve the question of the ground by rejecting Hegel's systematic reconciliation of reason and history in favor of a trans-rational eternality, their failure to make this eternality and its connection to historical actuality clear and comprehensible led to an even deeper and more trenchant form of nihilism. Hegel had understood historical actuality as the external manifestation of the dialectical development of reason and spirit. Kierkegaard and Nietzsche on the contrary had denied the capacity of reason to form or grasp historical actuality as a whole. The success of their critique of Hegelianism and their failure to articulate a viable alternative to it, however, left man with nothing but the flux of historical actuality on which to take his stand. They thus prepared the way for Dilthey and historicism.

In Dilthey's view the ultimately real is not to be found in a transcendent or immanent eternality but in the concrete actuality of life and life-experience. By life, however, he does not mean the particular life-experience of an individual human being but rather the agglomeration of life-experiences that characterize historical humanity. Each individual always exists within a certain historical horizon that determines the way in which he lives and interprets his own experiences. Man thus cannot simply rely upon his own individual experience in attempting to understand the natural world and human life because each man sees only partially and therefore imperfectly. What is necessary instead is historical study, which turns not to some supposedly "objective" account of the past but which imaginatively projects itself into the consciousness of past ages while recognizing at the same time the limits put on such a projection by the historical circumstances of its own time. On this basis Dilthey believed it was possible to isolate certain historical archetypes and thus to establish a basis for a rational science of the human spirit (*Geisteswissenschaft*). It is hard to see, however, how such a notion can resist relativism and nihilism. Dilthey argues that life is everywhere and always already organized and therefore meaningful, but his historicist assumptions call into question the basic principles at the heart of all forms of life. Moreover, he also calls into question the possibility of all immediate knowledge of the real and demands instead an apparently endless hermeneutic examination of the historical and epistemological accretions of meaning. Thus, to many critics Dilthey and historicism generally seem to obliterate the ground for all knowledge of what is simply true and to replace it with a relativism and nihilism that is intellectually debilitating and politically and morally corrosive. Among the foremost of these critics was Husserl.

Like Dilthey, Husserl was convinced that philosophy had to come to terms with concrete existence, but he did not believe that historicism or for that matter positivistic naturalism had really done so. In his view both were in fact constitutionally incapable of grasping existence because they were insulated from it by their own historical and epistemological presuppositions. It was thus necessary to turn away from both historicism and naturalism and to return "to the things themselves." Such a return was not, however, a new objectivism, for the real, as Husserl understood it, is discovered not in being but in consciousness. It is this truth that phenomenology attempts to reveal by tracing the various modes of being back to the fundamental structures of transcendental consciousness. Through such an analysis Husserl believed man could come to know what was simply true. Such a return to a Cartesian or Kantian beginning, however, necessarily runs the danger of subjectivism, and it was thus perhaps not accidental that Husserl was never able to successfully resolve the question of intersubjectivity, i.e., the question of the social basis of life and thought. Despite such difficulties, however, this thought represented a real challenge to all forms of historicism.

The German philosophical world at the beginning of the twentieth century was torn by these various conflicting schools of thought. Positivism, neo-Kantianism, historicism, and phenomenology all had their advocates and disciples, Nietzsche and Kierkegaard were read with a passionate intensity, and even Hegel had been re-discovered and rehabilitated. The philosophic landscape was thus much changed from the time of Hegel. This transformation was in large part due to the collapse of Hegelianism and the rise of the question of nihilism. The nineteenth century, which still lived in the remnants of the European tradition and the anticipation of the eventual triumph of reason and science, was, however, unable to grasp the real magnitude and seriousness of nihilism. The twentieth century on the contrary became all too horribly aware of this question as a result of the First World War, which like a great storm washed away all of the comfortable illusions of traditional European civilization. The War thus gave the contemporary philosophic debate a real meaning and urgency that it had previously lacked. It seemed to many that a new beginning had to be made, that in some way the philosophical presuppositions of modernity or perhaps even of the West itself had been monstrously defective and that consequently a new way of thinking that went beyond modernity and the West was needed. This was the problem that impelled thinking in the years following the First World War, and it impelled no one's thought so completely and so power-fully as that of Heidegger.

Heidegger was born in 1889 and thus raised and educated in the years preceding the War. His earliest works in fact reflect the scholarly debates of this period. He had received his philosophical education under the neo-Kantian historian and value-philosopher Heinrich Rickert, and from an early period had been attracted to the work of Dilthey and Kierkegaard and somewhat later to that of Nietzsche and Hegel. Indeed, his early thought has been characterized as the attempt to think the "is" of the Kantian categories as "life" in Dilthey's sense, i.e., as the irreducible historical facticity of human existence.[3] Heidegger's concern with such a reconciliation apparently arose in consequence of his encounter with phenomenology. While still a student in the *Gymnasium* he had become deeply interested in the question of Being as it appeared in the thought of Franz Brentano, an early and influential phenomenologist. It is thus hardly surprising that he soon became interested in the thought of Husserl, Brentano's student, or that he later became his friend and philosophical ally, when both he and Husserl were teaching at Freiburg. Heidegger's early thought thus became at least in one sense phenomenological.[4] What apparently appealed to him most about phenomenology, however, was not so much its methodology, which he later abandoned, but its imperative to return to the concrete actuality of human existence. Heidegger's attachment to phenomenology was always tempered by his profound sense of the necessity of seriously confronting the philosophical tradition. He saw the lack of such a considera-tion in Husserl as a serious drawback.[5] The attempt to reconcile the systema-tic thought of neo-Kantianism with the historical thought of Dilthey and Hegel under the rubric of phenomenology, i.e., to interpret time as the transcendental horizon for the question of Being and thus to open up the way to a new consideration of the ground, was the project of Heidegger's unfinished magnum opus, *Being and Time*.

The specific task of *Being and Time*, according to Heidegger, was to raise the question of the meaning of Being (*Sein*) through an analysis of human Being (*Dasein*) in terms of temporality.[6] Through this analysis of human historicity Heidegger hoped to reveal time as the horizon of Being itself. The goal of Heidegger's project in *Being and Time* was thus nothing less than the determination of the fundamental relationship of Being and noth-ing or, as Gadamer suggests, the demonstration that "Being itself is time."[7] In this way Heidegger hoped to overcome the basic presuppositions of Western metaphysics that had in his view led to nihilism. He was unable to complete the project to his own satisfaction, however, and consequently never published the decisive second half of the work. This failure was in part apparently the result of the Cartesian or Kantian presuppositions of his phenomenological methodology. As a result, the language of *Being and Time* and consequently Heidegger's analysis remained inextricably entwined in subjectivity and a subjectivistic metaphysics, which, as Heidegger himself later argued, excluded even the possibility of raising the question of Being as such.[8] The completion of the project of *Being and Time* could only be achieved by abandoning phenomenology and explicitly confronting the problem of subjectivity. For Heidegger this meant a decisive "turn" in his thought that manifested itself in the first instance as a thorough and unrelenting critique of modernity.[9]

Heidegger's Critique of Modernity

According to Heidegger, modernity is characterized by subjectivity, i.e., by the fact that in modern times man himself serves as the measure and ground of all truth and hence as the measure and ground of all ethical and political life. Modernity is thus also the realm of freedom, for the predominance of subjectivity frees man from the theocentric structure of traditional Christian society.[10] Truth ceases to depend upon the authority of revelation and finds its ground in man's own perception and reflection. Consequently, human life can no longer be founded upon claims of divine or traditional right but instead must discover a new basis in subjectivity itself, i.e., in the perceptions, feelings, opinions, and ratiocinations of man.

Heidegger does not mean to assert, however, that the truth which forms the basis of human life in modernity is merely subjective in opposition to the objectivity of science. Rather the universality of subjectivity is necessarily bound up with the universality of objectivity: the discovery of the self as the basis of truth and the subsequent legitimation of an ethics and politics based upon feelings, opinions, and desires has as its necessary complement the development of modern science, which establishes an objective criterion for all natural and historical being. There can thus be no subject without an object and no object without a subject, and modern man is fundamentally subjective not because he is incapable of objectivity but because he conceives of himself within the subject-object relationship. The dualism of subjectivity and objectivity thus constitutes the essence of modernity.

The source of this new conception of subjectivity, according to Heidegger, is Descartes' revolutionary reinterpretation of man and of the world in the formula *ego cogito ergo sum* as self-consciousness. The sort of truth that characterizes self-consciousness, i.e., certainty, thus becomes the standard in terms of which everything else is measured and legitimated. The ground that had hitherto been conceived as the idea of the good or the universal natural substance or the transcendent God thus appears in Descartes as the human subject. Henceforth man *is* only insofar as he perceives and thinks, and the world *is* only insofar as it can be thought or perceived. Man's humanity thus is thought to reside not in his membership in the polis or the church but in self-consciousness, and man is no longer conceived as a creature of the earth but as an independent being who can measure, conquer, and transform nature. Man thus becomes something *in* and *for* himself, capable of establishing laws and judging both man and nature on the basis of himself alone. Modern man consequently becomes free in a hitherto unknown way and sets out to liberate the world from superstition and error and to refound social and political institutions upon man himself. The Cartesian revolution thus propels man in a new direction and gives him a new task. The history of modernity, as Heidegger understands it, is the completion of this task.

Heidegger, however, does not mean to assert that subjectivity and hence modernity are simply Descartes' creation or even that Descartes is the historical beginning of modernity. The question of the ground in Heidegger's view is the fundamental question of all metaphysics ancient and modern and the specific answer that it receives in the thought of Descartes was prepared by a long historical tradition. The search for the ground as the *fundamentum absolutum inconcussum veritatis* already had a place in William of Occam's nominalist distinction of word and thing and was crucial to Luther's conception of the certainty of faith and Galileo's conception of mathematical certainty.[11] Moreover, this conception of freedom and its political consequences were already recognized by Machiavelli.[12] Descartes' precedence in Heidegger's view is not historical but ontological—he was the first to articulate the new relationship of man and the world, which remained implicit and unthought in Luther, Galileo, and Machiavelli. Descartes is decisive because he was the first to determine the relationship of knowing and being as a whole, i.e., to develop a method and system that explains the character of subjectivity and freedom ontologically.

Nor does Heidegger mean to assert that modernity is characterized by individuality. Subjectivity is not individuality. In fact, as a way of being, subjectivity in his view belongs as much to the We as to the I. Modernity frees man from the traditional dominion of the church and state insofar as it establishes a new ground for his existence in subjectivity, but the character of this subjectivity itself is not thereby determined. Thus, modernity creates a collective subjectivity as a necessary antipode to individual subjectivity. In fact it is only because man has become a subject that the question arises for him whether he ought to be an I or a We, a personality in a community or a mere group member in a body social, an individual economic actor or a class, a citizen or a human being.[13]

As the realm of subjectivity and freedom, modernity is the realm in which man becomes something in and for himself. The consequence of man's elevation above nature and community, however, is a rift or separation of

man and the world. The world of which he was hitherto a part thus becomes
something opposed to him. It is no longer a place in which he can dwell and
be at home, no longer an *ēthos* in which ethical and political life are
possible, but an alien entity which resists and threatens him.[14] In his uttermost being man thus becomes alienated from the world and is consequently thrown into uncertainty and insecurity. Modern man finds the
solution to this uncertainty and alienation not in a reintegration into the
natural world or the community but in the conquest of nature and its
subordination to the categories of subjectivity, i.e., in the objectification and
mastery of the alien other.

　　This objectification of nature, according to Heidegger, is achieved
through science and labor. Man is established in subjectivity as self-
consciousness. Self-consciousness, however, is nothing other than the consciousness of consciousness, i.e., in Descartes' terms I am that being that is
aware of itself as aware of the world; I am the thinking of thinking. The
ground that is sought in subjectivity thus depends not merely upon the
inner more or less formal self-certainty of self-consciousness but also upon
the certainty of the world that provides the substance of the self, i.e., of
thinking. The objectification of the world through science aims at a secure
determination of nature as the substantial complement of the formal certainty of subjectivity. This is achieved by the objectification and subordination of nature to the categories of subjectivity. Man reinterprets the world in
his image and comes to understand the world as a world-picture (*Weltbild*),
i.e., in terms of a scientific model. According to Heidegger, this rationalization of the world takes a number of different forms—the Enlightenment,
reason and its laws, the humanism of classicism, idealism, and even positivism—all of which, however, merely represent an objectivity commensurate
with human subjectivity, a system of laws that describe the necessary
motions of objects and hence allow for the prediction and subsequent
manipulation of nature to secure this subjectivity. On the basis of such a
world-picture the mastery of the actual world becomes possible. Here,
however, the application of human labor is necessary. Labor in this sense
completes what science begins insofar as it transforms nature into objects
for human use. It is this organization of labor under the leadership of
science to manipulate and transform the natural world in the interest of the
certainty and security of man as ground and standard of all truth and
therefore of all being that constitutes the essential activity of subjectivity and
hence the characteristic activity of modernity. Thus, insofar as man is
established in subjectivity, the scientist, *homo conscientia* as *homo scientia*,
and the worker, *homo faber*, replace the priest and the noble as the model
of man's humanity.[15] Henceforth, their activity becomes *the* human activity.

　　This objectification of the world, however, fails to overcome the alienation and insecurity that characterize and motivate modern man. Not only is
this task essentially unlimited, but it also continually brings man in conflict

with his fellows. This competition, however, is not in Heidegger's view the consequence of political or personal ambition, as Machiavelli or the ancients understood it, nor simply the result of a universal desire for self-preservation, as Hobbes might have characterized it, but the consequence of a new understanding of man's humanity and the subsequent attempt of men to realize it. To be a human being for modern man means to be a subject and hence to objectify the world through science and labor according to the categories of subjectivity. This is true, however, for all men: the humanity and freedom of each is bound up with his ability to master and objectify nature. This necessarily brings men into conflict with one another and imposes limitations upon their subjectivity and therefore upon their humanity and freedom. Thus, no single subject is able to overcome alienation and insecurity merely through the objectification of the natural world. Moreover, mutual restraint produces only universal dissatisfaction and frustration. This in turn undercuts mutual restraint and radicalizes the problem: man discovers that he himself is in danger of being objectified and enslaved, that he is both subject *and* object and consequently that he is in constant danger of losing his humanity altogether, his subjectivity, and his freedom.

For every man qua subject, every other man is both subject and object, both an opposing will and like the rest of nature a raw material that may be used and shaped by the will. The competition for the objectification of nature, i.e., for the conquest and exploitation of the earth, becomes in Heidegger's view the struggle of wills for mastery over one another and over the world as a whole. Man becomes human, therefore, insofar as he is able to subdue the will of others, i.e., insofar as he can treat them as objects or as means to his own ends, to his own security and freedom. This objectification of man comes to encompass all realms of human life. In the political realm it takes the form of a technical politics of power and control, which organizes man à la Machiavelli for conquest and rule, and in the economic realm the technical organization of men and machines which aims at the objectification and exploitation of nature. No realm of life can remain sacrosanct and no traditional social or political institutions can be tolerated because man's very humanity, as he understands it, is bound up with this transformation. All of those traditional institutions, which hitherto limited arbitrary power, are thus undermined and abolished by the demands subjectivity makes for its security and freedom. Thus, in a paradoxical fashion, the demand for freedom opens up the possibility of universal slavery and the pursuit of man's humanity produces a thorough inhumanity.

If Heidegger is correct, then any modern conception of morality or politics that seeks to secure human freedom on the basis of either a natural or a rational law that recognizes men as subjects and hence as ends in themselves is ultimately untenable because the natural and human rights that arise with subjectivity are put in jeopardy and ultimately overturned by subjectivity itself. Subjectivity entails subjugation whether to a single man or a majority, a party or a class, a state or a race, or to a general will that forces each "to be free." Thus, subjectivity, which frees man from traditional authority, creates in its stead a new bondage in many ways more terrible and universal than any of its predecessors. Subjectivity and modernity thus culminate in the will to power and the will to will, in nihilism and a totalitarian world technology.

The will to power, according to Heidegger, is the penultimate form of modernity. In it the distinction of subject and object dissolves. As Nietzsche puts it: "*this world is the will to power—and nothing besides! And you yourselves are also this will to power—and nothing besides!*"[16] The will to power thus makes possible the universal objectification of everything, for objectification becomes nothing other than the subordination of the will to itself. The end of the will is the subjugation of man and nature, i.e., power. This power, however, has as its end only the security of the will to will. The will to power is thus implicitly the will to will.[17] As such it is merely the means to further means with no end beyond itself and thus fundamentally nihilistic. The will to power, which rests upon the recognition that God is dead, thus passes over into the all-encompassing and all-establishing will (*Ge-Stell*) of an irresistible world technology.[18]

The advent of the will to power as the will to will opens up the possibility for the unlimited exploitation of everything. This occurs through the universal establishment of everything not merely as objects but as pure instrumentalities (*Bestände*) and through the subordination of all subjectivity and freedom to the overarching necessities of the will implicit in technology. Man is organized on a global scale by political, social, and economic agencies for production and consumption, and the earth itself becomes nothing but a reserve of energy and raw materials that are brought forth and directed by a technology that aims only at its own continuation and growth. The absolute technical state itself serves only to guide the total mobilization of human and natural resources for the unlimited exploitation and consumption of the earth. Politics along with all other institutions thus becomes an appendage of technology. In this "planetary imperialism" of technical organization subjectivity and modernity reach their end.[19]

With the advent of world technology freedom is extinguished. The general conception of technology as a tool in the hands of a self-determining humanity is in Heidegger's view a fundamental misunderstanding, for technology has a logic and necessity of its own that passes beyond human control. All men are governed by economic and technical necessities: the competition for the unlimited exploitation of the earth requires the objectification and subordination not just of some men to others but of all men to the world task. Man thus becomes human to the extent that he constitutes himself as a raw material that has no determinate characteristics, or as a pure instrumentality that can be used as momentary necessity dictates. Man becomes an interchangeable part.[20]

In the midst of this technological frenzy of production and consumption, of subordination and exploitation, man fails to recognize, according to Heidegger, that it is the very subjectivity and freedom he regards as the essence of his humanity that uproots him and casts him into uncertainty, insecurity, and alienation. Hence he does not recognize that all his striving only more completely obliterates his place in the world and his true humanity. Indeed, man and the world are thereby so transformed that the very possibility of a place, of an *ēthos*, and hence of an authentic ethics and politics is extinguished. Man who had a home in the world in the context of the polis and traditional life is at home in the modern world everywhere and nowhere: as a pure instrumentality man can adapt himself to anything. As *homo faber* man becomes mass man.[21]

Man's reaction to this universal homelessness and alienation in Heidegger's view is not a thoughtful hesitation and reflection upon his own being but an overly hasty decision to fabricate a place for himself, i.e., to objectify himself and his tradition in such a way that every place becomes a necessary place, determined by the inevitability of historical development. The science that achieves this is History (*Historie*). As the science of the *res gestae* History is the objectification of what has occurred. Insofar as it is an objectification, however, History is severed from history (*Geschichte*) itself, from the tradition of which it was a part and in which it had a place, and hence can be made and remade according to the momentary necessities of power and technological development. In this manner History not only fails to establish a secure place for man but indeed itself becomes an, if not the, crucial weapon in the struggle for power and thereby more thoroughly fosters human insecurity and alienation. History thus serves only as an apologetic and polemic for the various conflicting forces concerned with unlimited objectification and exploitation and thereby becomes entangled in this conflict itself.

The resulting disagreement about the Historical interpretation of history in Heidegger's view leads not to the abandonment of History but to a relativism that rests upon the recognition of the subjective element in all History. However, this does not resolve the question about the character of history but only gives rise to a thorough confusion, which further obliterates the truth of tradition and man's place in the world. This Historical confusion about history in Heidegger's view is Historicism. Modernity's response to Historicism, however, is not a return to or a reconsideration of the traditional but rather an ever more vehement attachment to a particular Historical interpretation and an increasingly comprehensive attempt to persuade and indeed to force others to recognize and accept its manifest truth. History thus becomes ideology and replaces philosophy, politics, art, etc., as the determinative explanation of human life.[22]

Ideology leads to a simplification of History. It purports to explain the Historically necessary way of objectifying, using, and exploiting the world and the Historically necessary social and political organization best suited to carry out this task. In the midst of modern uncertainty and confusion it tells man in Lenin's words "what is to be done" in order to overcome alienation and secure himself in the world. According to Heidegger, ideology thus resolves the confusion of Historicism through a *totalistic* explanation of man's origin and destiny, which provides a blueprint and imperative for political and economic action. This ideology manifests itself through the mass media as propaganda and journalism, which interpret and subordinate events within the Historical structure that ideology defines.[23] In this way ideology not only subordinates all individuals to its guiding interpretation of History but directs them daily according to the momentary demands of power and technological development. Ideology thus comes to form and transform human being without any concern for human freedom or rights or spirituality and hence serves only to further solidify the rule of the inhuman and the institutionalization of a universal slavery. Moreover, the exclusive and ever more fanatical claim of every ideology necessarily brings it into conflict with every other ideology. The result is a "propaganda war" or a "struggle of world views" to determine in Nietzsche's words "who shall be master of the earth," i.e., which ideological interpretation will direct the conquest and exploitation of man and nature. This struggle unfolds itself as world war and *homo faber* as mass man thus becomes *homo brutalitas*.[24]

This struggle in Heidegger's view is essentially a struggle to determine the character of the institutionalization of nihilism, i.e., which sort of political or social arrangement is best able to exploit nature and hence best able to overcome alienation and insecurity. World war is thus the necessary consequence of the establishment of man in subjectivity. War, however, does not decide anything because there is really nothing to decide and in fact only more completely encompasses man in the struggle for mastery while simultaneously obliterating the last vestiges of traditional life. Man is thereby delivered into unconditional and unlimited servitude through the total mobilization and organization of mankind for total war on the basis of the totalistic imperative of the prevailing ideologies. World war thus does not solve the problems of modern man and in fact only propels him into totalitarianism.[25]

Nor does war end in peace. The end of war is rather only a "cold war," a continuing ideological struggle that dissolves the whole distinction of war and peace. At the bottom of this apparently insoluble conflict and competition lies not the simple desire for economic advantage or military superiority or even political domination but rather universal homelessness and alienation that give rise to an unbearable uncertainty and insecurity that in turn motivate man in his fruitless technological quest for stability in and through the universal objectification of everything. There is thus a great danger in believing that this ideological dispute is really about politics or morality in Heidegger's view, for such a belief only reinforces the same striving for predominance and the same pursuit of universal objectification that is the source of the conflict itself.

The greatest danger thus is not nuclear annihilation but the delusion of peace. Peace in Heidegger's view has become indistinguishable from war and is in fact a preparation for it.[26] The horrors of war and nuclear annihilation are at least apparent, whereas peace is cloaked with the benign aspect of progress. This progressive peace, however, is continually upset by new economic, social, and political crises that mobilize men to develop ever new technical solutions.[27] Such "solutions," however, only further intensify alienation and insecurity. Indeed, the greatest danger to man in this sense is apparently prosperity, which conceals the nihilism of world technology. According to Heidegger, "the desolation of the earth is just as compatible with the attainment of the highest living standards of man as with the organization of the equality of happiness of all men."[28] While modernity may produce prosperity, it does so only by sacrificing man's true humanity as *homo humanus*, since it necessarily destroys the earth as earth, i.e., the *humus* of the *humanus*, and consequently sets man adrift in an infinite cosmos, a space age in which he has all the space, all the *Lebensraum*, he could desire, but in which he has no place that is peculiarly his own and hence is destined to continually transform everything into his own, into an object for his insatiable and unlimited will.[29]

Heidegger describes three concrete forms of world civilization at the end of modernity: Americanism, Marxism, and Nazism. In his view all three are avatars of subjectivity and nihilism and thus are metaphysically, although perhaps not morally or politically, identical. All are characterized by the dictatorship of the public over the private and by the predominance of natural science, economics, public policy (*Politik*), and technology. As such they represent the unlimited exploitation of man and nature by an institutionalized nihilism.[30]

In Heidegger's view it is not liberalism or democracy that is essential to Americanism but a particular form of subjectivity, i.e., logical positivism. Combined with psychology, psychoanalysis, and sociology and making increasingly greater use of cybernetics to facilitate the direction and coordination of affairs, it develops operational models to explain the nature of psychological, social, economic, and political phenomena. American philosophy thus abandons itself to the technological essence of modernity and indeed even understands itself as the handmaiden of science. In this sense, however, Americanism is really only a transplanted Europeanism that reconstructs all human understanding on the model of mathematical physics. Although man thus may develop an enormously complex world-picture (*Weltbild*) that renders events highly predictable through the application of a mathematical-statistical methodology, this science fails to reach the essence of either man or nature and in fact serves only to facilitate the technological exploitation of both. The reality of Americanism, according to Heidegger, is the industrial complex, which is the central agency of unfettered economic and technological striving. It is this agency that is responsible for the universal organization of the common man and that extends its rule throughout the world through foreign aid and the development of a world market.[31]

Marxism like Americanism is only another form of subjectivity and the opposition that is supposed on the Soviet side between bourgeois society and industrial society and on the American side between individualism and collectivism is metaphysically untenable. Communism is not only a party or a world-view and Americanism is not only a way of life.[32] Both are rather institutionalized forms of nihilism as technology. Heidegger does not mean thereby to deny that there are decisive moral and political differences between the two systems. The political and moral, however, are not in his view what is essentially at stake. The question is rather whether either of these systems offers an answer to the underlying nihilism that ever more explicitly characterizes modern life. That one seduces man from his true humanity with pleasure, happiness, and prosperity while the other relies upon coercion and indoctrination may be ethically decisive but does not preserve man's humanity. Nihilism, as Heidegger understands it, cannot be overcome by the replacement of God by reason, progress, or an economic socialism that establishes mere democracy but necessarily depends upon a transformation of the essence of man himself.[33]

All Marxism in Heidegger's view rests upon Marx's statement that "to be radical is to grasp the matter by its root. The root for man, however, is man himself."[34] Marxism is consequently the social production of society and the self-production of man as a social being. This is the essence of subjectivity as technology. Marx thus grasps Being as the process of production and believes that he thereby overcomes the subjectivism or idealism of Hegelian dialectic and replaces it with an objective and scientific dialectical material-ism. On this basis Marx can claim that previous philosophy has only inter-preted the world and that now what counts is to change it. Not only does Marx thereby fail to recognize that interpretation is always a transformation and that thought is merely the highest form of praxis but he is also blind to the necessarily conceptual basis of his own thought. Dialectical materialism thus represents the end of all philosophy, for all questions in Heidegger's view die in its net, and the end of politics, for politics becomes just another means of man's self-production.[35]

Both Americanism and Marxism fundamentally misconstrue human spir-ituality as calculative intelligence in the service of the objectification and exploitation of man and nature. This is also characteristic of Nazism.[36] Nazism in Heidegger's view aims at the creation of a humanity that is neither an individual nor a mass but a type, on the model of the Prussian soldier or the Jesuit. This type is the overman who has as his necessary complement the underman. This in Heidegger's view represents the end and reversal of modernity and indeed of metaphysics as such in which man as the rational animal becomes an *animalitas*, who recognizes a "higher" truth than reason, the truth of instinct. In this way subjectivity unfolds itself as the *brutalitas* of the *bestialitas*. At the end of modernity *homo sapiens* as *homo faber* establishes his being in Nietzsche's phrase *Homo est brutum bestiale* as the blond beast.[37]

Subjectivity, which is utterly dissolved in the necessity of the will to power and the will to will, appears in the absolute instincts of the *Führer* or leaders who articulate the subjective essence of race and establish the universal exploitation of all human and natural material through world mastery. These leaders solve the problem of values insofar as their determinations eschew reason altogether and rest upon their unthinking and unknowable instincts. The opinion that these leaders are merely egotistical and self-seeking, however, fundamentally misconstrues their significance. They are rather "the anger, that does not escape from the consequences of anger," the necessary response to the subjectivistic demand for direction and order, for certainty and security in a nihilistic world in which reason can no longer find a ground for choice. Their instincts rise above intellect, which is paralyzed by nihilism, to deed (*Tat*) and give the illusion of certainty and stability. What Nazism fails to recognize is that there is no essential difference between the overman and the underman since both have been reduced to beasts. The superrational and the subrational are substantively identical. Nazism's distinction of the two according to race is thus utterly arbitrary and hence in Heidegger's view only possible when subjectivity has become unconditional in a nihilism that overturns all standards of truth, morality, and right, when in Nietzsche's words "everything is permitted."[38]

Modernity, which begins in freedom, and the promise of science thus ends in nihilism, in world technology, totalitarianism, and total war. According to Heidegger, however, this disaster is not the fault of modernity. Modernity and modern metaphysics are in his view only the consequence of the unfolding of metaphysics and the West itself. Modernity leads to nihilism not because its own starting point is defective but because metaphysics itself is defective, because "metaphysics as metaphysics is authentic nihilism."[39] Plato's metaphysics differs from Nietzsche's only in that the nihilism that comes to light in the latter remains concealed in the former. One might well wonder, however, whether Heidegger does not overlook an issue of paramount importance here. If indeed the world and life are at heart irremediably nihilistic, it would seem that the proper response would be to cloak this nihilism in the shining fabric of myth or rationality so that this emptiness and its horrible consequences for human life might, at least by and large, go unnoticed, enabling most men to live relatively contented if fundamentally illusory lives. If such were indeed the case, then one might want to depreciate modern philosophy, which seeks increasingly to reveal such a nihilistic essence, and perhaps to foster instead an appreciation for the synthetic unity of ancient life. Although Heidegger is sympathetic to such a line of thought, he rejects it on three grounds. First, he believes that the contemporary world has succeeded in both revealing and covering up nihilism in such a way that, unless it is properly understood and overcome, the obliteration of human spirituality, which is already well advanced, will necessarily follow. The desire to obscure this nihilistic essence in the interest of humanity is thus too short-sighted, an opiate that relieves the pain while fostering a forgetfulness of the disease itself. Second, he does not believe that nihilism—at least as it is generally understood—is irremediable. Man may not be able to take effective action to ameliorate or resolve the problem of nihilism, but he can prepare the ground for such a resolution. Third, Heidegger believes that only on the basis of a real revelation or disclosure of the essence of nihilism, i.e., of the relationship of Being and nothing, is a true ethics and politics possible. Nihilism thus cannot be overcome by merely rejecting modernity in favor of antiquity but necessarily depends upon overcoming both modernity and antiquity and that means overcoming metaphysics and the West itself.

Heidegger's Critique of Metaphysics as the History of Being

The reinterpretation of Being as history or time presupposes the liberation of thought not only from the horizon of subjectivity but from the horizon of metaphysics as a whole. Overcoming metaphysics, however, is no mean task. Metaphysics has in fact become so pervasive in Heidegger's view that there is no realm of life or thought that is not subject to its categorical dominion. Metaphysics thus cannot simply be cast aside or rejected, and any attempted rejection can only serve to obscure and thus fortify the power of metaphysics over human life. Nor can it be simply negated, since every negation remains subliminally dependent upon its opposite for its substance and meaning. A mere negation of metaphysics thus remains entangled in the essence of metaphysics in the very moment it proclaims itself as a liberation from metaphysics. This in Heidegger's view was the fate of Nietzsche's thought. It is necessary to go beyond a mere rejection or negation of metaphysics and come to terms with its essence in order to liberate man from it and counteract its power over human life. This task Heidegger characterizes as the destruction of metaphysics or ontology. Its goal is the demonstration that metaphysics is nihilism.

Heidegger of course does not mean to assert that metaphysics is intentionally nihilistic and in fact argues that metaphysics always aims at overcoming nihilism. Metaphysics fails, however, because it fails to discover the true ground. This very failure, however, is hidden from metaphysics itself because metaphysics fails to grasp its own essence. To overcome nihilism and metaphysics it is thus first necessary to think what metaphysics leaves unthought, i.e., to come to terms with the unperceived essence of metaphysics itself and to demonstrate how this unthought essence pervades and determines the West.[40]

What metaphysics leaves unthought, according to Heidegger, is Being, and it is thus that it is nihilistic. The blame for this does not lie with metaphysics, however, but with Being itself: metaphysics fails to think Being only because Being itself withdraws and does not allow itself to be thought. From this perspective metaphysics and the West are characterized and determined as nihilism by the *absence* of Being. The attempt to come to terms with the essence of metaphysics and to demonstrate that metaphysics is fundamentally nihilistic is, therefore, also the attempt to come to the recognition of Being itself and to an understanding of the way in which Being has always secretly guided and determined the course of metaphysics and the West. The attempt to liberate man from metaphysics is thus fundamentally the attempt to establish him in the history of Being, i.e., in the history in which Being remains the unthought and unperceived horizon of all human possibilities.

This history in Heidegger's view is the result of the original revelation of Being and its subsequent withdrawal and concealment. It begins with the Greek experience of this revelation, which is then concealed in the thought of Plato and Aristotle, further obscured by Latin antiquity and medieval Christianity, and finally and utterly forgotten by modernity.[41]

This process of concealment or withdrawal itself occurs in and through the bifurcation of Being and being and the ever more encompassing interpretation of Being in terms of being. While Being thus does not simply disappear it is always thought only in terms of beings, i.e., as what lies behind beings or at their heart or what is other than or prior to them. The original experience of Being itself thus is lost, and man comes increasingly to experience only beings and to assume that their Being is self-evident and tautological. The ground of beings in Being thus appears in a vague way, but its very obviousness leads man to neglect and forget it. The history of the West is determined by this bifurcation of Being and being and the ever-greater concealment of Being within it. It ends with the complete withdrawal of Being and the corresponding predominance of being in the explicit nihilism of technology and totalitarianism. (For a schematization of this process see the diagram at the top of the following page.)

Metaphysics and the West begin with the experience of Being itself. This experience, however, is fundamentally different than the experience of beings. Being appeared for the Greeks not as just another being or entity but as the abyss, as a fundamental question or aporia that erupted out of ordinary everyday life and encompassed man in all its mysteriousness. This mysteriousness in turn evoked man's wonder and thus brought him to think. This thinking opened up a new world, brought new gods, a new ethics, a new politics, and a new conception of man's humanity—in short,

Pre-Socratic	Being (nature, cosmos, truth)	
Metaphysics Greek:	*Being* ⟵⟶	*beings* (appearance, becoming)
Plato	the forms, the good	objects of opinions, appearances
Aristotle	substance, substratum, what-Being	activity, completion, that-Being
Christian:		
Roman	idea, essence	actuality, existence
Christian	ground, infinite, creator	causality, the finite, creature
Modern:		
Early modern	subject, represen-tation ⟶	object, actuality ⟙
Nihilism	being (will, technology)	

this experience of the question of Being gave birth to the Greek world and through the Greeks to the West itself.

In speaking of the question of Being, however, Heidegger does not mean some vague question *about* Being but rather the explicit question which Being itself poses, the question *as* which Being *is*.[42] This question is "What is being?" and Western history, as Heidegger understands it, is nothing other than man's attempt to answer it. Insofar as the question itself impels man toward answers, the question, and that means Being itself, is forgotten. The history of the West is thus the ever-greater forgetfulness of the original question of Being, and the epochs that comprise this history are the consequence of the particular ways in which Being withdraws and conceals itself.

Each epoch is thus a particular form of misrepresentation or error that reveals the truth about answers, i.e., about beings, but disguises the truth about the question, i.e., about Being itself, and the sequence of epochs that comprise this history is determined by the degree of this misrepresentation. It would be a mistake, however, to see this development as dialectical in the ordinary sense of the term. Every epoch and ontology in Heidegger's view conceals as much as it reveals and is thus fundamentally insufficient. He denies, however, that it is this insufficiency that gives rise to the new ontology and argues instead that this transformation is a consequence of the further removal of Being itself as a question in favor of its answers. Each epoch or ontology is determined by the particular relationship of Being and being. The transformation of this relationship brought about by the withdrawal of Being out of this relationship thus necessarily undermines this ontology. The various transformations of Western ontology and thus the various epochs of Western history arise not out of defects or contradictions in the prevailing ontology but out of the changing manner in which Being both reveals and conceals itself.[43]

This dualism of question and answer, of revelation and concealment, that is the source of historical motion, appears for the Greeks as a struggle or *gigantomachia* of Being and being, or of Being and appearance, or, in Nietzsche's terms, of the real and apparent worlds. At the beginning, however, the Greeks experience this as a struggle within Being itself.[44] Being for them is, on one hand, the mysterious and sudden shining-forth of the incomprehensible and overpowering that produces conflict and disorder (*chaos, polemos, eris, pyr, phainesthai, deinon, moira, apeiron*) and, on the other, that which gathers everything together into a unified order or whole (*hen, eon, einai, emmenai, esmenai, logos, harmoniē, philia, dikē, pan, archē, chrēon*). The twofold of both these elements they understand as cosmos (*kosmos*), nature (*physis*), and especially truth (*alētheia*), all of which in Heidegger's view capture the fundamentally dualistic character of Being as both revelation and concealment.[45]

Being in this sense is likewise understood as the source of man's humanity as human Being. Man is human for the Greeks insofar as he is capable of thought and that means of speech. He comes to think and speak in the fundamental sense, however, only when he is struck by the mystery and wonder of Being. Man in this sense is used by Being, which always comes to be only through man. In being used by Being, however, man becomes human as the *zōon logon echon*, i.e., 'life that has speech' or, as it was later translated, the rational animal. Man is thus the place (*Da*) at which Being (*Sein*) comes to be and hence is human Being (*Dasein*). Man's humanity in this view, then, resides not in his passions or intellect or in his connection to his fellows through ethics, politics, or morality but originally and decisively in his connection to Being.

Insofar as human Being is bound up with Being, it is also caught up in the struggle in the heart of Being itself, between the question of Being and its various answers. For the pre-Socratics this struggle is carried out in art or what Heidegger often calls language (*Sprache*), and it is through art or language that the question of Being and its various answers determine the structure and character of Greek life, the character of the gods and the polis, the temples and tragedies, the games and philosophy.[46] With this conception of art Heidegger does not mean to assert the preeminence of poetry and tries in fact to show that there was no sharp distinction between poetry and philosophy, on one hand, and poetry and all the rest of the arts, on the other, at this time.[47] Indeed, the confrontation with the question of Being in his view is fundamentally a communal enterprise that involves poets, sculptors, architects, thinkers, and statesmen, all of whom take part in establishing the laws, customs, and institutions that characterize this world. What is crucial is not the particular form of activity but the openness to the question of Being that makes such an experience possible and the authenticity of the response that makes the answer meaningful. It is the experience of Being and this experience alone that involves man in the struggle to determine the ontological horizon of the world and that is the source of the wonder that evokes the creative thought that is capable of such a determination. As human Being man thus creates a new ontology and a new world for himself in response to the question posed by Being itself. Through his experience of Being he becomes a creative artist in the widest sense of the term and thus creates not merely beautiful things but an entire life and world.

A comparison to Nietzsche is enlightening. Nietzsche too argues that art is the source of all values and hence of all horizons and ontologies. In Heidegger's view, however, Nietzsche's understanding of creativity is fundamentally anthropomorphic and subjectivistic. For Nietzsche creativity is the exercise of the will of the individual who establishes new values through the projection of his inner state upon the world. He thus creates the world in his own image, and it is thus nothing but an objectification of his own will. Heidegger understands creativity on the contrary not as an assertive expression of the will but as the authentic response to the question which Being poses for man. Man is thus not a demigod or overman who paints his soul upon the heavens but a human Being (*Dasein*) who carries out the commission of Being (*Sein*) given in and as the question of Being. The particular character of the world that is thus brought into view is not the projection and universalization of the self but the unfolding of Being. Heidegger thus concludes that man's struggles only reflect the basic struggle in Being itself.[48]

The foremost creation of the Greeks and the foundation of their world was in Heidegger's view the polis.[49] He understands the polis, however, not in the modern sense as the place where the business of state is transacted but, taking his clue from Hölderlin, as the place of the revelation of Being and thus as the place at which gods and men take up relationship to one another, as the place at which man first recognizes his earthly mortality in opposition to the heavenly immortality of the gods.[50] It is in this sense that the polis is the source of man's humanity as human Being. The polis itself, however, arises in response to the question of Being. The Greeks in Heidegger's view understood this revelation as *chaos*, as the yawning openness, out of which everything arises and within which everything subsists. *Chaos* in this sense is the source of destiny that gives shape to the world. As such, it is, on one hand, the *whole*, that is greater than all its parts and, on the other, the *holy* (*das Heilige*, from the Indo-European root *kailo-,* 'uninjured,' 'whole'), that is older than time and beyond both gods and men.[51] As such it decides over both gods and men, whether they are, who they are, how they are, and when they are. The question of Being that appears in and as *chaos* or the abyss thus determines man's place in conjunction with or in opposition to the place of everything else, but especially with respect to the gods. Indeed, man's earthly mortality can only be understood in conjunction with their heavenly immortality. Insofar as man is determined with respect to the gods he has a particular place or *ēthos* that is his own and thus becomes capable of ethics. This place of the revelation of Being at which the relationship of men and gods is established is the polis. "Out of the severity of a comprehension that poeticizes, thinks, and builds they [the Greeks] were first able to approach the gods in a brightly structured presence. That is their founding and building of the polis as the place of the occurrence of history which is determined by the holy."[52] The polis in this sense is always the place of the gods and is characterized in its laws and institutions by the particular pantheon that has been revealed by poets, sculptors, thinkers, and statesmen in response to the revelation of Being. In this place the debate among men about what is pious and impious, great and small, valiant and cowardly, noble and ignoble, master and slave takes place. The medium of this debate is art or language, which thus establishes a rank order among human actions that culminates in the heroic life of fame and glory. This hierarchy is in turn the overpowering order of justice (*dikē*) which determines and regulates customs, actions, and opinions and thus gives man a home as human Being.[53]

The pre-Socratic experience of Being, however, is in Heidegger's view fundamentally tragic. The experience of the abyss of Being is the source of wonder and thus thought. It gives birth to politics and ethics but at the same time also opens up the fundamental mysteriousness of existence and casts man out of the everyday realm in which the prevailing order is accepted as a given. Those who are struck by Being in this way become preeminent as creators and founders but "become at the same time *apolis,* without city and place, alone, alien, without a way out in the midst of being as a whole, at the same time without statute and limit, without structure and order because as creators they must first ground all this."[54] Like Antigone and Oedipus, or for that matter Heracleitus, they are beyond good and evil, pariahs cast out not by their fellows but by their experience of the abyss of Being, which calls everything into question and directs them in a new and as yet uncharted direction. The experience of Being for the early Greeks is thus in Heidegger's view the experience of homelessness and nothingness that drives them to the attempt to establish a new home, a new *ēthos,* and hence a new ethics and politics through the articulation of new gods, heros, virtues, and laws, according to the clue given them by the particular character of the revelation of Being itself in and as the question "What is being?" Like Heracleitus such men seem apolitical, but this is only because they are not concerned with some immediate public use like those within the polis. They are concerned with what is far more important, the ground of the polis itself in Being. Thus, whatever public opinion may think of such men and however resolutely they may seem to abandon political life, their attendance upon the question of Being and the gods is the source of all ethics and politics and thus the authentic political act. In this heroic-tragic sense, battered, blinded, and cast out, they thus represent for the Greeks the highest human possibility.[55]

The tragic age in which such heroic figures have meaning and significance, however, is short-lived and comes to an end with the disappearance of the revelation and experience of Being. The reasons for this disappearance lie in Being itself. Being is always only as a question or aporia, i.e., as the abyss of Being. As this abyss, Being strikes man, evokes his wonder, and directs him toward a particular realm of answers. Being thus reveals a new realm and order of life, a new ontology and hence a new historical world. In the midst of its answers, however, the question of Being itself withdraws, is concealed, and thus forgotten. The pre-Socratic world is characterized by the continual reappearance or reassertion of the question of Being in opposition to the realms of answers, i.e., in opposition to the worlds it has engendered. Like Oedipus, the Greeks of the tragic age move in Heidegger's view from one riddle to another, continually struck by Being and cast into homelessness, continually constructing a new home through their art. This world ends when the question becomes submerged in its answers and fails to resurface as a question, i.e., when Being itself withdraws in favor of its answers. This eclipse of the pre-Socratic world and the original experience of Being is thus not the fault of man, not due to the replacement of mythology or music by philosophy, as Nietzsche argues, but the consequence of the withdrawal of Being itself.[56] The struggle of Being and being thus ends with the triumph of being not because it is stronger than Being but because Being itself as the question that opens up or reveals the realm of being retreats into concealment and oblivion. Why this occurs is in Heidegger's view dark and mysterious; that it occurs is the central and decisive fact of all Western history, is indeed the source of Western history as such.

According to Heidegger, Being involves concealment or hiddenness in two ways: first, insofar as it directs man to one realm of answers and hence to one interpretation of the world, it closes off all other interpretations, and, second, insofar as it directs man to answers at all, it directs him away from the question itself. The character of Western ontology as a whole rests upon the first sort of hiddenness, in the character of the question of Being itself. Being appeared for the Greeks in and as the question "What is being?" and thus directed them toward the realm of the what. In asking what things are, the Greeks ceased to ask who they are and failed to ask how or why or when or where they are. All of these other questions subsequently were conceived as subsidiary to and derivative from the what-question.[57] Being as the what-question thus gave birth to philosophy and the West but at the same time closed off the mythological or theological realm as well as all other fundamental ontological possibilities. In this sense the truth of Being remained hidden even from the pre-Socratics.[58] They experienced Being not as the question per se but as the what-question and thus did not recognize it as only one sort or mode of revelation. Even this one-sided experience of Being was lost, however, when the question itself was submerged in its answers. This second sort of hiddenness, however, also lies in Being itself, for as a question Being directs man to answers and hence leads him to neglect the question of Being itself. To remain in the vicinity of the question of Being it is necessary to pose it ever more sharply and profoundly, but it was this that the Greeks failed to do. They merely accepted Being as the question and did not ask about its truth. Consequently, they became concerned with the realm of beings that Being opened up and hence no longer concerned themselves with Being itself.[59]

This withdrawal of Being as a question begins with the Sophists and culminates in the thought of Plato and Aristotle. Characteristic of this decline in Heidegger's view is the disappearance of creative thought and its replacement by mere polemics and intrigue. This is particularly apparent in the Sophists, who were the first to understand appearing, which for the early Greeks had characterized the revelation of Being, as mere appearance. They thus opened up the chasm between the real and apparent, which subsequently became the fundamental characteristic of metaphysics. The sophist Antiphon, for example, argued that only the basic elements really were and that all else was appearance and illusion. This means in Heidegger's view that anything *more*, and that means Being itself, is mere appearance, thus subject to change, and consequently not ultimately real. Insofar as the original experience of Being was thus lost, the direction it gave to thought and life became obscure. Logos, which had established this direction in and through art or language, thus became a searching for direction in and as dialectic.[60]

While Being as a question directs man toward answers and thus withdraws from consideration itself, it does not completely close off the possibility of an experience of this question, since there is nothing to prevent man from following it in its withdrawal and lingering in its mysteriousness. Of all the Greeks, however, only Socrates followed this path: "Through his entire life, even into his death, he did nothing other than set himself in the tailwind of this withdrawal (*Zuges*) and hold himself there. Thus he is the purest thinker of the West."[61] The pre-Socratics were struck by the question of Being and lived in its *presence*. Beginning with the Sophists, however, Being withdrew in favor of its answers. Socrates thus experienced only the *absence* of Being in his experience of the various answers to that question. He thus had to follow the withdrawal of this question through a dialectical examination of answers or opinions that led back to and opened up anew the mysterious and aporetic ground of all opinions in Being itself. Socrates thus never wrote anything but remained in the great wind of logos and let himself be blown by it, while all of his successors sought refuge from it in the windshadows of literature, in the dogma of answers.

While Socrates sought a solution to the problem posed by the Sophists in a return to the question of Being, Plato turned to the answers themselves and sought to establish a ground for the distinction of true and false answers in a doctrine of real and apparent beings.[62] Insofar as he turned out of the question, he fell prey to the forgetfulness of Being that had already characterized the Sophists. The withdrawal or concealment of Being that occurs in Plato's thought, however, is more subtle, since Being does not simply disappear into mere appearance but reappears in conjunction with appearance or being as the Being of beings. This, however, is only a more thorough concealment of Being, for insofar as Being appears at all it is not missed and thus not called into question but always and everywhere overlooked, recognized but recognized only as something self-evident and tautological and hence as something unworthy of investigation. In disappearing as a question Being thus reappears as the highest answer, as the ultimate or final ground of beings. Henceforth, the question of the ground becomes the central question of metaphysics and the West.

While Plato in Heidegger's view does not entirely reject the pre-Socratic view of truth as revelation (*alētheia*), he proposes in its stead a new doctrine of truth based upon a new conception of Being. The truth for the pre-Socratics resided in the mysterious and aporetic, and wisdom consisted in dwelling in the vicinity of this mysteriousness, in the vicinity of the abyss of Being and in repeatedly being struck by it. Plato, too, in Heidegger's view recognizes the aporetic but in contradistinction to both the pre-Socratics and Socrates aims not at revealing it as the truth but at resolving it through the recognition of Being as presence, of Being as the eternal and unchanging, in contradistinction to the ephemerality of being or becoming.[63] Being (*Sein*) itself, however, is thereby always understood only in terms of being, i.e., as the negation of being. It is conceived as everything that being is not: being is subject to change, therefore Being must be unchanging; being is many, therefore Being must be one; being is bodily, therefore Being must have no part in body. To use terminology that only later becomes appropriate, the essence *is* only as the negation of existence. Plato, however, assumes exactly the reverse, i.e., that it is the unchanging forms or ideas that are truly real and that make possible the limited Being of beings, just as these beings make possible images or illusions.[64] On this basis Plato is able to articulate an ontology or hierarchy of beings in terms of their proximity to Being itself, i.e., to the idea of the good, which as the idea of ideas or the Being of beings is the ultimate source of the possibility of everything.

This ontology, according to Heidegger, determines the character of human life for Plato. It is the order of natural justice (*dikē*) and thus the proper order of political life. The political in this sense does not arise out of the creative chaos of the question of Being but rests upon the theoretical determination of its answers. Correct action thus depends upon theory, upon having seen the ideas and hence upon an education (*paideia*) that turns man around from the sensible to the intellectual, from ephemeral appearances to an eternal reality.[65] The highest human possibility is thus no longer the heroic life of fame or glory that arises out of the courageous confrontation with nothingness but the life devoted to theory, the life of the philosopher.

Human life thus becomes a fundamentally philosophical or metaphysical striving for the correct knowledge of the hierarchical order of beings. Such a striving, however, is always only a striving for *answers* that in Heidegger's view turns away from the *question* of Being itself, away from the mystery and wonder that characterized early Greek life and that fostered the creative struggle of poets, thinkers, and statesmen to encounter and contain Being. With Plato myth and logos and thus tragedy and philosophy part company, and original Greek life comes to an end.[66]

Heidegger, however, does not blame Plato for this transformation but attributes it to Being itself. Here the crucial difference between Nietzsche and Heidegger becomes apparent. For Nietzsche the Greeks of the tragic age derived their vitality and their art from the contradiction of their passions. This conflict of the passions, however, exhausted them and led them to seek a refuge in reason. Poetry or music, which was the highest expression of this conflict, was thus destroyed by philosophy and that means by Socrates and Plato. The gods of the Greeks and the political life they represented thus died because the Greeks themselves became too weak to cultivate and sustain them. For Heidegger, on the contrary, the responsibility for this collapse lies not with man but with the "gods," i.e., with Being, which withdraws from the realm of experience and conceals itself in the dualism of Being and being. Being thus disappears as a question and returns as the highest unquestioned and unquestionable answer. Heidegger in contrast to Nietzsche thus exculpates Plato and all of his successors from the crime of nihilism. The responsibility for the nihilism that lies at the heart of metaphysics and the West in this sense lies with Being. This withdrawal, however, does not mean that Being ceases to exercise its determinative power over beings. In fact, the reverse seems to be the case, for it is the withdrawal of Being itself in favor of beings that determines the particular ontological structure or character of an age. The presence of Being as the fundamental question undermines all ontologies, calls every ontological determination into question. In its presence all ontologies are thus overthrown. The character of an age thus depends upon the particular revelation of Being *and* its withdrawal, upon the original impulse given by the question of Being and the forgetfulness of the question as a question, which allows this impulse to be carried out. The absence of

Being and the forgetfulness of this very absence thus in Heidegger's view remain the determinative ground and source of metaphysics and ontology. Nihilism as the absence of Being is thus the inner logic of the history of the West.

At first glance Aristotle appears to be an exception to this forgetfulness, since he seems to reject the Platonic conception of Being and to return to the earlier pre-Socratic notion. However, while Heidegger suggests that Aristotle recognized Being as a question and was thus "more Greek" than Plato, he concludes that Aristotle too falls prey to the dualism of Being and being that characterizes metaphysics.[67] In his early thought Heidegger apparently believed that Aristotle had come to terms with the concrete facticity of human existence in his conception of action (*energeia*) but admitted already in *Being and Time* that even Aristotle failed to clear away the darkness that arises out of the dualism of Being and being and the attendant hierarchical distinctions and interconnections. Thus, while Aristotle may stand above all other metaphysicians, he still ultimately defines Being in terms of what-Being (*to ti esti*) and that-Being (*tode ti*) or what was later characterized as essence and existence. Thus, while he rejected the idea of the good and tried to think the manifold senses of Being in terms of a unity of analogy, he was unable to think the truth of Being as the question that opens up and directs man to being.[68]

While the forgetfulness of Being begins with Plato and Aristotle, they remain within the horizon opened up by Anaximander, Parmenides, and Heracleitus. They are in fact the great conclusion of the initial revelation of Being, since the question of Being remains the impetus for their investigations even though they do not consider this question itself. Their answers and the ontology they establish thus are the final embodiment of the Greek experience of Being. Like the pre-Socratics they experience Being in terms of art and understand all beings as the product of some making. For Plato ideas, artifacts, and images are made by the god (*theion, phytourgos*), the craftsman (*demiourgos*), and the poet, respectively, and even theorizing is a sort of making (*poeisis*). For Aristotle as well the model for all coming into being is art (*technē*) as a revelation of being.[69] For the pre-Socratics art was the realm in which the struggle of Being and being (appearance, becoming) occurred, and it was through art that poets, thinkers, and statesmen constructed a world in response to the chaos of Being. In this respect they followed the clue given them by the *question* of Being itself. With Plato and Aristotle this sense of making became a sort of conscious planning based upon the observation of eternal models or ends. It was thus fundamentally subservient to the conception of Being as presence and consequently to the guiding *answer* to the question of Being given by metaphysics. The question of Being, which in Heidegger's view is the true source of creativity, thus retreats, and art consequently degenerates into mere imitation or indeed into the imitation of an imitation of a supposed eternality.

The second phase in the withdrawal of Being and thus the second epoch in the history of Being is characterized by the translation of Greek ontology into Latin by the Romans and its consequent embodiment in Christianity. The metaphysical dualism of Being and being had already become embedded in language in the thought of Plato and Aristotle, first in the Platonic distinction of nouns and verbs and then in the solidification of these and further distinctions in the Aristotelian categories, which were themselves institutionalized by the Stoics and the Alexandrians. This was augmented by the distinction and separation of logic, physics, and ethics at the hands of Xenocrates and the Perapetetics.[70] Despite these transformations and the increasing withdrawal and forgetfulness of Being, the connection to the mystery and wonder of the original experience of Being was preserved in the language itself. The translation into Latin, however, further obscured the experience of Being, since it obliterated even this subliminal connection. The dualism of Being and being thus appears, on one hand, as idea (*idea*) and actuality (*actualitas*), and as essence (*essentia*) and existence (*existentia*), on the other. Moreover, the name for Being itself, i.e., *physis*, 'the shining forth,' is replaced by *natura*, 'nature,' which implies birth and growth. The sense of Being as a sudden and inexplicable revelation thus is concealed, and it appears instead as a natural process of action and reaction, as a chain of causes and effects (*Wirkungszusammenhang*).

This new ontology in Heidegger's view unfolds itself in its fullness as imperial Rome.[71] Man, as he is understood by the Romans, i.e., as *homo romanitas*, is the embodiment of virtue (*virtus*). Virtue, however, consists in a recognition of the hierarchy of beings and is attained by education, by what the Greeks called *paideia* and what the Romans understood as *humanitas*.[72] Man for the Romans thus becomes human as the rational animal, not, however, in the Greek sense as life that has logos or speech but as the animal which is capable of a categorical understanding that correctly distinguishes the ontological hierarchy. The highest human possibility in such a world is thus school philosophy, which masters the dogma, i.e., the doctrinal answers embodied in the prevailing ontology.[73]

With the Roman Empire the metaphysical dualism of Being and being thus loses touch entirely with Being itself. The institutionalization of ontology as dogma is the exclusion of the question of Being. According to Heidegger, this chasm, which is opened up between Being and being, is the space into which Christianity settled.[74] Christianity is the result of a new revelation of Being that transforms both man and the world by establishing both in relationship to God. This new revelation, however, is in fact only a further withdrawal of Being out of nature and into transcendence as the divine ground of all beings. This further withdrawal opens up anew the ontological question that ancient metaphysics had answered with its distinction of Being and appearance, or essence and existence, because with this further withdrawal the essence reveals itself as a mere nothing and the ground disappears. Man is cast into the abyss and confronted with some sense of the original mystery and wonder evoked by the question of Being.[75] This experience of Being, however, is the experience not of its presence but of its even greater absence and thus leads not to a creative rebirth of the tragic age but to a further radicalization of metaphysics.

The vitality of this revelation, which appears as the longing for an absent or dead God, is dissolved when Christianity comes to depend first upon Scripture, which turns from the question of man's relationship to God into dogmatism, and then upon metaphysics and the categorical understanding that metaphysics fosters. Christianity thus loses touch with the original revelatory experience of the absence of Being. The apostles John and Paul, Augustine, Aquinas, and Luther, according to Heidegger, originally experienced Being as the abyss of God but became entangled in metaphysics as soon as they attempted to explain this experience and its meaning for human life.[76] In fact, the only Christian thinkers who were able to remain in the vicinity of this abyss were mystics such as Meister Eckhart who rejected metaphysics and logic in favor of contradiction and tautology. While they, like Socrates, were able to follow Being in its withdrawal, they were unable to articulate this experience in a way that was generally accessible and hence were unable to offer a real alternative to dogmatic Christianity.

The institutionalization of Christianity under the rubric of a neo-Platonist conceptualism thus effectively extinguished the original Christian experience of Being as a revelatory enigma and replaced it with the dogma of a metaphysically interpreted scriptural revelation. The result was a new ontology and a new historical world that remained within the general horizon of ancient metaphysics but which found its center not in the question of Being as truth (*alētheia*) or in nature but in a transcendent God who had created both man and nature and who had revealed himself in and as Christ. As the ground and source of beings, God as Being is understood as the highest and most real being (*summum ens*). Being itself is thus more completely interpreted in terms of being and hence retreats even further from human life. This movement of the center also produces a corresponding movement throughout the conceptual framework of metaphysics. The idea of the good is replaced by God as the highest good (*summum bonum*), the conception of substratum by God as the underlying ground (*subiectum*), action (*energeia*) by actuality (*actualitas*) and causality (*causalitas*) with God conceived as the first cause (*causa prima*). Art (*poeisis*) becomes the divine creativity (*creatio*) of an uncreated God (*ens increatum*) who produces a creation (*ens creatum*) in which man on the model of the craftsman (*demiourgos*) becomes the finite maker (*ens finitum*) who continues the making of the infinite maker (*ens infinitum*).[77] Christianity thus preserves the Platonic ideal of a hierarchy of beings but recognizes these not merely as ontological distinctions but as extensions of divine substance and thus also as moral distinctions. Man is thus fundamentally characterized not by a questioning that arises out of the experience of the abyss of Being but by faith, i.e., by the abandonment of all questioning. The highest human possibility is not the philosopher but the priest or saint who lives not by questioning but by faith alone. Thus, despite its manifest reliance upon philosophical categories and concepts, there is no Christian philosophy in Heidegger's view.[78] Nor for that matter is there even true knowledge, for the ground, i.e., God, remains by definition incomprehensible save through Scripture. The basis of human life is thus the *certainty* of faith, a certainty that takes its substance from Scriptural revelation as it is grasped and explained by a Platonized theology. In this certainty of faith, however, both the Greek and the original Christian experience of the abyss or question of Being are concealed, and Being itself shines only dimly through the divine creator and his creation. It is within this horizon that modernity arises.

Modernity, as we previously noted, begins in subjectivity with the subject-object relationship and ends in the nihilism of world technology, totalitarianism, and total war. The responsibility for this disaster thus seems to lie at least at first glance with modernity and especially with the rejection of traditional Christian life and the ancient metaphysical ontology that underlies it. Heidegger admits that modernity turns against faith and Christian ontology but attempts to show that this is only the result of a further withdrawal of Being within an essentially unchanged metaphysical horizon, that modernity arises out of a new revelation of Being that places man at the center of all being but that man is not thereby freed from metaphysics but only more deeply entangled in it.

The revelation of Being that characterizes modernity in Heidegger's view is the result of a further withdrawal of Being itself in which man replaces a disappearing or dissolving God as the ground of all being and hence as the center of all ontology. This withdrawal first manifests itself as the universal doubt of traditional authorities and that means ultimately of Scriptural revelation and the theocentric ontology that underlies it. Man discovers the answer to this new question not in a return to nature as the ancients understood it but in the objectivity of natural science and the subjectivity of the will. Modernity ends with the explicit recognition of the dissolution and death of God and thus with the complete predominance of science and will as they are manifested in world technology and totalitarianism. The ultimate consequence of this most distant withdrawal of Being, however, is not thus an even greater bifurcation of Being and being, or of the real and apparent worlds, but the abandonment of Being altogether in favor of being, a turn away from the essential and real in favor of the actual. Even this rejection of Being as the Being of beings, however, remains fundamentally entangled in the metaphysical essence of Christianity: the certainty of faith becomes the certainty of self in introspection, divine creativity becomes world technology, and man himself thus becomes the highest being, the prime mover, and final end of existence. Even in its conclusion in atheism and nihilism, modernity in Heidegger's view thus remains fundamentally Christian and hence fundamentally metaphysical.

Each revelation of Being, according to Heidegger, propels man in a new direction. Each revelation, however, appears within a particular ontological horizon or tradition and thus appears as a reinterpretation of this tradition or ontology. The character of the ontology, which arises out of each revelation of Being, is thus determined, on one hand, by the character of the old ontology and by the particular character of the revelation itself. The horizon of Western ontology rests in this sense upon the original revelation of Being in the question "What is being?" and the guiding Platonic answer that understands Being in terms of being as what in the truest sense is, i.e., as presence. The succeeding revelations that determine the different epochs of Western history all occur within this horizon and do not call the basic understanding of Being as a what or as presence into question. They are instead the result of the withdrawal of Being as the ground or Being of beings. This withdrawal undermines the prevailing answer to the original question of Being, which depends upon a particular understanding of the relation of Being and being. Each further withdrawal of Being thus appears as the loss of the ground and leads to an ever-greater reliance upon being. Each epoch in the history of the West is thus in Heidegger's view only a further radicalization of the Platonic premise that drives man ever more completely into answers and thus into being. The history of the West is thus the history of growing error (*Irre*), of the forgetfulness of Being and the growing predominance of being. The end of modernity, which is characterized by the final triumph of being in the doctrine of the will and nihilism, is thus the end of metaphysics and of the West itself.[79]

Being, which had been understood as truth (*alētheia*), nature, God, and subjectivity, is understood at the end of modernity as nothing, as just another value or being. In this way the original experience of Being is completely forgotten and the impulse it gave the West is thus at its end. In this end the mystery and wonder that Being evoked are completely swallowed up in the self-certainty of subjectivity in and as the will to power and an unfettered totalitarian world technology. Moreover, man who had already passed from hero-artist to philosopher to saint degenerates even further as scientist, worker, and brute. The modern world and modern man are in this sense the last phase in the withdrawal of Being and are characterized by an unprecedented darkness and barbarism, a darkness so black that it even lacks the light to understand itself as darkness and indeed conceives of itself as Enlightenment, as the brightest and most glorious epoch in human history.

Heidegger, like Kierkegaard and Nietzsche, turns against this Enlightenment view and attempts to reveal the darkling character of modern life, to indicate the numinous or chthonic power that is part and parcel of our illumination. He does not draw our attention to this brooding nihilism, however, only to provoke our disgust with ourselves or to plunge us into despair but rather to reveal the very depths of this darkness as the source of light, in order to show us that nihilism is only the forerunner of Being, to demonstrate that "where the danger is, there salvation also grows," that this world-midnight that in his view has darkened our world with its unprecedented horrors, its violence, its inestimable pain and unavoidable despair does not merely follow the dusk of God and metaphysics but also precedes the dawn of Being. Such a task, however, can be completed only in and as the demonstration that the nothingness of nihilism is itself the clearest and highest revelation of Being within a world utterly characterized by being, that in short Being is nothing, that Being is history or time. Such a demonstration depends not upon the history of Being, i.e., not upon an account of metaphysics, but upon a revelation of the nihilistic essence of metaphysics as Being.

The Revelation of Being as Nihilism and History

Nihilism, as Heidegger understands it, is the basis for a new revelation of Being itself. Nihilism is the triumph of being and the consequent obliteration of the Being of beings. This obliteration of Being, however, is also the obliteration of the distinction of Being and being and thus of metaphysics. Metaphysics had hitherto presented an insuperable obstacle to the consideration of Being itself, since it always conceived of Being in terms of being as the Being of beings. As this Being of beings, Being always appeared and was taken for granted as something obvious. Hence, it was never itself called into question and thus never investigated. With the advent of modern nihilism, this barrier to the reconsideration of Being itself is removed. The triumph of being in nihilism is thus nothing other than the most distant withdrawal of Being in and by which it completely severs itself from being and preserves itself in its purity and unity. With the obliteration of metaphysics in nihilism, the revelation of Being itself thus once again becomes possible.

In this sense our age is presented with the possibility of an experience and understanding that has not been available to the West since the pre-Socratics, the possibility of experiencing Being in all its primordial purity. Our possibilities are thus the same as those of the early Greeks—we can again experience the truth in all its fullness as the abyss of Being, we can wrestle with the question that speaks out of this abyss, and we can apparently also approach new gods and found new political communities and ways of life. The world-midnight in which we find ourselves is thus the basis for a new revelation of Being that passes beyond the ontological horizon and hence the misconceptions and hiddenness of the West. Nihilism in Heidegger's view is thus the ground not for despair but for our highest hopes.

Nihilism in this sense is the dark side of Being. As such it represents the first phase of the revelation of Being itself. Ordinarily nihilism is understood as the doctrine that nothing is, i.e., not that absolutely nothing is, which would be absurd, but that there is no ground of beings. Heidegger, however, wants to understand nihilism as the realization that the ground is nothing, i.e., no-thing and thus no being. Nihilism is thus not the assertion of groundlessness per se but only the assertion that the ground cannot be a being and cannot be understood in terms of beings. This, however, only means that the ground is something other than being, and for Heidegger this means Being. Nihilism is thus the implicit recognition of Being itself. It is merely implicit, however, because Being is recognized only by its complete absence. It is to be sure no longer disguised as the Being of beings but has not yet revealed itself in its own right. It is not pure presence but a pure absence that shatters all ontologies and propels man, on one hand, toward a complete reliance upon beings in modern science and technology and, on the other, toward the question of Being itself in its unity and purity.

Heidegger thus seeks to interpret nihilism in terms of the primordial, pre-metaphysical conception of Being, which understands nothing as one form of Being. This in his view is the true meaning of Heracleitus' conception of nature (*physis*) as that which "loves to hide," or, as Heidegger translates it, as that which "inclines itself to self-concealing," and of the Greek conception of truth (*alētheia*) as dis-closure or un-hiddenness that is decisively dependent upon closure and hiddenness.[80] Nihilism in this sense is the complete self-concealment or closure of Being that brings Being itself and not merely being or the Being of beings into question. Nihilism thus directs authentic thinking to Being itself as the fundamental question. As a question rather than an answer, Being thus necessarily appears as chaos or the abyss that undermines all ontology and therefore all ethics, politics, and religion. The advent of nihilism signals in this sense the passing of metaphysics and the West and thus opens up a path for a return to the premetaphysical and pre-Western perspective. Thus, Heidegger sees in nihilism the possibility for the rapprochement of East and West, for in the Orient, "nothing [is] the word for Being." This is analogous to his own insight that "nothing, as the other to being, is the veil of Being."[81]

This, however, is not merely a return to pre-Socratic or pre-Western conception of Being. The pre-Socratics, to be sure, understood Being as a question or abyss but accepted this abyss as the fundamental fact and hence did not recognize that this abyss was only one particular revelation of Being. They thus thought that the question "What is being?" was the fundamental question and did not investigate it in its own right. As a result they fell prey to an even deeper hiddenness in the question itself, which led them to believe that in understanding *what* something was they had exhausted all of its possibilities. With the end of metaphysics in modern nihilism, there are no more answers to this question, and for the first time the question itself comes into question. It is in this sense that Heidegger believes that we can approach Being itself. Being, which hitherto was understood as the Being of beings and thus as the final and highest answer, now appears in its truth as the original and fundamental question. In this sense it is no longer conceived in terms of the what as presence but as the question that opens up the whole realm of the what, i.e., the realm of beings, and that thus determines *how* these beings are *what* they are. This is the truth that nihilism reveals: that Being is not a *what* but a *how*, a no-thing that opens up and grounds the whole realm of the what and everything within it. Nihilism, which is the revelation of Being as the how of beings, is thus in Heidegger's view the greatest event in the history of the West because it allows us to grasp Being more profoundly and more primordially than even the pre-Socratics, to recognize Being in its truth not merely as a question but as questionality itself, to recognize in short that Being is time or history.

This understanding of Being thus passes beyond the West itself and in fact is a return to or retrieval of the primordial meaning of Being implicit in pre-Western or mythical thinking. Heidegger asserts, for example, that "Mana is the most general character of Being, the 'how', into which the actuality of all human Being falls . . . the 'how' of all mythical actuality, i.e., the Being of beings;" and that "*kosmos* means . . . the how, in which being and indeed being *as a whole* is."[82] It is this primordial how that Heidegger sees in nihilism and that he hopes to show in the essence (*Wesen*) of history.

In nihilism, however, Being as the how appears not as mana or cosmos but "as simply not-being, as nothing" and thus occurs in its purest form by not occurring, by not revealing itself.[83] This is not a defect, however, but the highest revelation of Being itself, liberated entirely from the what and appearing in the purity of its otherness, as that which is essentially other than all being. "Being does not have its like. What stands against Being is nothing and perhaps nothing is itself in essence for Being and only its messenger."[84] Heidegger's "return" to the pre-metaphysical is thus not a return to a specific concrete historical mythology or ontology but a return to the essence (*Wesen*) of the primordial that shines forth out of nihilism. This essence in his view is history as destiny.[85]

History (*Geschichte*) for Heidegger is not a causal series within being or the unfolding of human freedom but the destiny (*Geschick*) of Being itself. *Geschichte* originally meant 'providence' or 'that which happens' and therefore 'a happening'. Heidegger, however, wants to go beyond this meaning to its apparent source in the past participle *geschickt*, 'sent', from *schicken*, 'to send', from which *Geschick*, 'destiny', and *Schicksal*, 'fate', also derive. As a participial noun *Geschichte* thus means 'the sent'. *Ge-*, however, is a collectivizing prefix in German, for example, *der Berg*, 'the mountain', *die*

Berge, 'the mountains', and *das Gebirge*, 'the mountain range'. Heidegger wants to identify the *Ge-* prefix in *Geschichte* as collectivizing and thus to understand history as the collection of what has been sent and delivered into the present. As this sending, history (*Geschichte*) is the destiny (*Geschick*) in which Being gives itself (*es gibt Sein*) to man as the disclosure, as the truth or how of being.

Heidegger understands destiny here in terms of the Greek *Moira*, 'the deadly', 'the unspeakable', and, according to Hesiod, the offspring of night.[86] It is the dark and mysterious essence of change that, according to Parmenides, reveals or discloses being as a whole without revealing itself. This destiny is Being as the how of being that remains unperceived because it does not appear in its own right but instead always holds to itself.[87] It is precisely this holding-to-itself that renders Being as destiny incomprehensible. It establishes the horizon of beings but remains beyond that horizon.

Being in this sense, according to Heidegger, is epochal. The Greek word for holding-to-itself is *epechein*. By holding to itself in and as destiny Being thus determines the *epochē* or epochs of the history of Being. This holding-to-itself, however, is nothing other than the withdrawal of Being as a question that, as we have seen, opens up the realms of answers, the various ontologies with their attendant ethics and politics that have constituted Western history. It is in this sense that Being is destiny and, in keeping with a subsidiary meaning of *epechein, prevails over* being by determining how being can be.

In holding to itself, Being thus becomes history (*Geschichte*) because it sends (*schickt*) the truth and establishes the horizon in which beings stand as the destiny (*Geschick*) of a particular people or generation within which individuals find their own fate (*Schicksal*). It is not the individual who is historical, i.e., who stands in and is the recipient of the destiny of Being as the particular truth of being, but the community or polis. Indeed, in the truest sense it is not the individual but the polis that is human Being.[88] *Why* Being holds to itself or withdraws in a particular way and thus appears as a particular sort of truth that gives rise to a particular ethics and politics is unknowable. Destiny is *Moira*, the offspring of night: Being as the source of truth does not itself stand in the light of truth, is not itself disclosed. The particular historical sending has its origin in Being, as the destiny of Being, and hence cannot be understood as the result of a causal series or the consequence of willful human or divine action. Indeed, in one sense it cannot be understood at all: *Moira* is beyond both gods and men and in weaving its threads weaves both into its tapestry. What turn it takes, what new form is woven, remains unknowable. Thus history is not subject to rational laws nor can it be predicted by extrapolating from past events. Nor is this destiny even subject to natural laws. In fact, natural law itself in Heidegger's view is subordinated to this destiny and thus, as in the case of

Newtonian physics, *becomes* true and by implication can also become false.[89]

This understanding of history as the destiny of Being must not, however, be confused with Historicism. Such thinking is not historical in the ordinary sense of the term, i.e., it does not think the order in or of events. It does not produce the *historia rerum gestarum*. Nor is it a relativism that recognizes itself as fundamentally limited by its own historical context. It is rather thinking according to the history of *Being*, i.e., it thinks what is as the giving and hence the gift of Being, of that which is beyond all historical contexts. Heidegger's "historicism" is thus much more akin to the "historicism" of Paul the Apostle or Augustine than to that of Dilthey and Croce.[90] As Pöggeler has pointed out, "Over against that form which modern historical thinking takes . . . there arises a way of experiencing 'the historical' which Heidegger has assimilated on the model of primitive Christian faith."[91] As Heidegger himself remarks, "If the eternity of God allows itself to be philosophically 'construed,' then it can probably only be understood as more original and 'infinite' temporality."[92] Heidegger's "historicism" thus is not the historiciza- tion of Being but in a sense the eternalization of history and time. It does not treat Being as an object subject to change but as the source and form of change itself. History (*Geschichte*) as the destiny of Being is thus the unfold- ing of eternity, not however of an eternity of presence but of an eternity that is in a mysterious and incomprehensible way the source and essence of change itself.

The similarity to Hegel in this respect is clear, but the differences are crucial. For Hegel the revelation of the eternal as the concealed ground of the historical is the consequence of spirit's dialectical process of self- reconciliation that is completed in the perfect self-consciousness of the parousia of the absolute. This process itself is fundamentally rational and necessary. For Heidegger history is kairetic, therefore unpredictable and, even in retrospect, fundamentally incomprehensible. Each historical epoch is determined by a unique revelation of Being, by the appearance of a particular sort of nothingness or aporia that directs man's speculations and activity in a new direction and thus establishes a new ontology. All other ontological possibilities and the ethical and political standards they entail are subsequently reinterpreted within this new ontology and hence lose any independent claim to truth. Each age thus believes that it has the truth and consequently regards all other ontologies as mere superstition or specula- tion. Moreover, each age is *right*; it *does* have the truth. In contradistinction to Hegel there is thus no dialectical development toward a final or absolute truth. Rather history is a collection of the various projections of eternity upon temporality. Each is unique and incommensurable with all others, and yet each is an expression of the eternal, of Being itself as the *how*, as the destiny of beings.[93]

Nihilism, as it appears in our time, is in Heidegger's view the *kairos* of a new revelation of Being.[94] As such it is the advent of a new epoch, a new ontology, and a new ethical and political world. Nihilism is thus the moment of transition, the night after the sunset of being, i.e., of God and metaphysics, and before the sunrise of Being itself. Thus, "the region of completed nihilism constitutes the limit between two world ages."[95] Our age is the world-midnight, too late for God and too early for Being. It is, however, also the moment of revelation itself. The historical world of beings is revealed to us in the light of metaphysics. This light has its source in the guiding question of metaphysics—"What is being?"—and thus in Being itself as this question. As the source of light, however, Being itself remains unillumi-nated and hence concealed, closed, forgotten. Thus, it is preserved for the darkest hour, for the world-midnight when the darkness itself, when the "nothing" can be perceived as the source of light.[96] The highest truth thus appears not as the bright and glorious conclusion of a long and arduous historical development but as the mysterious beginning that establishes the horizon of such a development. The truth for both Hegel and Heidegger thus arises out of the experience of nihilism. In contradistinction to Hegel, however, Heidegger does not try to show the way in which this nothingness serves as the basis for differentiation and mediation, i.e., as the Being of beings, which in his view serves only to conceal Being itself, but to demon-strate that this nothing, this abyss of nihilism, is the purest and highest revelation of Being itself.

The advent of explicit nihilism in Heidegger's view thus presents us with the possibility of the experience of Being itself that points us beyond metaphysics and indeed beyond the West itself. This possibility presents itself as a fundamental question that demands a more fundamental answer than the West has ever discovered. Moreover, this answer must be qualita-tively different than all metaphysical answers or grounds. "The essential answer is only the beginning of responsibility in answering. In this answer the question awakens more originally. Thus the genuine question is also not overcome in the answer that is discovered." Knowing in the realm of Being, according to Heidegger, does not consist in the categorization and system-atization of being. This was the fateful error to which Greek thought succumbed when it was unable to pose the question of Being more radical-ly, and it is this error that has characterized metaphysics ever since. In explicit nihilism, however, "questioning is no longer only the pre-condition of the answer that is overcome in knowing, but questioning itself becomes the highest form of knowing."[97] This way of questioning is the way that Heidegger seeks to follow.

The nihilism that opens up this way, however, also opens up another way, the way not of Being but of being, not of history and destiny but of History and technology. The end of metaphysics in the complete withdrawal of

Being is, according to Heidegger, the source of nihilism. Nihilism in this sense appears as the utter separation of Being and being. The authentic response in his view is the turn onto the path of Being as a question. This path, however, involves a confrontation with nothingness, with anxiety, boredom, and meaninglessness with no guarantee that this confrontation will produce anything other than anguish. The other path, the path of being, is both more accessible and more inviting. It is the path not of questions but of answers, and it promises not pain and suffering but pleasure and prosperity, not homelessness and alienation but a secure and useful life in the context of a progressive and humane society. It is Heidegger's aim, however, to reveal the disasters that wait upon this path and the spiritual death that is its necessary end. Heidegger thus hopes to turn man away from the path of being, from the path of technology and History, and onto the path of Being, the path of history and destiny.

For Heidegger the appearance of History and the development of the Historical sciences in the nineteenth and twentieth centuries is the proof that the Western tradition has come to an end and that man is in danger of losing his connection to his concrete historical actuality. Heidegger understands History in terms of the Greek *historia*: "The word 'History' (*historein*) means: to investigate and make visible, and thus names a sort of representation."[98] Thus, History claims to give the determinative representation of history. It understands what has been as what is past. As past, however, it is completed, hence whole, and consequently a possible object for observation, mastery, and exploitation. Thus History explains the past as a chain of effects, i.e., as an objectified occurrence, and explains the present and thus itself as the product or effect of past events. There is, however, no agreement about the character of History, and indeed, as we have seen, it is torn to pieces by conflicting ideological interpretations because its determination is the chief means of establishing and maintaining the security and stability of every form of organization of the masses, of every regime and politics, in the continual flux of fundamentally undifferentiated being and the constant struggle for survival and power vis-à-vis all other beings in the universal pursuit of objectification.

History (*Historie*), as Heidegger understands it, is fundamentally bound up with technology and like technology is a manifestation of the essence of subjectivity that aims at the objectification and subordination of everything. "With the completion of modernity history delivers itself up to History which has the same essence as technology."[99] This History, however, does not merely legitimate modern technology with a doctrine of progress but also sets conscious and "Historically necessary" goals for technological striving. The conjunction of History (or ideology) and technology thus seems to open up the possibility for man to master and plan his own future by freeing him from the bonds nature and natural necessity have placed upon him and hence by allowing him either to choose his future from all the human possibilities made available to him by History or to attain his true humanity in and through the fulfillment of his Historically ordained task.

Heidegger thus admits that at the end of modernity History replaces metaphysics as the principle mode of human understanding, but he argues that this "replacement" is in fact merely the completion and transmographication of metaphysics, only the last step in the long process of forgetting or neglecting Being and history, which begins with metaphysics itself. Thus, "history as Being, indeed coming out of the occurrence (*Wesen*) of Being, remains unthought."[100] History (*Historie*) always understands history as an objective causal series of beings or states of being, and does not suspect that history is the occurrence of Being itself. Hence, History, especially in conjunction with philosophy, feels the need to establish its own ground among beings, either in some highest or most fundamental being or as the product or consequence of the historical process as a whole in order to secure its own claim to truth.

The modern attempt to establish an ontological ground for history in Heidegger's view is thus nothing other than the attempt to secure all being within the horizon of human subjectivity, within the subject-object relationship, whether on the basis of absolute spirit, as in Hegel, or the great affirmation of the eternal recurrence by the overman, as in Nietzsche. Nietzsche's great Yes like Hegel's absolute, however, is fundamentally the negation of a negation that does not come to the source of the negation, i.e., to the nothing itself. Nietzsche thus merely completes the task Hegel began of transforming the *contradiction* of Being and becoming (being, appearance) into the *ground* out of which everything arises and upon which everything rests. This is, however, nothing other than the acceptance and affirmation of the dualism that lies at the heart of metaphysics itself. Nietzsche and Hegel and for that matter Marx thus remain entwined in metaphysics as dialectic, in the "dictatorship of the questionless. In its net every question suffocates."[101] Hence, they constitute the completion of metaphysics and nihilism. They do not come to the question of Being and nothing and hence do not truly understand history. The attempt to ground history Historically thus succeeds only in obscuring history itself. Hence, despite its claims to liberate or enlighten mankind, History actually only undermines the basis for human life in history and Being and in its radicalized forms as Historicism and ideology produces totalitarianism and total war.

There is, according to Heidegger, no overcoming nihilism in the commonly understood sense. Rather he proposes a step back out of metaphysics and History and into the history or destiny of Being. Through this step back Heidegger wants to prepare man for what he believes is the coming conflict of the question of Being, "the setting-apart-from-one-another of the power of being and the truth of Being."

> The highest decision, which can be made and which each time
> becomes the ground of all history, is between the guiding
> power of being and the rule of Being . . . It is never made and
> completed by a man. *Its* result and issue decides much more
> *about* man and in another way about god.[102]

This decision cuts one history off from another, the history of Being from
the history of being and metaphysics. Both of these in a sense lie side by side
within our past and it is up to us which one we appropriate as *our* tradition,
which one will serve as the basis for our future, whether we will march
forward on the path of technology and History into the world of the last man
ruled either by the unfettered necessities of economic development or the
conscious and all-encompassing technological politics of totalitarianism, or
whether we will discover a different path that leads us not to answers but to
questions, not to technology but to thinking, not to the realm of the last man
but to Being and human Being, to an authentic ethics and politics, and thus
to a rebirth of human spirituality.

The decision between the path of being and the path of Being is, thus, the
crucial decision for human life.[103] This is the reason, according to Heidegger, that "we brought the question about Being into connection with the fate
of Europe, where the fate of the earth is being decided, whereby our
[German] historical human Being proves to be the middle for Europe."[104]
The question is the question of the fate of Europe and the world, which is
not something already decided but which turns on the decision made about
the question of Being itself. The conclusion that Heidegger draws about our
success in this decision is, however, ominous. "The question, how it stands
with Being, reveals itself also as the question, how it stands with our human
Being in history, whether we *stand* or only stagger. Seen metaphysically we
are *staggering*."[105] The question of Being is thus not merely a crucially
important theoretical question but the decisive and determining question
of Western civilization itself. It is indeed the question whether there shall be
a West, whether there shall be human Being or only a wasteland populated
by tool-using brutes, by the last men living under the mantel of Americanism, Marxism, or Nazism.

The transformation of nihilism thus depends upon the recognition of
Being as the how of beings and hence as time or history. We have seen that
for Heidegger this means the recognition of history as the kairetic sending
or destiny of Being, of *Moira* that as the abyss or question of Being directs
man to a realm of answers and thus establishes an epochal horizon of
beings. In this way Being establishes the ontology or tradition within which
man always finds himself. Being itself, however, does not appear within this
tradition. In fact the ontology or tradition can only be insofar as Being itself
as the fundamental question remains out. The revelation of Being itself in
the kairos or moment of vision undermines every ontology and tears man

out of every tradition. Every tradition is a selection of what is relevant out of the past on the basis of a particular goal. Every authentic goal, however, is established in and by Being itself as a question. The revelation of Being always propels man in a new direction, toward a new goal and a new future that is discontiguous with what he hitherto has understood as his tradition. In establishing a new future the revelation of Being also establishes a new past, a new tradition that is appropriate to or commensurate with this future. Being thus unfolds itself not merely forward but also backward out of the kairos. Each revelation of Being gives rise to a new history or tradition and every history is thus a selection or re-collection of what has been, according to the new goals and standards that Being establishes. Thus history is always collected out of what has been forgotten (*lēthē*) by Being as a question. Being itself is thus truth (*alētheia*) as the un-forgetfulness or un-hiddenness that "grants new insights to remembrance."[106] Being in this sense is man's heritage as the collected occurrence (*Ge-Wesen*) that constitutes tradition.[107] The particular character of any tradition does not arise naturally, nor does it correspond to the character or genius of the people, nor is it created by law-givers or overmen but is in fact the consequence of the revelation and unfolding of Being itself as a question and thus as history or destiny.

Modern Historical thought, however, does not recognize history as the history of destiny of Being and hence conceives of what has been as merely past. Heidegger does not deny that there is a past as History understands it but argues that what is truly past, for example, everything that is mass-produced and mass-consumed, is historically meaningless. The meaning of what has been in his view is only evident and is in fact only disclosed or remembered in terms of the goal or end established by the question of Being. In this way History reverses history and understands the present not as an accumulation or collection of what is relevant in the past with a view to a particular future but as the necessary consequence of a past and unalterable, although perhaps not fully comprehended, causal series, and the future as the necessary consequence of the present.

The only historical necessity in Heidegger's view is the necessity or need (*Not*) of Being itself. In the first instance, Being is the horizon or worldhood of the world, to use the language of *Being and Time*, into which man is thrown and within which he always finds himself. Second, Being necessitates and directs man by the claim it makes upon human Being in and as a question. This historical necessity Heidegger understands in terms of the Greek *chrēnai. To chrēon*, according to Heidegger, is the oldest name for the Being of beings and already thinks what Homer and Parmenides later thought as *Moira* or destiny. It does not imply force and compulsion but is that which gives everything its own essence (*Wesen*) and maintains it in this essence.[108] In this sense Being directs man as the epochal destiny or tradition that hands him his fate. There is thus always a world or tradition within which man finds himself that limits and determines his possibilities. This tradition, however, just is the unceasing arrival of Being as the specific horizon or disclosure of possibilities. Being, however, is not merely the past that is thrown up by tradition as world but also the question that has always already directed man toward a specific goal and opened up the tradition or disclosed the world on the basis of the possibilities needed by man to attain that goal. Being thus is a twofold historical necessity (*Not*) as the "has been" and "not yet," as tradition and futurity.[109]

Modern nihilism, however, seems to free man from both his tradition and his future and thus to establish the regime of utter necessitylessness. This nihilism, as we have seen, is the result of the complete withdrawal of Being. Being disappears as a question and consequently seems not to necessitate. According to Heidegger, however, it continues to necessitate even in this extremity, not, however, by opening up a particular tradition or realm of possibilities but by opening up *all* possibilities, or, as Nietzsche proclaimed, by releasing a world in which "everything is permitted." This in Heidegger's view is the result of the disappearance of Being as the Being of beings, as the specific *how* of beings, and its subliminal reappearance as the pure how, no longer in terms of beings but as time or history. The necessity-lessness that characterizes nihilism is in this sense the realm of the pure how, the regime of pure means, the realm in which everything is understood in terms of its use and *only* in terms of its use.

From the perspective of metaphysics, nihilism seems to be the realm of necessitylessness and meaninglessness. This, however, is a misperception.

> The necessitylessness as the concealed, most extreme necessity of Being rules, however, in the age of the darkening of being and the confusion, the violence of humanity and its despair, the disorder of will and its impotency. Limitless suffering and measureless pain and sorrow announce the world-condition and are everywhere silent as the fullness of necessity. Likewise, the world-condition in the ground of its history is necessityless. This, however, according to the history of Being, is its highest and most concealed necessity. For it is the necessity of Being itself.[110]

What is necessary is to grasp this concealed necessity in the apparent necessitylessness that nihilism opens up, which in turn requires the authentic experience of nihilism itself.[111]

Such an authentic experience of nihilism, however, depends in Heidegger's view upon man's recognition that his own death is inescapable and inevitable. This is the recognition that there is an absolute limit to human life and hence a real necessity. This necessity, however, appears from the perspective of metaphysics as the nothingness of death, as utter annihilation, and consequently as necessitylessness, indeed as the source of all necessitylessness and meaninglessness. From the perspective of Being, however, death appears as the *inevitable* possibility and hence as the "proof" that everything is *not* possible, that even in the most radical nihilism there is a certain limit and order that determines how what is can be. In this way "death as the shrine of nothing conceals the occurring (*das Wesende*) of Being itself."[112] This recognition of death as one's ownmost possibility is thus the presupposition of the comprehension of the necessity of Being as history, of the necessity of the history of Being as the continual and unceasing determination of how what is is, as the truth or disclosure of the occurrence of beings.

Man, however, generally fails to grasp the necessity of his own death because he is blinded by his "anxiety about anxiety."[113] This blindness arises in the face of nothing, i.e., in the face of the absence of Being. Man's failure to face nothingness, however, entails his further entanglement in inauthentic nihilism, technology, and History, and the danger of losing his possibility of Being. Thus, according to Heidegger, this blindness may even be more dangerous in the long run than the despicable adventurism of the brutal hunger for power. This blindness is, moreover, not merely an individual blindness but a collective blindness that encompasses our entire civilization in the form of optimism (or for that matter pessimism).[114] This optimism takes the form of a Historical or ideological assurance of the inevitability of technological and human progress and thus even more thoroughly conceals the purposelessness and hence necessitylessness that such a conception of infinite progress entails. It thus obscures the experience of Being in nihilism itself.

Heidegger argues that man can only come to a true understanding of nihilism when Being has reached the limit of its withdrawal. He apparently believed that the abyss of World War II represented this most extreme withdrawal. The strength of inauthentic optimism even in the face of the abyss opened up by the horrors of this cataclysm, however, apparently led him to doubt that Being had attained its most extreme withdrawal and that humanity had yet exhausted its most abysmal possibilities.[115] If, however, man can grasp the finitude of his own Being and thus come to understand himself as human Being rather than as a subject and can thus confront the question of Being itself in and as the necessary nothingness of death, then in Heidegger's view he could understand what is according to the history of Being. Man then could understand Being as disclosure, as the determinative how of what is, and hence as history. This is the possibility that Heidegger sees not merely for overcoming modernity but for transforming the West itself—that man come to recognize not *what* is but *how* what is is, not being as History but Being as history.

In this light the question of the ground of history, i.e., "What is history?" reveals itself as an insoluble question, not because there is no answer but because the question itself misdirects thought into an inappropriate realm. The question seeks to understand history as a what, for example, as a causal series, or as the unfolding and enfolding of absolute spirit, or as the dialectical development of the means of production, or as the conjunction of the will to power and the eternal return. In Heidegger's view, however, history is not a what but a how, indeed *the* how of what is, that which determines the what, which determines how being is. Thus, to demand a ground of history, i.e., a what that underlies history, is to demand a ground for the source and determination of all grounds. There is no such ground, however: history as Being is groundless since it has no ground, ungroundable since it is the source of all grounds, and abysmal since it undermines all grounds. Heidegger's interpretation of history as Being does not, however, thereby cast all being into the abyss of nothingness. Rather it constrains what is within its own limits and recognizes a mutual reciprocity of the how and the what. Heidegger does not mean to obliterate all being in a mystical union with Being but to put each in its proper place. Thus, "the forgetfulness of Being is the forgetfulness of the distinction of Being from being."[116] Heidegger's history of Being is not the historicization of all being but rather a delineation and determination of two realms within which man dwells. Heidegger's complaint arises because in his view the entire realm of Being has been usurped and its truth obliterated in modern man's headlong and ultimately disastrous rush into being.

What is necessary in Heidegger's view is not a ground for history but a recognition of the historical necessity of Being itself through the recognition of human finitude. In the contemporary world of nihilism, man turns one way and then another, is drawn in one direction and then another by his attraction to new possibilities amid the apparently limitless pool of such possibilities opened up or disclosed by a nihilism in which everything is permitted. All of these turnings, however, are enclosed within the horizon opened up by the concealed question of Being. Human Being is thus constantly turned into the necessity of Being, brought face to face with the uncanny, with homelessness, with death, and hence with the inauthenticity of its everyday life. The turn that Heidegger proposes is a turn out of History and metaphysics, i.e., out of dogma, out of the answers to the question of Being and into the question itself.

The necessity of Being in this sense is the openness or freedom of the truth (*alētheia*) that liberates all being to be itself, i.e., that establishes the limit and horizon of the various realms of being and Being and gives to each its own.[117] This liberation is thus the establishment of the how of what is, which frees the what itself to be being, i.e., frees it to be itself and from the necessity of being what is not, i.e., Being, history, the divine, etc. This freedom to be occurs through the appropriation of the necessity of Being that appears in the kairetic revelation of tradition. The freedom of beings to be arises in the authentic experience of history as the tradition and destiny of Being that opens up the world as a whole and thus is the source of all grounds.[118]

This freedom is thus not freedom in the ordinary sense. It is not a first and hence grounding cause, not freedom from or to something, nor the freedom of spirit over nature, nor even the freedom of the "I think" that encompasses both spirit and nature, but the freedom of Being itself, the freedom to be *as* or *how* one is.[119] The ordinary understanding of causality derives in Heidegger's view from being and understands what occurs as the consequence of a particular relationship between beings. Freedom as the how of human being is understood metaphysically in terms of this causality, either as its analogue or as its absence or negation. Even idealism only understands freedom within the mutuality of the freedom and necessity of beings and ideas. This misunderstanding arises in Heidegger's view as a result of the metaphysical misunderstanding of Being as presence, i.e., as a result of a particular misunderstanding of Being in terms of time. Freedom, as he understands it, rests upon a reinterpretation of Being as time or history in the fullest sense, a kairetic understanding that apprehends the past, the present, and the future out of the moment of vision, the moment in which Being appears as a goal-establishing question.

The history of Being is thus the destiny that has arrived and is occuring all around us, the heritage of Being that constitutes the fullness of our moment of existence. When we understand this history of Being as *our* tradition, as the claim made upon us by Being, as the question that presents us with a new future and a new past, we are freed to be what we already are, freed as the place (*Da*) of the occurrence of Being (*Sein*) to be human Being (*Dasein*). The whole conception of natural causality and its antithesis to freedom, which is based upon the conception of time as the measure of the motion of beings and thus as linear and irreversible, is consequently set aside in favor of the how of causality as the how of Being that unfolds itself backward and forward out of the kairos. That this how appears as both freedom and necessity is not an indication of its contradictory or dialectical character but of an ontological transformation that establishes a new realm in which this contradiction no longer applies. It is in this sense that Heidegger can claim to have overcome the central contradiction that seemed to necessitate a ground for history—he does not establish such a ground but instead attempts to show that it is not needed and indeed that the attempt to establish it must necessarily fall short of its objective.

This understanding of Being as history opens up the possibility of a true dwelling and therefore of a true ethics and politics because it allows man to be himself, to be human Being. Man cannot escape from technology and a technological politics through a return to nature, antiquity, or God. Indeed, there is in Heidegger's view no possibility of such a return, for the technological and Historical are not something into which man has fallen and from which he can therefore extricate himself but rather the manifestation of the fact that man himself has become *homo faber*. Man cannot escape his fundamental psychological, social, and political problems because he cannot escape himself. Moreover, not only can man not escape from this modern world but he cannot really change it. Any attempt to transform himself or his world only more securely establishes him in the Historical and technological as *homo faber* and indeed as *homo brutalitas*. The most important step for man is thus the step out of his incessant activity, the step back into the acceptance of the necessity of the necessitylessness of nihilism, of History and technology, that recognizes this necessity as the necessity of Being itself. This is not, however, a fatalism that accepts the status quo, nor is it Nietzsche's *amor fati*; it is rather a turn into Being itself as the question, as the aporia that first opens up the possibility for true thinking, a turn for man out of his existence as *homo faber* and into the freedom of human Being.

From one perspective this must appear to be diminution of man, the denial of his essential power and creativity. Insofar as man's humanity is thought to reside in his Promethean or Faustian character such a conclusion is inevitable. Heidegger, however, sees this Faustian struggle, which characterizes modern man and which is thought to constitute the human essence, as the unfolding of subjectivity and thus as the source of nihilism. Man's humanity in his view does not lie in the unlimited striving of human subjectivity but in the recognition of human limitation and the ultimate dominion of that which transcends this limitation and establishes it as a limitation. It is hubris of Prometheus and Faust that characterizes man today, a hubris, however, which while it does not draw down upon man the wrath of the gods, draws man's vision down from the heavens and fastens it upon the earth so securely that he becomes blind to both Being and the gods and thus to his own true humanity as human Being. Man can come to dwell and hence be truly ethical and political only when he can truly *be*, and he can only *be* when he grasps the finitude of his own Being, i.e., that he is mortal. Such an understanding, however, is only possible when he also recognizes the immortal. Through such a recognition of the necessary relationship of man and the gods, of the earth and heaven, what Heidegger in his late work calls the fourfold, he hopes that man will comprehend the futility of Faustian striving and abandon the attempt to establish a technologically secure realm of and for human subjectivity. If man can understand the futility of trying to overcome homelessness through technology and the struggle it engenders, man opens up the possibility for a return to an authentic dwelling as human Being.

This dwelling and the ethics and politics that it makes possible are not a denial of the modern technical and political world but the recognition of Being as the necessity of and in this technical and political edifice. This recognition, however, is nothing other than the freedom of man to accept his own essence as human Being.[120] Man is not a god. He cannot himself ultimately create or order what is. The attempt to do so in fact consequently undermines human Being itself and man's place or role in the world as the shepherd of Being. The technical mastery of nature and man destroys the possibility of a true ethics and politics and replaces them with Historicism and ideology, with technology and totalitarianism. An authentic politics is thus only possible when history itself is understood as the history of Being, as the how of what is. Such an understanding, however, cannot come merely from man, for in the epoch characterized by Historicism and ideology there is apparently no Being to stand under. Man must step back from this world and into the question of Being itself, out of the futility of Faustian striving and into an attendant and preparatory waiting by the abyss for the revelation of Being itself. We like Socrates must in Heidegger's view follow Being in its uttermost withdrawal. In the midst of the frenzied struggle for the conquest and exploitation of man and the earth we must, like the early Christians, go into the catacombs and there amid the bones of our past await the revelation of Being and the resurrection of this past. What form this revelation will take, however, is unknowable.

In keeping with his renunciation of History and Historicism, Heidegger thus offers no prognosis for the future. There is in his view no inevitable or irresistible necessity that impels man toward one particular goal. This does not mean that man has no goal. Rather, man dwells in the *question* of his goal, i.e., in the question of Being as the question of the character and relationship of the *has been*, i.e., the tradition, and the *to be*, i.e., the goal, as they appear in the *is*, i.e., the kairos. Man's place or role in the world arises out of his dwelling within this question and his attendant listening and corresponding to it. It is this question, this aporia, that is in Heidegger's view the true kairos, the occasion or moment of vision in which man's destiny within the history of Being is revealed. *How* man is to *be*, the character of the ethical and political constellations of human Being can be apprehended only within the kairos of this aporia.

In this light the question with which we began, i.e., "What is history?" finds no answer in Heidegger's thought. History for Heidegger is fundamentally bound up with Being, which is a question. The answer to our question is thus itself a question. Heidegger's examination indicates that our question itself may be wholly inappropriate and in fact positively misleading. Heidegger, however, thereby redirects our questioning toward a realm that is today still unexplored. The consequences of this redirection of the question of the history for human life and politics have scarcely been perceived and certainly have not been adequately comprehended.

Critique and Conclusions

For Heidegger history begins with the early Greeks and ends with the explicit nihilism of late modernity. It is in his view the history of an error. The origin lies in the initial Greek mistake in grasping Being on the basis of the what-question as presence and the solidification of this misunderstanding in the thought of Plato and Aristotle. The history of the West is nothing other than the deepening of this error, a wandering ever further into the darkness of a blind alley that leads only to the ruin and desolation of the universal exploitation of the earth and the unlimited degradation of man by world technology and ideological totalitarianism.

The source of this error and the responsibility for its consequences, however, do not lie in man, according to Heidegger, but in Being itself as destiny. Insofar as every revelation of Being involves and indeed rests upon concealment, Being is necessarily the source of error. In the first instance this is the concealment of the question in the answers, but more fundamentally it is the concealment implicit in the question itself that, in the case of the West, directs man solely toward the realm of the what and thus excludes all other possibilities of Being. Consequently, the truth of Being as the *how* of beings is not recognized.

The full meaning of this concealment and forgetfulness, however, only becomes apparent at the end of modernity in explicit nihilism and world technology. Both of these are the manifestation of the complete but utterly concealed predominance of Being as the pure how, i.e., as history or disclosure, but are completely misunderstood by metaphysics (in its final form as History and natural science) as the realization of the unadulterated hegemony of being. The solution to nihilism in Heidegger's view thus lies in the revelation of Being as the *how* of beings, i.e., of Being as history and destiny, through the destruction of metaphysics and the reinterpretation of the history of the West as the history of Being. This leads not to a transformation of the West that involves the abandonment of technology or modern science but to a reinterpretation of their significance and thus of their meaning for human life. In this way Heidegger hopes to establish man authentically in the present through the revelation of the hitherto concealed goal and tradition that determine the character of the world and of human life. Within the context of this authentically understood present an authentic dwelling and hence an authentic ethics and politics will thus once again become possible. Nihilism for Heidegger is thus the advent of a new revelation of Being that is more original than anything the West has ever known and that thus, if properly understood, can provide the basis for a new and harmonious relationship of man and the world.[121] It is the goal of his thought to open up the way to such an authentic understanding.

We must ask, however, whether this reinterpretation of history is correct and whether it provides a real solution to the problem of nihilism. One might well wonder in the first instance whether Heidegger does not distort history, unreasonably collapsing antiquity and modernity and in particular whether his claim that nihilism is the result of metaphysics as a whole and thus ultimately of early Greek but more fundamentally of Platonic thought is sufficiently grounded.[122] Is nihilism the result of the ancient interpretation of

Being as presence on the basis of the what-question, as Heidegger maintains, or is it not the result of the rejection or abandonment of this position in modernity in favor of actuality and history, i.e., of Being as becoming. From this perspective, the *how* that Heidegger wants to see as primordial and thus pre-metaphysical appears as a peculiarly modern question and nihilism thus as the necessary result of the rejection of the eternity of Being and the futile attempt to discover a ground to replace this in history or becoming itself. In this sense Heidegger's thought appears to be not a return to or retrieval of the primordial and pre-metaphysical but only a radicalization of modernity that conceals itself as such a retrieval, a surrender to history and the nihilistic essence of the how that goes beyond even historicism. From this perspective Heidegger's project appears as a heroic attempt to establish a last absolute in the face of modern nihilism that, however, ultimately serves only to complete the destruction of the true basis for a solution in the retrieval of the thought of antiquity. One might thus want to argue that what is necessary is not a rejection of all metaphysics, ancient and modern, but a renewed appreciation of ancient thought and those strains of modern thought such as the natural rights teaching of Locke and Hobbes that most resist this surrender to history and historicism.[123]

The strongest indication of the insufficiency of Heidegger's attempt to collapse antiquity and modernity into a single history of Being is the apparent inadequacy of his interpretation of Plato. Heidegger, as we have seen, was deeply concerned with overcoming historicism and relativism. It is thus somewhat surprising that he turns against Plato, who would seem to be his natural ally in such an endeavor.[124] In Heidegger's view, however, it is Plato who establishes the ground for relativism and value-philosophy in his doctrine of truth as correspondence and Being as the idea of the good. It is this Platonic metaphysics that establishes the horizon for the West and thus lies at the end of modernity in the thought of Nietzsche, Marx, and Dilthey. To overcome relativism and nihilism it is thus necessary in Heidegger's view to overcome Plato.

Such a conclusion, however, rests upon a manifestly one-sided and peculiarly narrow interpretation of Plato that locates the essence of the Platonic teaching in the doctrine of the forms, particularly as it is presented in Book VII of the *Republic*, and that thus neglects the ambiguous presentation of this teaching and the manifest importance of the political and moral questions that underlie it.[125] There is no simple teaching in Plato. Rather, the dialogue form is essentially ambiguous and gives rise not to answers but to questions. The attempt to discover a Platonic ontology thus obscures the extent to which Plato fosters the aporetic and questionable. Thus the conception of truth and the definitive ontology that Heidegger uncovers in Plato's thought must at least be qualified, if not totally rejected, because of Heidegger's failure to locate this teaching in the larger and more fundamental context of dialectic as such. Moreover, not only is it unclear whether Plato is ultimately committed to *this* ontology but it is also question-able whether ontology is central to his thought at all. In many ways political and moral questions seem to determine its structure and character. If this is indeed the case, then it is at least possible that the character and status of all ontology is fundamentally subsidiary to and dependent upon political questions. The dialogues in this sense seem to be aimed not so much at the determination of a single true answer to the ontological question in re-sponse to the relativism and conventionalism of the Sophists but rather at a demonstration that all prevailing answers, if closely examined, lead only to contradiction and aporiae and that what is thus necessary is an openness to the mysterious character of existence. In this sense, Plato's project strikingly resembles Heidegger's own attempt to reawaken a fundamental question-ing with the crucial difference that Plato takes extreme care to distinguish politics and philosophy in such a way that he can pose the most extreme and revolutionary theoretical questions without undermining political stability and moderation.

It is, however, perhaps not entirely fair to criticize Heidegger for such a misinterpretation. In fact such criticism only accuses Heidegger of doing imperfectly what he does not do at all. The complaint that he is unfaithful to the text or insufficiently sensitive to the context fundamentally misunder-stands the intention of his project, which aims at recovering not what was thought but what was left unthought, not the intention of the author but the intention of Being itself as the dark and incomprehensible destiny that operates in and through the text and the context. This of course does not mean that we cannot criticize Heidegger's interpretations but only that we cannot criticize him merely on a textual or contextual basis. Instead, we must determine whether his whole mode and conception of interpretation is valid and whether it can achieve the goal he sets for it.

Heidegger's conception of interpretation is fundamentally bound up with his conception of Being and history. It is concerned not merely with the right or wrong reading of a text or historical situation but with the fundamental ontological transformation that occurs in or through this text or situation. It is in this sense that he wants to distinguish his method from mere interpretation as hermeneutics.[126] His hermeneutical stance derives from the revelation of Being. This revelation, as we have seen, unfolds itself both forwards and backwards, establishing both a new goal and a new tradition appropriate to this goal. The means by which this new tradition comes to be is hermeneutics. Heidegger thus strives to think not what was thought, i.e., not the "Historical" truth, but what was left unthought, what indeed could not be thought because it was concealed by the prevailing goal and tradition. Heidegger's retrieval of past thought thus always is the establishment of a new tradition that is necessarily at odds with the old one and that thus always fails to "do justice" to it. Interpretation or hermeneutics is in this sense an act of creation that is carried out in response to the revelation of Being itself and that thus rises above the constraints imposed by the demand for historical accuracy.

There are, however, certain problems with this whole approach.[127] In the first instance a determination of what was left unthought would seem to presuppose the antecedent retrieval of what was actually thought. Without such a retrieval it is difficult to see how Heidegger could know that he has really come to the unthought, and in fact he would thus necessarily run the risk of casting aside his most trustworthy allies or of falling into errors that he himself condemns. Therefore, while one cannot demand of Heidegger that he actually produce an accurate interpretation of what was thought, one can perhaps hold him responsible for confusing the thought and the unthought. In such questions Heidegger often seems to overlook the distinction of the public teaching and the private or "secret" teaching so characteristic of ancient thought and simply to adopt the public teaching as *the* teaching. In a sense, he may, however, have some justification for this, since he is concerned not with the real teaching but with the history of Being and thus with the reception and transmission of that teaching. Thus, even if Plato's esoteric teaching were more or less similar to that of Heidegger, this teaching would in Heidegger's view be historically meaningless. In this sense Heidegger often seems to be concerned not with a text but with what "happens" in the text, i.e., not with the intention of the author but with the text as a historical event.[128]

It is only fair to admit, however, that a method of interpretation that relies upon this distinction of a public and a private teaching has dangers of its own that are akin to those of Heidegger's hermeneutic methodology. The most obvious of these is the danger that the "discovery" of a "secret" teaching is in fact nothing more than the fanciful projection back upon a thinker of intentions and ideas that are alien to him. The interpretation of silence is always treacherous regardless of whether that silence is understood as the unspoken or as the unthought.

Heidegger's defense in face of the objection that he fails to produce a true or even adequate interpretation of the intention of the author or the meaning of the text or event, however, is more radical: not only is it unnecessary or inappropriate to try to recover the original meaning of a text or an event, it is in fact impossible, since the being, and thus the meaning or significance, of every text and event is dependent upon the ontology that is itself characterized by the prevailing revelation of Being. The original meaning thus is no longer retrievable because both the text and the context no longer are as they were. The entire past is always created anew out of every revelation of Being, and it is through interpretation, i.e., through hermeneutics, that this re-creation is carried out.

Hermeneutics, as Heidegger understands it, thus rests upon the assumption that there is no eternal truth which can be grasped everywhere and always nor even an absolute moment out of which the whole can be completely comprehended. Man always seeks to understand or interpret the past on the basis of a particular revelation of Being. Insofar as this revelation rests upon concealment and this is particular and partial, the horizon of understanding and interpretation derives from the ultimately real. Whether Heidegger ought to be characterized as a historicist or relativist is thus not easy to determine. Every age in his view understands the truth and therefore understands Being. Each revelation, however, is exclusive and conceals all other ontological possibilities. Each age therefore only understands one way of Being and always necessarily reinterprets the truth of all other ages in terms of its own revelation. Thus it would seem that Heidegger's thought does lead to historicism and relativism.[129] Yet, each age in his view does understand the truth of Being and thus the fundamentally real. Indeed, Heidegger even asserts that all philosophers say the same thing in different ways. In this sense he seems to retrieve thinking from historicism and relativism.

In any case, Heidegger wants to deny the more rudimentary historicist claim that each man is a child of his time and cannot rise above it. This claim made by Hegel and later by Marx and many others assumes that man is fundamentally determined by his historical circumstances, by an objective world that limits his possibilities in numerous and inescapable ways. In Heidegger's view, such a conception rests upon a mistaken view of man within the subject-object relationship. Man, according to Heidegger, is fundamentally bound up with and characterized by his relationship to Being. His possibilities are thus the possibilities of Being, and these are fundamentally unlimited. While man by his own power cannot overleap his age, he can follow Being wherever it leads. In fact, if Heidegger is right, the possibilities opened up by the revelation of Being are *never* present in the prevailing tradition and must always be retrieved from another tradition that unfolds itself out of the revelation itself. While man is thus crucially dependent upon Being as fate or destiny, he is not subject to historical necessity, and there is no historical limit upon human possibilities.

It might be objected here that each new revelation always occurs within the context of a prevailing tradition, that, as Heidegger himself argues, man is always thrown into a world, and consequently that the new world and tradition that this revelation opens up will in many ways be necessarily dependent upon the possibilities inherent to, if not explicit in, the prevailing tradition. Heidegger in part seems to grant this point at least with respect to the epochal character of the history of the West. With respect to the revelation of Being itself that he sees in modern nihilism, however, he takes a more radical position. Each revelation of Being is unique and directs man to a realm that is fundamentally different than all others. Metaphysics directed man to the realm of the what, and nihilism seems to direct him to the realm of the how. Such a redirection thus does not necessarily depend upon the possibilities that are present in the prevailing realm. This new

tradition lies side by side with the old but can only be grasped as a
possibility on the basis of a new revelation of Being, which in a way switches
human Being onto a new track that runs parallel to the course it has
previously followed but that moves in an entirely different dimension
toward an entirely different goal. Such a tradition in Heidegger's view is
thus the farthest of the far *and* at the same time the nearest of the near.[130]

Being in this sense reveals itself in and as a goal or imperative that directs
man to a new future and opens up for him a past to correspond to this
future. His task is twofold: to strive toward this goal, and to constitute a past
appropriate to it. The latter is the task of hermeneutics. As Löwith has
pointed out, however, Heidegger's project like that of Marx appears in this
light as a peculiar sort of futurism or millenarianism that is dependent upon
Judeo-Christian eschatology.[131] Unlike Marxism, however, it does not point
to a single, necessary future but recognizes the continual, if intermittant,
revelation of new futures by Being itself. The hermeneutical establishment
of a tradition on the basis of a new revelation of Being thus begins to
resemble the simple justification or legitimation of an arbitrary goal established by an essentially capricious human imagination. Heidegger argues, of
course, that this retrieval or reinterpretation of the past is achieved on the
basis of the revelation of Being, but it is difficult to see the basis for
distinguishing and differentiating such a revelation from human caprice or
spontaneity.

In this sense the difference between interpretation and creation seems to
dissolve, and one is tempted to see Heidegger in the same light as Nietzsche,
Gadamer, and Derrida. Indeed, there is some reason to believe that Heidegger intends at least to blur, if not to dissolve, this distinction. The lack of such
a distinction, however, leads to several difficulties. First, there are no rules
of the game that allow one to differentiate an authentic revelation from
mere caprice. Each revelation may be characterized by concealment and
thus error, as Heidegger argues, but how are we to distinguish ontological
error from mere everyday mistakenness? Moreover, how are we to determine what is relevant in the past, what is to be chosen and retrieved?
Heidegger argues that this arises out of the revelation of Being itself, but he
does not divulge the principle of selection that guides his discussion of the
history of Being.[132]

It is thus crucial to Heidegger's argument that man be able to distinguish
a true revelation of Being and thus the authentic claims of true prophets
from the capricious and often demagogic claims of false prophets. Here,
however, Heidegger's argument rests on woefully weak grounds. His "standard" arises out of the experience of Being and is, despite Heidegger's
protestations, at least in one sense subjective. In *Being and Time* it is
understood in terms of anxiety in the face of personal death and in the later
works as the experience of the horrible beauty or attractiveness of nothingness, of the awful abyss of Being that speaks its silent speech out of nihilism.

This of course, as Heidegger often seems to maintain, may be the essential characteristic of an authentic moment of vision that is always unique and intelligible only in terms of itself.

Even if we grant his basic hermeneutical premise, however, it is not clear that Heidegger has achieved such a hermeneutical transformation or even that he has adequately established the outlines of such a transformation. While it would certainly be an exaggeration to characterize Heidegger's account of history as fanciful or capricious, it may not be unjust to characterize it as partial and insufficient. This becomes perhaps most apparent when one considers the absence of any extended discussion of the relationship of the history of Being and the actual history of beings. In fact, it is not even clear that there is any relationship between the two. While this seems unlikely in light of Heidegger's discussion of such topics as the authentic destiny of a people, it is not impossible. Such statements might employ everyday terminology for ontological purposes that have no relation to concrete life.[133] If this is the case, one might justly accuse Heidegger of political or ethical irresponsibility in failing to make this distinction clear. If it is not the case and Heidegger recognizes a conjunction of the two realms, one might then complain that this conjunction is insufficiently spelled out. In point of fact, Heidegger almost entirely neglects the consideration of actual history and historical causes without ever explaining why they are unimportant or how they derive from the prevailing revelation of Being.

This radical separation leads to a real ambiguity in Heidegger's conception of history that has disastrous consequences for his account of social and political life. The center of this problem is a fundamental lack of mediation between the ontological realm of authenticity and the everyday realm of inauthentic life.[134] Heidegger's plunge into the abyss of Being like Spinoza's adherence to substance and Schelling's journey to the absolute leaves him far from everyday experience. He thus runs the danger of producing only a night in which all cows are black, of isolating and articulating a Being that has absolutely no meaning for ordinary human experience. What, for example, is the relationship of the history of Being to actual history, replete with its multiplicity of political, social, and psychological causes? Does the revelation of Being provide new objects for the passions, as Hegel seems to argue? Or liberate new passions, as Nietzsche claims? How does it reconstitute the structure of our concerns? Does it only work through artists, thinkers, and statesmen who transform our everyday lives with the violence of their works?[135] Or is it a dark and incomprehensible destiny that like some collective hysteria overpowers populations?

Heidegger describes two possible paths for man: the path of authenticity, and the path of inauthenticity. While he may be able to show how authenticity arises out of or occurs in the context of inauthenticity, can he equally well show the reverse, i.e., how ordinary life arises out of the revelation of Being? Even granting this, we must wonder whether all of human life is exhausted by these two paths, or whether politics, for example, is only inappropriately understood in terms of readiness-to-hand, presence-to-hand, and destiny.[136] If authentic communal life is always bound up with a people, what is the relationship of peoplehood and the political? Must each people express itself politically? Moreover, what exactly is a people? Is it a language-community in Wittgenstein's sense, or is it bound together by *Blut and Boden*?[137] In any case, it certainly cannot be unified by a historical tradition because it is precisely such a tradition that each revelation of Being establishes.

These questions become crucial in light of Heidegger's amalgamation of such apparently diverse political systems as the United States, the Soviet Union, and Nazi Germany. This amalgamation almost inevitably leads one to the conclusion that he is either simply wrong or at best politically naive. To be sure, he asserts he is only concerned with the metaphysical character of these systems and not with their moral or political character, but one has to wonder how significant moral or political differences can be, if they are more or less epiphenomenal. Moreover, even if Heidegger does believe that they are decisive on the level of being, one might still fault him for failing to explain the basis of ordinary life and its relationship to Being. Even without criticizing his interpretation of Americanism, which relies exclusively on positivism and neglects entirely the founding principles and the structures of social and political life, or his interpretation of Marxism, which is only concerned with an analysis of Marxist theory and generally eschews an analysis of its concrete institutional embodiment, one might ask whether Heidegger does not depend all too often upon an analysis of a particular scientific or philosophic system that predominates in these regimes without considering whether this predominance is necessary or accidental and indeed whether it is at all commensurate with the character of the regime itself. Heidegger of course disclaims such a concrete political analysis, but even so one must wonder why the prevailing form of philosophy or ideology should be more characteristic of a regime than its institutional arrangement and what the relationship is between its place in the history of Being and its political character.

This failure to adequately explain the relationship of the history or destiny of Being to actual history and politics has been the source of some of the most strident and vitriolic criticism of Heidegger's thought. His denial of the efficacy of the will and his assertion of the predominance of destiny seem to demand a fatalistic relinquishment and submission to the revelation of Being while opening the door to opportunism and passion.[138] Marxist interpreters in particular have attacked this acceptance of thrownness or destiny as a sort of quietism or pessimism that is in fact reactionary and ultimately fascistic.[139] This criticism, however, is unfair to Heidegger because he nowhere counsels the mere acceptance of the status quo. Even in the absence of Being he recognizes the necessity for a *preparatory* waiting that involves the destruction of metaphysics and a preparation of language for a revelation of Being. Moreover, the acceptance of destiny is by no means a sort of quietism. On the contrary, it has much in common with the millenarianism of Marxism itself. Man must accept the fate that is parceled out by the revelation of Being, but this "acceptance" is in fact resolute action in the service of the goal that Being establishes, a service that stretches itself forward through concrete political and technological action and that stretches itself backward through a hermeneutical reconstitution of the tradition. The disagreement arises here because Marxists see such a "theoretical" response as antagonistic to practical political activity, while Heidegger understands theory as the highest form of praxis.

The real danger that the disjunction of the history of Being and actual history and politics entails is not quietism but rather revolutionary fanaticism.[140] History, as Heidegger understands it, does not move forward gradually and regularly but spasmodically and unpredictably. Mankind is thus not gently turned toward a new future that is among the possibilities already present in its tradition but is wrenched out of its historical world by the nothingness of Being and cast toward a new goal that is utterly alien to this tradition, a goal so alien that it requires the construction of a new tradition to make it comprehensible. It is a submission to this truly revolutionary reconstitution of the world in accord with the revelation of Being that Heidegger sees as necessary to the salvation of the earth and man's humanity.

Moreover, a concern with the mundane decisions of everyday life, with economics, politics, and morality, not only is historically meaningless but is detrimental to an authentic and resolute response to the revelation of Being. The only answer to nihilism is a whole-hearted acceptance of the abyss as the first and highest ground, as a new dispensation that may not establish *the* millenium but certainly establishes *a* millenium. Heidegger's conception of Being as history or destiny thus leads to a disdain for everyday problems, for morality, ethics, and politics that turns instead to an inner purification with a view to the authentic experience of the revelation of Being.

This is likewise the innermost character of the task Heidegger establishes for man. This task has three separate but interrelated aspects. It is, first, the destruction of all metaphysics from Plato to Nietzsche and thus the destruction of all values and standards that metaphysics has established. It is certainly true that this destruction is also a reappropriation of metaphysics, but this is an emasculated metaphysics that has lost all of its authority and hence any claim to determine what is true or just.[141] The destruction of metaphysics is in this sense the revelation of metaphysics as nihilism and consequently the liberation from metaphysics into the openness of the nothing. The second aspect of this task is a resolute dwelling in the vicinity of this abyss, an attendant waiting in the absence of Being for its explicit revelation. In concrete terms this means a resolute confrontation with our own finitude in experiences of anxiety, anguish, boredom, homelessness, and meaninglessness. We must, in other words, first prepare ourselves for the experience of Being by purging ourselves of all past metaphysical standards and valuations, of all categories of logic, of all distinctions of natural kinds, of all our conceptions of justice and right, of freedom and necessity, of causality, indeed of every idea, structure, and institution with which we are familiar. We must come to regard these as the nihilistic manifestation of the withdrawal of Being. Second, we must then like Socrates and the medieval mystics follow Being in its withdrawal, plunge as it were into the absence of Being, into the abyss and wait there neither hoping nor despairing for the speaking of the silent sound of the revelation of Being itself. Finally, we must, then, resolutely and appropriately respond to this revelation by submitting ourselves to the imperative that it establishes and resolutely following wherever it may lead.

This way that Heidegger sketches for mankind is not, however, without its dangers. These are rooted in the problem of distinguishing a true revelation from the mere projection of passions or despair. In the first place, the experience of the abyss of Being that Heidegger believes is necessary to such a revelation destroys all metaphysics and thus all standards of judgment while at the same time fostering a state of mind that is, to say the least, "anxious" for a new revelation and new order for human life. Having abandoned the categorical reason of metaphysics for something approaching a pure intuitionism and the orderly world of everyday experience for the terrors of the abyss, man thus is liable to fall prey to the most subterranean forces in his soul or at least is in danger of mistaking the subrational for the superrational.[142] Here perhaps lies a clue to Heidegger's initial attraction to "the inner truth and greatness of National Socialism." Moreover, not only does this sort of openness find it difficult to distinguish between that which rises above and that which falls below reason, it also is apparently unable to distinguish between good and evil and indeed tacitly admits that both are present in every revelation of Being. Here again we see the disastrous consequences of the lack of mediation between Being and being and the failure to distinguish differences among beings. Whatever is not Being is merged into the undifferentiated unity of the everyday. Certainly, the differences in the order and dignity of human possibilities are thereby too quickly merged or too casually neglected.[143]

Moreover, Heidegger seems to maintain that there is no standard of responsibility for authentic thought, since it is wholly given up to the service of Being. This leads to the unsettling conclusion that a thinker can practice evil with impunity. As Heidegger himself remarks, "He who thinks greatly, errs greatly."[144] Is this a tacit justification of his attachment to Nazism? One has to wonder whether Heidegger properly understood the story of Oedipus for which he shows such a deep respect. If Oedipus represents the authentic confrontation with the abyss of Being, as Heidegger maintains, must we not also accept the poetic conclusion, that the man who seeks to answer this riddle necessarily entangles himself in the most heinous crimes and the most horrible degradations? Here Heidegger might well have taken a lesson from the Greeks. Or must we perhaps conclude that Heidegger was all too well aware of this lesson but nonetheless chose to run the risks that such a confrontation with nothing entailed? Even if this is the case, however, one must still wonder on what basis Heidegger could make such a decision.

Heidegger of course would argue that all objections of this sort arise out of an entanglement in values and thus in subjectivity. He believes that man's humanity is undermined and ultimately obliterated by such an understanding and that man's salvation thus depends on the recognition of his true nature as human Being, which is fundamentally bound up with and dependent upon his experience of Being. The grounds for the demonstration of this connection in Heidegger's thought, however, remain obscure. Indeed, Heidegger's fundamental argument is more radical and goes beyond choice altogether. In this view man does not choose between Being and being but is himself "chosen," struck and overcome by the mystery of Being, overwhelmed by a destiny that he can neither resist nor direct. Being in this sense seems to be a dark and numinous power before which men are powerless and from which they can hope only for grace (*Huld*) and salvation.[145] In this manner Heidegger seems to return to a mythic and almost anthropomorphic conception of Being, to a faith that seeks to overleap nature and become one with Being itself.[146]

It is perhaps this strain that is most disturbing in Heidegger's thought, since it seems to betoken an unwillingness to concern itself with the concrete problems of human life, a world-weariness that seeks to escape from boredom and meaninglessness through a radical leap into a nothingness that phoenix-like reconstitutes itself as Being. Here lies the danger of all existentialist openness with its "radical choice" and "commitment": those who peer too long into the abyss become too willing to accept whatever is disgorged and seldom even ask whether their new god is not in fact some horrible beast "slouching toward Bethlehem to be born."

Thus, we are driven in the end to ask whether there is not in fact another way out of nihilism than the dangerous path that Heidegger presents. He himself believes that he has demonstrated that his is the only path, that all other paths and indeed that the Western tradition itself leads only to the nihilism of world technology, totalitarianism, and total war. We have tried to show that there is at least room to doubt that his analysis is correct. Whether there is indeed an alternative that will release us from the necessity and the dangers of Heidegger's way, however, depends upon the capacity of thinking to draw upon the wellsprings of its own experience and to find its way back to the simple experience of wonder that once was and perhaps still is the true source of philosophy. It is this question that remains to be answered.

List of Abbreviations

Hegel

Aph	Aphorismen aus Hegels Wastebook
D	Differenz des Fichteschen und Schellingschen Systems der Philosophie
E	Enzyklopädie der philosophischen Wissenschaften
Fhps	Fragmente historischer und politischer Studien
GP	Vorlesungen über die Geschichte der Philosophie
GW	Glauben und Wissen
L	Wissenschaft der Logik
Mag	Dass die Magistrate von den Bürgern gewählt werden müssen
NS	Nürnburger Schriften
PC	Die Positivität der christlichen Religion
PG	Vorlesungen über die Philosophie der Geschichte
Ph	Wissenschaft der Phänomenologie des Geistes
PR	Grundlinien zur Philosophie des Rechts oder Naturrecht und Staatswissenschaft im Grundrisse
PRel	Vorlesungen über die Philosophie der Religion
RB	Ueber die englische Reformbill
VB	"Vertraulichen Briefen"
VD	Die Verfassung Deutschlands
VW	Versammlung der Landstände des Königreichs Wurttemberg

Heidegger

Ar	Aristotles, Metaphysik Theta 1–3
ED	Aus der Erfahrung des Denkens
EM	Einführung in die Metaphysik
HD	Erläuterungen zur Hölderlins Dichtung
HW	Holzwege
N	Nietzsche
PL	Platons Lehre von der Wahrheit. Mit einem Brief über den "Humanismus"
Sp	"Nur ein Gott kann uns retten," Spiegel interview
SD	Zur Sache des Denkens
SG	Der Satz vom Grund
SZ	Sein und Zeit
Th68	Séminaire tenu par le Professeur Martin Heidegger sur la Differenzschrift de Hegel
Th69	Séminaire tenu au Thor en septembre 1969 par le Professeur Martin Heidegger
US	Unterwegs zur Sprache
VA	Vorträge und Aufsätze
VS	Vier Seminare
WD	Was Heisst Denken?
WG	Vom Wesen des Grundes
WM	Was ist Metaphysik?
WW	Vom Wesen der Wahrheit

Kant

KrV	Kritik der reinen Vernunft

Notes

Chapter 1

1. Homer *Iliad* 18. 501; Hippocrates *Ius iurandum* 41 628L; for a discussion of Hippocrates' usage of the term, see Ernst Fränkel, *Geschichte der griechen Nomia agentis* (Strassburg: Trübner, 1910), p. 218; Thucydides *The Peloponnesian War* 2. 74. 3; for the general usage of the word as 'umpire' or 'judging witness,' see Manu Leumann, *Homerische Wörter* (Basel: Reinhardt, 1950), p. 278; Hesiod *Works and Days* 792; Sophocles *Electra* 840; Heracleitus 35, in Hermann Diels, *Die Fragmente der Vorsokratiker*, ed. Walter Kranz, 6th ed., 3 vols. (Berlin: Weidmann, 1959–62), 1:159; Bacchylides, *Odes* 8. 44; *Homeric Hymns* 32; Plato *Cratylus* 406b. See also Heracleitus 40, 129, in Diels, *Fragmente*, 1:160, 180–81.

2. For an excellent discussion of Herodotus's project and its problematic relationship to history as we understand it today, see Seth Bernadette, *Herodotean Inquiries* (The Hague: Nijhoff, 1969). See also Hartmut Erbse, "Der erste Satz im Werke Herodots," *Festschrift Bruno Snell*, ed. Hartmut Erbse (Munich: Beck, 1956), pp. 209–23.

3. Aristotle *Rhetoric* 1360a37; see also 1359b32; see also Pseudo-Aristotle *Oeconomica* 1346a26–32; *De mundo* 395b16; 396a20; *De plantis* 818b28; *De mirabilibus auscultationibus* 833a12; Polybios *Histories* 1. 57. 5.

4. Plato *Phaedo* 96a7–9; *Cratylus* 437b; Theophrastus, *Opera*, ed. Friedrich Wimmer, 3 vols. (Leipzig: Teubner, 1854–62), 3:172, 174. For its further development in Latin, see Karl Keuck's excellent *Historia. Geschichte des Wortes und Seiner Bedeutung in der Antike und in den romanischen Sprachen* (Emsdelten, Germany: Leuchte, 1934; dissertation, Münster, 1934). All translations unless otherwise noted are my own.

5. This generally meant that historians limited their accounts to events that occurred within their own lifetimes, often traveling extensively to inspect the places they described and to question local inhabitants about events and customs.

6. Aristotle *Metaphysics* 980a17–27.

7. For a fuller discussion of this see Hannah Arendt's illuminating "The Concept of History: *Ancient and Modern*," in her *Between Past and Future: Six Exercises in Political Thought* (New York: Viking, 1961), pp. 41–90.

8. Aristotle *Poetics* 1451b.

9. Epictetus *Manual* 5. 1.

10. Arendt argues that this is an attempt to emulate nature. Arendt, *Between Past and Future*, p. 43.

11. See R. G. Collingwood, *The Idea of History* (Oxford: Clarendon, 1946), pp. 17–28.

12. See Cicero *De legibus* 1. 1,5; *De oratore* 1.52; 2. 15. 63; and 62; 3. 211; *Brutus* 42, 262; *Ad familiares* 5. 12. 4; *Ad Quintum fratrem* 1. 1. 10. See also Pliny *Epistularum* 1. 1. 1; Juvenal *Satires* 1. 2. 103; Servius *Aeneid* 1. 373.

13. See Keuck, *Historia*, p. 22.

14. The so-called historical sections of the Old Testament cannot properly be termed history or histories. It is an attribution of modern times that has led to this concept of the "historicism" of ancient Jewish thought. 'Chronicle' (*dibre ha-jamīn*) literally means 'happenings (or words) of the day'; the narrative sections of the Old Testament are called *ketubīm*, 'the written'; and the genealogies *tol*'dot*, 'register', 'report'. The more subtle argument, that ancient Jewish thought is essentially historical because the concept of being, expressed by the word *hajah*, 'do', 'work', is itself historical, likewise is insufficient. The Old English verb *béon*, which became 'be' in Middle and Modern English, originally meant 'to grow', 'to become', yet one would scarcely want to argue that English theological and philosophical thought is therefore essentially historicistic, although this argument would be much easier to defend than the former. In the New Testament the word *historein* appears only once, and then only in the sense 'to see in order to become acquainted with'. Galatians 1:18.

15. The first attempt to combine Judeo-Christian and ancient histories was undertaken by Sextus Julius Africanus in the third century. His work served as a model for the *Chronicles* of Eusebius of Caesarea, which was later enlarged by St. Jerome. This work was the model for nearly all Byzantine chronicles and provided much of the material for medieval histories. The decisive articulation of the basis of Christian history, however, was St. Augustine's *The City of God against the Pagans*, which was adapted and enlarged by his pupil Paulus Orosius in his *History against the Pagans*. This work was the model for nearly all medieval histories, such as Bede's *Ecclesiastical History of England* and Otto of Freising's *The Two Cities*, as well as the histories of the Reformation and Counter Reformation, down to Bousset's *Discourse on Universal History* in 1681.

16. "Christianity recognized, corresponding to its spiritual stance, only *one* historical source and that was the Bible, the Old and New Testament and the Acts of the Apostles. This collective work was called by the Church Fathers the Sacred History or also the Divine History." Keuck, *Historia*, p. 97. Even Joachim of Floris must be included in this characterization. Although he in one sense turns to an examination of actual historical events, he does so always with a view to discovering the allegorical truth of revelation. On this point Löwith goes astray in his otherwise excellent *Meaning in History* (Chicago: University of Chicago Press, 1949), pp. 145–59.

17. This view is not universally shared. Marc Bloch, for example, has even argued that the Middle Ages were supremely interested in history. See his monumental *Feudal Society*, trans. L. A. Manyon, 2 vols. (Chicago: University of Chicago Press, 1961), 1: 88–102. What he calls history, however, is either the intrinsic traditionalism of a static society or a concern with Providence and one's location in the divine order between Creation and Parousia.

18. For a discussion of this transformation from a semantic point of view, see Reinhart Koselleck's *Vergangene Zukunft: Zur Semantik Geschichtlicher Zeiten* (Frankfurt: Suhrkamp, 1979).

19. Thomas Hobbes *Leviathan* 1. 9. 40.

20. Löwith makes a similar argument in *Nature, History, and Existentialism, and Other Essays in the Philosophy of History*, ed. and intro. Arnold Levinson (Evanston: Northwestern University Press, 1966), pp. 21–29, 136–54. As he points out, Roger Bacon saw the modern conquest of nature as the only way to the universal Christian state. Meinecke sees this not as a secularization of Christianity but as a rebirth of neo-Platonism. Friedrich Meinecke, *Historicism: The Rise of a New Historical Outlook*, trans. J. E. Anderson (London: Routledge & Kegan Paul, 1972), pp. 6–10, 17–18, passim.

21. Gottfried Wilhelm Freiherr von Leibniz, *Philosophische Schriften*, ed. C. J. Gerhardt, 7 vols. (Berlin: Weidmann, 1875–1890; reprint, ed., Hildesheim: Olms, 1960), 6:612.

22. Voltaire, *Dictionaire philosophique*, ed. R. Naves and J. Benda (Paris: Garnier, 1967), p. 14.

23. Löwith holds Christianity responsible for this transformation, but this seems an overly historical explanation that fails to grant modernity a real originality of its own. See Löwith, *Nature, History, and Existentialism*, p. 149.

24. It is this "discovery" of history as the *res gestae* and not merely the development of a critical science of history, i.e., of a scientific *historia rerum gestarum*, that is peculiarly modern and the source of what is often called historicism. J. G. A. Pocock, Julian Franklin, George Huppert, Donald Kelly, and Arnaldo Momigliano have persuasively traced the development of the science of history back to the sixteenth century, but they go crucially astray in their assumption that this is the source of historicism. See J. G. A. Pocock, *The Ancient Constitution and the Feudal Law* (New York: Norton, 1957); Julian Franklin, *Jean Bodin and the Sixteenth Century Revolution in the Methodology of Law and History* (New York, Columbia University Press, 1963); George Huppert, *The Idea of Perfect History* (Urbana: University of Illinois Press, 1970); Donald Kelly, *Foundations of Modern Historical Scholarship* (New York: Columbia University Press, 1970); Arnaldo Momigliano, *Studies in Historiography* (New York: Harper & Row, 1966).

25. Ernst Troeltsch later grouped these thinkers together under the title "historicists" in his important *Der Historismus und seine Ueberwindung* (Berlin: Heise, 1924).

26. For an excellent discussion of Condorcet's life, work, and influence, see Keith Baker's *Condorcet: From Natural Philosophy to Social Mathematics* (Chicago: University of Chicago Press, 1975). Odo Marquard sees this accelerationism as the revenge of religion on the Enlightenment in the form of a reborn Biblical eschatology. See Odo Marquard, *Schwierigkeiten mit der Geschichtsphilosophie* (Frankfurt am Main: Suhrkamp, 1973).

27. This is the *historische Rechtsschule*. The name first appeared in the group's own *Programmschriften* of 1814/1815 and was later carried over as the name for the "older" and "younger" Historical School of National Economy. The Historical School also included B. G. Niebuhr, J. Grimm, et al., and drew upon the work of Herder, Montesquieu, Möser, and Hegel.

28. The influence of Burke upon the Historical School has long been recognized, and while his Romanticism allies him with them he is rather suspicious of the people or *Volk* and more apt to rely upon the aristocratic virtues of the Old Regime than the popular spirit, although he appeals to it on occasion.

29. Karl Marx and Friedrich Engels, *Marx-Engels-Werke*, ed. Manfred Kliem et al. (Berlin: Dietz, 1956–), 3: 18, 43.

30. Ibid., 1:545.

31. The term 'historicism' was already used by Novalis, but until the middle of the nineteenth century it was rare. In 1848 Braniss used the term to name all speculative philosophy of history in order to distinguish it from both naturalism and determinism. Christian Julius Braniss, *Die Wissenshaftliche Aufgabe der Gegenwart als leitende Idee im akademischen Studium* (Breslau: Maske, 1848), p. 120. It was generally a term of opprobrium in the nineteenth century with the interesting neutral usage by Werner to characterize the work of Vico, from which the word itself is today most generally derived and understood. Karl Werner, *Giambattista Vico als Philosoph und gelehrter Forscher* (Vienna: Braumüller, 1881), passim. In the twentieth century the word takes on an increasingly broader signification, so that at its extreme, for example, in Meinecke, it means little more than historiography. Troeltsch, however, who identified historicism with relativism, gave the word its most widespread contemporary connotation. Here the term will be used in a more narrow and technical sense to characterize the thought of Dilthey, Croce, and their followers, such as Robin G. Collingwood,

who was largely responsible for the propagation and popularization of historicism in the English-speaking world. See his *Essays on the Philosophy of History*, ed. and intro. William Debbins (Austin: University of Texas Press, 1965).

32. Leo Strauss later articulated a similar view. See his *Natural Right and History* (Chicago: University of Chicago Press, 1953), pp. 9–34.

33. See, for example, Frantz Fanon, *The Wretched of the Earth*, pref. Jean Paul Sartre, trans. Constance Farrington (New York: Grove, 1965).

34. See, Löwith, *Nature, History, and Existentialism*, pp. 157–60.

35. See Karl Raimund Popper, *Poverty of Historicism* (London: Routledge & Kegan Paul, 1957), pp. 159–61.

36. See Patrick Gardiner, *Theories of History* (New York: Free Press, 1959), pp. 344–475, and especially Carl Hemple, "The Function of General Laws in History," pp. 344–56, and William Dray "'Explaining What' in History," pp. 403–8.

37. It must be admitted that a good deal of this criticism is also motivated by a real and sensible revulsion in the face of Nazism and Bolshevism. Karl Popper's critique in the *Open Society and its Enemies*, 4th ed., 2 vols. (Princeton: Princeton University Press, 1963) is illustrative of this position and its flaws, foremost of which is a profound ignorance of the thinkers it criticizes.

Chapter 2

1. Aristotle *Metaphysics* 1003a20, 1028a10–20.

2. Ibid., 981b28–983a26, 997a; Aristotle *Nichomachean Ethics* 1141a8; Plato *Republic* 509a.

3. For a comprehensive discussion of the teleological nature of causality in Aristotle, see Helene Weiss's profound *Kausalität und Zufall in der Philosophie des Aristotles* (Basel: Falken, 1942).

4. See Leibniz, *Philosophische Schriften*, 2:62; 4:232; 6:127, 602, 611–13; 7:299.

5. Jean-Jacques Rousseau, *Discours sur l'origine et les fondements de l'inégalité parmi les hommes*, in Marcel Raymond (Paris: Gallimard, 1959–), 3:132 (hereafter cited as *Inégalité*).

6. Ibid., p. 122.

7. In this light George Armstrong Kelly concludes that "Rousseau attempted the first methodical liaison between the sense world of process and individual psychological tensions, a sort of 'phenomenology'." G. A. Kelly, *Idealism, Politics and History: Sources of Hegelian Thought* (Cambridge: Cambridge University Press, 1969), pp. 28–29.

8. *Inégalité*, 3:123, 127, 133, 219.

9. Ibid., pp. 192–93. The amelioration of this diremption, in view of the character of self-consciousness, can follow in one of two ways: either through the generalization of the self, i.e., the general will of the *Social Contract*, or through the isolation of the soul from society as in the *Émile* or the *Reveries*.

10. Ibid., p. 164.

11. It is in this sense that self-consciousness, bringing about the degeneration of natural soul in the political realm, also opens up the possibility for the redemption of both the soul and the political realm in the unity of the general will.

12. See Rousseau's letter to Philopolis (Charles Bonnet), *Oeuvres complètes*, 3:230–36.

13. *Inégalité*, 3:165. The soul thus also comes into evil or vice and thence to the arts or sciences as Rousseau had already argued in the *First Discourse*. Rousseau's

conception of the human capacity for perfectibility is thus only in the most superficial sense indicative of any real human progress. In fact Rousseau's use of the term is generally ironic.

14. Immanuel Kant to Garve, 26 September 1798. Immanuel Kant, *Gesammelte Schriften*, ed. Königlich Preussischen Akademie der Wissenschaften (Berlin: Reimer, 1900–), 12:257–58. On the decisive importance of the antinomy for Kant's thought, see also 4:338, 341 n.; 10:252; 18:60–62; and Hans Feist, *Der Antinomiegedanke bei Kant und seine Entwicklung in den vorkritischen Schriften* (Borna-Leipzig: Noske, 1932; dissertation, Berlin, 1932), esp. pp. 3–17. Kant does not begin as is often argued, apparently merely on the basis of a misinterpretation of the argument in the "Preface" to the *Prolegomena*, with the epistemological problems of the "Transcendental Aesthetic" but with the antinomy. On this crucial point, see Immanuel Kant, *Kants Prolegomena*, ed. Benno Erdmann (Leipzig: Voss, 1878); Carl Siegel, "Kants Antinomielehre im Lichte der Inaugural Dissertation," *Kant-Studien* 30 (1925): 67–86; Norbert Hinske, "Kants Begriff der Antinomie und die Etappen seiner Ausarbeitung," *Kant-Studien* 56 (1965): 485–96; Heinz Heimsoeth, "Zum Kosmotheologischen Ursprung der Kantischen Freiheitsantinomie," *Kant-Studien* 57 (1966): 206–29; and his *Atom, Seele, Monad* (Wiesbaden: Steiner, 1960).

15. Immanuel Kant, *Kritik der reinen Vernunft*, ed. Raymond Schmidt (Hamburg: Meiner, 1956) p. A424/B452 (hereafter cited as *KrV*).

16. It must not therefore be concluded, however, that the antinomy is a contradiction of two different human capacities, reason and understanding. This common misunderstanding confuses the contradiction that arises from the mistaken use of two human capacities for a contradiction of the capacities themselves.

17. Georg Wilhelm Friedrich Hegel, *Differenz des Fichteschen und Schellingschen Systems der Philosophie*, in *Werke in 20 Bänden*, ed. Eva Moldenhauer and Karl Markus Michel, 20 vols. (Frankfurt am Main: Suhrkamp, 1970–71), 2:9 (hereafter cited as *D*).

18. *D*, 2:20; see 2:27. Ritter argues that diremption is only decisive for modernity in Hegel's thought. Joachim Ritter, *Hegel und die französische Revolution* (Frankfurt am Main: Suhrkamp, 1965), pp. 45, 58. This, however, seems too narrow a construction. Diremption for Hegel is the chief characteristic of all human history. Despite its shortcomings, however, Ritter's work is one of the most important considerations of Hegel's thought in the last twenty years.

19. *D*, 2:21

20. *D*, 2:22–23.

21. In the 150 years since his death, the political significance of Hegel's thought and especially its relationship to the French Revolution and English political economy has received varying and often contradictory interpretations. It has been characterized as a doctrine of liberation and revolution, as a system for the bureaucratic organization of modern economic life, as a philosophy of German nationalism, and even as an idealist metaphysics with a fundamentally theological intention that consequently has little to do with political life. Beginning with the Left or Young Hegelians, many have characterized Hegel as a proponent of radical or revolutionary social change. For a consideration of this development in the nineteenth century, see Karl Löwith, *Von Hegel zu Nietzsche. Der revolutionäre Bruch im Denken des neunzehnten Jahrhunderts* (Zürich and New York: Europa, 1941). In the twentieth century Herbert Marcuse has argued that German idealism and especially the philosophy of Hegel is the theory of the French Revolution and that however bitter Hegel's criticism of the Terror, he remains a proponent of the principles of the Revolution. Herbert Marcuse, *Reason and Revolution: Hegel and the Rise of Social Theory* (London: Oxford University Press, 1955), pp. 3–7, 179. György Lukàcs adds that when Hegel became estranged from Revolutionary ideals because of the Terror, "he found his way out of the labyrinth and back to dialectics with the aid of the compass provided by political economy and in particular the economic condition of England." György Lukàcs, *The Young Hegel: Studies in the Relations between Dialectics and Economics*, trans. R. Livingstone (Cambridge, Mass.: M.I.T. Press, 1975), p. xxvii. Jürgen

Habermas concludes in this light that Hegel wants to revolutionize actuality without revolutionaries and thus overcomes the Revolution by establishing it as the basic principle of his thought. Jürgen Habermas, *Theorie und Praxis: Sozialphilosophie Studien* (Neuwied and Berlin: Luchterhand, 1963), pp. 105–6. Thus, Ernst Bloch can argue that even if Hegel's later philosophy was more reactionary he was never a Romantic nationalist and never a supporter of the Restoration. Ernst Bloch, *Subjekt-Objekt: Erläuterungen zu Hegel*, 2d ed. (Frankfurt am Main: Suhrkamp, 1972), pp. 244–59. (Despite their ideological prejudices these works avoid the Leninist reductionism of someone like Wilhelm Raimund Beyer who pushes this view of a revolutionary Hegel to its absurd extreme. W. R. Beyer, *Hegel-Bilder: Kritik der Hegel-Deutung* [Berlin: Akademie, 1967], pp. 89–100.

In contradistinction to this "revolutionary" interpretation of Hegel, the Right and his liberal detractors have attempted to portray him as a conservative nationalist. Rudolph Haym, whom Beyer has characterized as the father of the reactionary and imperialistic view of Hegel, argues that Hegel's attachment to the Revolution, which Haym calls "the great tragedy," was both momentary and uncharacteristic, a student's intoxication that was fundamentally at odds with the philosophical system of the otherwise completely unrevolutionary Hegel. He thus concludes that Hegel's system "became the scientific abode of the Prussian restoration" and that the *Philosophy of Right* was both antiliberal and anti-Republican, favoring in fact a limitation of individual freedom to secure stability and a measured order. Rudolph Haym, *Hegel und seine Zeit: Vorlesungen über Entstehung und Entwicklung, Wesen und Werthe der Hegel' schen Philosophie* (Berlin: Gärner, 1857; reprint ed., Hildesheim: Olms, 1962), pp. 32, 359, 380–83. In this vein Carl Michelet concludes that it was thus not the French Revolution but English institutions that were decisive for Hegel's conception of freedom. Carl Michelet, *Hegel, der unwiderlegte Weltphilosoph* (Leipzig: Duncker & Humblot, 1870; reprint ed., Aalen: Scientia, 1970), pp. 46–49. Franz Rosenzweig admits, on the contrary, that Hegel's philosophy grew out of Rousseau and the Revolution and that it is thus forged of the metal of freedom but concludes that Hegel's conception of freedom differed fundamentally from that of Robespierre and the Revolutionaries, residing not in the general will of individuals but in the rational will of the state. Rosenzweig thus concludes that Hegel's call for freedom and reason is in fact a call for men to subordinate themselves to the state. Hegel thus is understood as the spiritual father, or at least the midwife, of the Bismarckean state. Franz Rosenzweig, *Hegel und der Staat*, 2 vols. (Berlin: Oldenbourg, 1920; reprint ed., Aalen: Scientia, 1962), esp. 2:243. Oskar Negt thus concludes that "Hegelian philosophy serves as the theoretical and practical refutation of the Marxist theory of revolution," and Giovanni Gentile goes so far as to claim Hegel as the spiritual father of Fascism. Oskar Negt, *Aktualität und Folgen der Philosophie Hegels* (Frankfurt am Main: Suhrkamp, 1970), p. 11; Giovanni Gentile, "Il concetto dello Stato in Hegel," in *Verhandlungen des 2. Hegelkongresses vom 19. bis 22. Oktober 1931 in Berlin*, ed. B. Wigersma (Tübingen: Mohr, 1932; Haarlem: Willinz, 1932), pp. 121–34. Hubert Kieswetter thus argues that there was a direct development from Hegel to Hitler, and Karl Popper discovers in Hegel the true enemy of the "open society." Hubert Kieswetter, *Von Hegel zu Hitler: Eine Analyse der Hegelschen Machtstaatideologie und der politischen Wirkungsgeschichte des Rechtshegelianismus* (Hamburg: Hoffmann & Campe, 1974); Karl Popper, *The Open Society and its Enemies*, 2: 27–80.

In opposition to these views of Hegel as a liberal revolutionary and a conservative nationalist is the view of Hegel as a metaphysician-theologian. Theodor Haering, for example, sees the fundamental tendency in Hegel's thought in his "spiritual monism," which represents his theological-pedagogical intention. Thus, as Ritter has remarked, the roll of the French Revolution slips into the background in Haering's interpretation. Theodor Haering, *Hegel: Sein Wollen und sein Werk. Eine chronologische Entwicklungsgeschichte der Gedanken und Sprache Hegels*, 2 vols. (Leipzig: Teubner, 1929 and 1938; reprint ed., Aalen: Scientia, 1963). In this vein H. S. Harris tries to show that Hegel's early thought, far from being concerned with Revolution, as Lukàcs and others argue, aimed at establishing a folk religion. H. S. Harris, *Hegel's Development: Toward the Sunlight* (Oxford: Clarendon, 1971). Even Emil Fachenheim, who argues that we must try to find and maintain the middle in Hegel's thought, comes to the conclusion that the relationship of human experience to absolute thought is the central problem of Hegel's philosophy. Emil Fachenheim, *The Religious Dimension in Hegel's Thought* (Bloomington: Indiana University Press, 1967). This interpretation reaches its extreme in Heidegger and Fink who understand Hegel's thought as onto-theo-logy. Martin Heidegger, *Hegels Phänamenologie des Geistes* (Frankfurt am Main: Klostermann, 1980), and "Hegels Begriff der Erfahrung," *Holzwege* (Frankfurt am Main: Klostermann, 1950), pp. 105–92 (hereafter cited as *HW*); Eugen Fink, *Hegel: Phänomenologische Interpretation der "Phänomenologie des Geistes"* (Frankfurt am Main: Klostermann, 1977). The interpretation presented here attempts to chart a middle course between the Scylla of the Right and the Charybdis of the Left without losing itself on Calypso's metaphysical island.

22. Hegel, *Vorlesungen über die Philosophie der Geschichte*, in *Werke*, 12:529; see also p. 521 (hereafter cited as *PG*). One should note that while Hegel's assertion here is far from restrained it is also little short of the truth: Klopstock, Wieland, Schiller, Herder, and many others welcomed the Revolution and the humanistic transformation they believed in would work upon Europe. See Dieter Henrich, "Leutwein über Hegel," *Hegel-Studien* 3 (1965): 39–77; and Otto Pöggeler, *Hegels Idee einer Phänomenologie des Geistes* (Freiburg: Alber, 1973), pp. 21–22. The first chapter of Pöggeler's work as well as Ritter's *Hegel und die Französische Revolution* should be consulted for an alternative and more biographical account of Hegel's relationship to the French Revolution. Each in its way is an alternative to Lukàcs's *The Young Hegel*.

23. Hegel, *Wissenschaft der Phänomenologie des Geistes*, in *Werke*, 3:436 (hereafter cited as *Ph*). For the generally similar reaction of German literary and political opinion see Kelly, *Idealism, Politics, and History*, pp. 86–88.

24. Hegel, "Die Positivität der christlichen Religion," in *Werke*, 1:203 (hereafter cited as *PC*). This would seem at least on the surface to directly contradict Hegel's assertion in the *Philosophy of Right* that the owl of Minerva only takes wing at dusk, i.e., that philosophy can only understand what is already completed. The discrepancy of these two assertions has often been pointed out, generally in order to prove that in his late works Hegel is less revolutionary and more reactionary or quietistic and therefore either more or less sensible (depending upon the commentator's political persuasions). Löwith has produced perhaps the best argument to demonstrate the compatibility of these two statements. He argues that philosophy for Hegel is always bound by its time but that as knowledge of the eternal is always beyond its time. Karl Löwith, "Aktualität und Inaktualität Hegels," in *Hegel-Bilanz: Zur Aktualität und Inaktualität der Philosophie Hegels*, ed. R. Heede and J. Ritter (Frankfurt am Main: Klostermann, 1973), p. 5. This suggestion offers a plausible solution. We might also note that philosophy even in the *Philosophy of Right* seems always to encapsulate and deliver over one age to the next. In this sense we ought to remember that when the owl of Minerva takes flight all other birds go to sleep.

25. *Ph*, 3:432–33; *PG*, 12:524–27.

26. Hegel, *Vorlesungen über die Geschichte der Philosophie*, in *Werke*, 20:307 (hereafter cited as *GP*); *Grundlinien der Philosophie des Rechts oder Naturrecht und Staatswissenschaft im Grundrisse*, in *Werke*, 7:400 (hereafter cited as *PR*).

27. Hegel, *Die Verfassung Deutschlands*, in *Werke*, 1:583 (hereafter cited as *VD*); *PG*, 12:528; *GP*, 20:296–97.

28. *PG*, 12:528–29; *GP*, 20:297. It has been recognized at least since Tocqueville that the French Revolution was preceded not by harsh or repressive governmental measures but by minor reforms aimed at alleviating the most obnoxious abuses. Hegel is not concerned, however, with the merely historical truth. He recounts rather the development of consciousness or spirit, which in his view can be recaptured not through a determination of the objective facts but by a consideration of the self-understanding of each age. In this sense the errors are at least as important as the facts and may in fact reveal the underlying truth about that age, i.e., its own peculiar prejudice. More on this below in Chapter 4.

29. *GP*, 20:331; see also *Ph*, 3:432–35; *PR*, 7:80–81, 400; Hegel, "Ueber die englische Reformbill," in *Werke*, 11:127 (hereafter cited as *RB*); *PG*, 12:529; *GP*, 18:358; 20:292, 297.

30. *Ph*, 3:435–36.

31. Hegel, "Aphorismen aus Hegels Wastebook," in *Werke*, 4:546–47 (hereafter cited as *Aph*); *Enzyklopädie der philosophischen Wissenschaften*, in *Werke*, 10:177 (hereafter cited as *E*); *Vorlesungen über die Philosophie der Religion*, in *Werke*, 16:246; 17:312 (hereafter cited as *PRel*); *Ph*, 3:437; *PG*, 12:322. Hegel's revulsion is also apparent in his letter to Schelling of 24 December 1794: "That Carrier has been guillotined you will know . . . This case is very important and has revealed the complete infamy of the Robespierrites." *Briefe von und an Hegel*, ed. J. Hoffmeister and F. Nicolin, 4 vols. (Hamburg: Meiner, 1969–79), 1:12. Nor was Hegel appalled merely by the tyrannical Committee of Public Safety: the rapacious attack of the French army upon the southwestern German states discredited the Revolution even among many of its most ardent supporters, among them Hegel. *VD*, 1:610; *Briefe*, 1:57–58. See also Karl Rosenkranz, *G. F. W. Hegels Leben* (Berlin: Duncker & Humblot, 1844; reprint ed., Darmstadt: Wissenschaftliche Buchgesellschaft, 1977), p. 91; Erwin Hölzle, *Das alte Recht und die Revolution* (Munich: Oldenbourg, 1931); and Pöggeler, *Hegels Idee*, pp. 47–49.

32. *GP*, 20:331–32; see also *Ph*, 3:437; *PR*, 7:52; and Hegel, "Fragmente historischer und politischer Studien," in *Werke*, 1:433 (hereafter cited as *FhpS*). This, according to Hegel, is not true rational freedom but the empty idea of freedom characteristic of the understanding.

33. Hegel, "Ueber die wissenschaftliche Behandlungsart des Naturrechts," in *Werke*, 2:476.

34. *PR*, 7:339. Hegel had already developed this idea of bourgeois society in Jena. See Hegel, *Jenaer Systementwürfe III*, ed. R. Horstman (Hamburg: Meiner, 1976), in *Gesammelte Werke*, 8:267–70. On Hegel's theory of bourgeois society, see the essays by Manfred Riedel, Rolf Peter Horstmann, and Siegfried Blasche, in *Materialien zu Hegels Rechtsphilosophie*, ed. M. Riedel, 2 vols. (Frankfurt am Main: Suhrkamp, 1974), 2:247–337.

35. *PG*, 12:537.

36. *GP*, 20:299.

37. *GP*, 20:425; see *PG*, 12:534–35; see *GP*, 20:79, 91.

38. *PG*, 12:537.

39. Ibid.; see *PR*, 7:399, 442; *E*, 10:342; *PG*, 12:535.

40. Hegel, "Vertraulichen Briefen," in *Werke*, 1:258 (hereafter cited as *VB*); "Versammlung der Landstände des Königreichs Wurttemberg," in *Werke* 4:476, 484 (hereafter cited as *VW*); *PR*, 7:341, 537–38; *RB*, 11:85–86.

41. Hegel's first acquaintance with national economy arose through his reading of Sir James Steuart's *An Enquiry into the Principles of Political Economy*. He later became acquainted with the works of Adam Smith, Say, and Ricardo. *PR*, 7:346–47. See also *VW*, 4:473–74; *PR*, 7:538.

42. See *PR*, 7:349, 353–54, 389–90, 395, 493. In his critique of the English Reform Bill, Hegel raises the question whether resistance to the rationalization of English law and right might not engender the same sort of confrontation of *hommes à principes* and *hommes d'état* that was in his opinion a primary cause of the French Revolution. *RB*, 11:127–28.

43. *GP*, 20:292; see also p. 295. As Shlomo Avineri remarks, "To Hegel, Natural Law failed to find a middle way between Hobbes and Robespierre." Shlomo Avineri, *Hegel's Theory of the Modern State* (Cambridge: Cambridge University Press, 1972), p. 83. This book is probably the best study of Hegel's political philosophy in English and one of the best in any language.

44. See Hegel, *Briefe*, 1:185; and H. S. Harris, "Hegel and the French Revolution," *Clio* 7 (1977): 5–18.

45. *PR*, 7:440.

46. *VD*, 1:572.

47. *PR*, 7:460.

48. *RB*, 11:83–84. Such a transformation had been foreshadowed in Hegel's view by the American Revolution and especially the principle of no taxation without representation. *VB*, 1:258. For an excellent discussion of Hegel's critique of the English Reform Bill, see Avineri's *Hegel's Theory*, pp. 208–20.

49. Hegel, "Dass die Magistrate von den Bürgern gewählt werden müssen," in *Werke*, 1:273 (hereafter cited as *Mag*).

50. *GP*, 20:68; see *E*, 10:401; *PG*, 12:494; *GP*, 18:12; 20:298.

51. *VD*, 1:439, 453–54, 465–67, 478, 515–16, 525; *Aph*, 2:546; *PG*, 12:425.

52. *VD*, 1:516, 518, 544, 546.

53. *PG*, 12:497; see also p. 490.

54. *RB*, 11:123, 128.

55. *VD*, 1:511, 575.

56. The word *Stände* has several different senses, all of which Hegel apparently means to convey: the *estates* within bourgeois society, the *estates general*, especially of the Holy Roman Empire, and hence the *states* that they represent. *Stände* will be translated here as 'states' but the subsidiary meanings must not thereby be forgotten.

57. *VD*, 1:505, 542, 570, 576, 596, 598; *Aph*, 2:564. According to Rosenkranz, Hegel hoped through his critique of the German constitution to become Germany's Machiavelli, i.e., to preserve Germany as Machiavelli had attempted to preserve Italy from political disintegration and ruin. Rosenkranz, *Hegels Leben*, p. 236; see also *VD*, 1:554–58. He saw the German states unable to defend themselves from foreign interference just as the Italian states in Machiavelli's time had been unable to unite to resist foreign intervention. The military disaster of the wars against the French solidified Hegel's opinion that "Germany is no longer a state." *VD*, 1:453, 461; see also *Aph*, 2:546; and Rosenkranz, *Hegels Leben*, pp. 235–46. The true fiber of a state is measured in his view not in times of peace but in times of war, when it is called upon to act as a whole in defense of itself as a state, when the citizens are called upon to sacrifice their private interests and ultimately their particular lives for the public or general good. In this, according to Hegel, the Germans had failed utterly. That the disintegration that this failure made evident might be remedied seems to have been his hope. He soon became convinced, however, that such a project was hopeless and consigned his manuscript to a desk drawer. No immediate salvation was possible and indeed the idea of a German nation-state was in his view dead. Nonetheless, a general and beneficial reform might be effected. The project to which he dedicated himself, however, was not to reconstitute the old Empire but to provide the ground for a spiritual unity within which rational and just states could subsist. This is especially clear in his commentary on the meeting of the estates general in Württemberg in 1815/1816 to consider a new constitution. In his view since the institutionalized anarchy that was nonsensically called the German Empire had come to an end, it would be possible to found new constitutional states. Unfortunately, as he himself points out, all too many members of the old estates had still not learned the lesson of the French Revolution. They were, to be sure, not "taken in by the blind cries for freedom," but they also believed they would be able to retain their old feudal rights and privileges. While political conditions were thus favorable in Hegel's view to the establishment of rational states in Germany, what was necessary was the education of the people in the principles upon which such states were to be based. He believed that the tendencies to particularism and nationalism could thus be avoided by the articulation of such an overarching theoretical ground. *VW*, 4:505–8. This is the ultimate teaching of his systematic philosophy: not objective spirit, i.e., not the person, family, society, or state, but absolute spirit, i.e., art, religion, and philosophy are fundamental. The attempt to establish a universal state could lead in his view only to the most wretched despotism. It is in this light that his attack upon Fries and Romantic German nationalism in the "Preface" to the *Philosophy of Right* must be understood—all doctrines that rely upon the *immediate* expression of nationalistic *feeling* or the will of the *Volk* bypass and hence undermine the moderating effect of mediating institutions and ultimately destroy all real liberty. Thus, Hegel himself stood far from the fervor of

Nazism and far even from the rational universal state that Alexander Kojève attempts to uncover in the *Phenomenology*. Alexander Kojève, *Introduction à la lecture de Hegel* (Paris: Gallimard, 1947), pp. 147–54.

58. *GP*, 20:311; see also Hegel, "Glauben und Wissen," in *Werke*, 2:304,314 (hereafter cited as *GW*); *PG*, 12:525; *GP*, 20:276–77,281, 308, 344.

59. Hegel, *Wissenschaft der Logik*, in *Werke*, 5:14 (hereafter cited as *L*).

60. Hegel, *Nürnburger Schriften*, in *Werke*, 4:100–101 (hereafter cited as *NS*); *L*, 6:441. In the Nürnburg lectures the order of phrases in the last sentence is in one instance reversed without, however, changing the sense.

61. *GP*, 20:357.

62. For a more comprehensive discussion of Kant's rather ambiguous conception and evaluation of the French Revolution, see Peter Burg, *Kant und die Französische Revolution* (Berlin: Duncker & Humblot, 1974); and Kelly, *Idealism, Politics and History*, pp. 153–58. Regardless of his ultimate evaluation of the Revolution, it is clear that in his Critical thought, which was completed before 1789 there is no indication that he would view such a revolution as morally justifiable.

63. *GW*, 2:320.

64. *L*, 5:59.

65. *GP*, 20:359.

66. *GW*, 2:318.

67. For a comprehensive discussion of Kant's conception of history, see William Galston's fine *Kant and the Problem of History* (Chicago: University of Chicago Press, 1975); and Yirmiahu Yovel's clear-sighted *Kant and the Philosophy of History* (Princeton: Princeton University Press, 1980).

68. *GW*, 2:320. See also *E*, 8:142–47. Hegel expressly identifies this mathematical concept of an infinite progression as "the bad infinity," which he distinguishes from his own notion of "the affirmative infinity," which takes the form of a continual circular self-discovery. *L*, 5:156–71, 262–76.

69. *E*, 8:127–28.

70. Martial Gueroult's assertion that "Hegel's judgement of the antithetic of pure reason is thus point for point faulty" is correct but misleading. Martial Gueroult, "Hegels Urteil über die Antithetik der Reinen Vernunft," in *Seminar: Dialektik in der Philosophie Hegels*, ed. Rolf-Peter Horstmann (Frankfurt am Main: Suhrkamp, 1978), p. 287. A close examination of Hegel's critique of Kant's antimony doctrine leads one to the conclusion that Hegel's misconstructions are in fact intentional and systematic, aimed not at reproducing or even fairly representing Kant's doctrine or at criticizing this doctrine on its own grounds but at demonstrating the true and unarticulated essence of the antinomy.

71. *KrV*, p. A61/B86.

72. Ibid., p. B805.

73. *L*, 5:39.

74. *NS*, 4:190; see also p. 101.

75. *E*, 8:128.

76. Maluschke Günther argues that Hegel misses Kant's point that human thought is limited by and to experience when he attempts to dissolve the antinomy into forms of thought through a categorical analysis. Maluschke Günther, *Kritik und Absolute Methode in Hegels Dialektik, Hegel-Studien*, Beiheft 13 (1974):145. This, however, is not entirely fair to Hegel. Hegel does not miss this point but denies the validity of its ground, arguing on the contrary that without a true phenomenological ground there can ultimately be neither a rational phenomenal realm nor a concretization of the noumenal realm, i.e., that without such a ground there can be neither natural science nor morality.

77. *L*, 5:52.

78. *GW*, 2:432–33.

Chapter 3

1. In his voluminous study, H. S. Harris tries to show that Hegel's early thought aimed at the foundation of a folk or civil religion. H. S. Harris, *Hegel's Development*. In this respect he operates under the general influence of Fachenheim who sees religion as central to Hegel's thought and in opposition to Lukàcs who sees the religious element in Hegel's early thought as camouflage for underlying political and economic concerns. Emil Fachenheim, *The Religious Dimension*; Lukàcs, *The Young Hegel*.

2. Love in this context is understood as that which turns man toward the beautiful and the divine. See Plato *Phaedrus* 243d–57c; Rosenkranz, *Hegels Leben*, pp. 45–46, 58, 59; and Pöggeler, *Hegels Idee*, pp. 335–36.

3. *D*, pp. 83–88. For a concise account of Fichte's political philosophy and its importance for Hegel's thought, see Kelly, *Idealism, Politics and History*, pp. 218–85.

4. *L*, 5:18. For a fuller consideration of this point, see Werner Marx, *Hegel's Phenomenology of Spirit*, trans. Peter Heath (New York: Harper & Row, 1975), pp. ix–xiv; Otto Pöggeler, "Die Komposition der Phänomenologie des Geistes," in *Materialien zu Hegels Phänomenologie des Geistes*, ed. H. Fulda and D. Henrich (Frankfurt am Main: Suhrkamp, 1973), pp. 329–34; and Hoffmeister's "Feststellung des Textes," in Hegel, *Phänomenologie des Geistes*, ed. G. Lasson and J. Hoffmeister (Hamburg: Meiner, 1952), pp. 575–81.

5. Wilhelm Windelband, *Geschichte der neueren Philosophie*, 3d ed., 2 vols. (Leipzig: Breitkopf & Härtel, 1878–80), 2:311. Dilthey was one of the first to turn to the *Phenomenology* and he is often credited with beginning the Hegel revival, although he wrote little on Hegel. Wilhelm Dilthey, *Gesammelte Schriften* (Leipzig: Teubner, 1921–), 4:vii, 157, 217; and "Fragmente aus W. Dilthey's Hegelwerk," *Hegel-Studien* 1 (1961): 128–34. This so-called Hegel renaissance, which included such figures as Kroner, Glockner, Haering, Marcuse, Lukàcs, and Kojève, generally believed that the *Phenomenology* presented a vibrant new possibility for understanding the dynamic character of human life and history. See in this regard H. Fulda and D. Henrich, eds., *Materialien zu Hegels Phänomenologie des Geistes*, pp. 23–27; and Otto Pöggeler, "Perspektiven zur Hegelforschung," in *Stuttgarter Hegel-Tage 1970*, ed. Hans-Georg Gadamer (Bonn: Bouvier, 1974), pp. 79–81. On the character of the *Phenomenology* as an introduction to Hegel's system, see Hans Friedrich Fulda, *Das Problem einer Einleitung in Hegels Wissenschaft der Logik* (Frankfurt am Main, Klostermann, 1965), pp. 22–25, 79–115.

6. On the title, see Friedhelm Nicolin, "Zum Titelproblem der Phänomenologie des Geistes," *Hegel-Studien* 4 (1967): 114–23; and Otto Pöggeler, "Die Komposition," pp. 339–85.

7. *Ph*, 3:32.

8. *KrV*, p. A490/B518.

9. Friedrich Wilhelm Joseph von Schelling, *Sämmtliche Werke*, 14 vols. (Stuttgart and Augsburg: Cotta, 1856), div. I, 1:382–83.

10. As Pierre-Jean Labarrière has pointed out, however, spirit must always be understood from the perspective of consciousness, as general or universal consciousness. Pierre-Jean Labarrière, *Structures et mouvement dialectique dans la phénomenologie de l'esprit de Hegel* (Paris: Aubier-Montaigne, 1968), p. 25.

11. See W. Marx, *Hegel's Phenomenology*, p. 53.

12. See Pöggeler, "Die Komposition," p. 334; and Jean Hyppolite, *Genesis and Structure of Hegel's Phenomenology of Spirit*, trans S. Cherniak and J. Hekman (Evanston, Ill.: Northwestern University Press, 1974), pp. 3–4. W. Marx presents probably the best counter-argument. See W. Marx, *Hegel's Phenomenology*, pp. xii, 53–54. His argument is aimed, however, at demonstrating that the "Preface" does not contradict but in fact materially supports the argument of the *Phenomenology* proper. See pp. 15–16. There is also some question

whether the "Introduction" is intended as an introduction to the work as a whole or only the first three chapters. See Hyppolite, *Genesis*, p. 4. This argument is bound up with a larger argument about the composition and consistency of the work as a whole. However, it is at least in one sense trivial. Even if the "Introduction" was originally intended only as the beginning of the shorter *Experience of Consciousness*, the fact that it was retained by Hegel as the beginning to the *Phenomenology* indicates that he at least saw some consistency with the larger argument. It is of course possible that the work got out of hand and Hegel went astray, but there is no more evidence for this than there is that any writer goes astray when he changes his mind or revises his work.

13. Of all the commentators, only Eugen Fink and Ulrich Claesges have any notion of the structure of the "Introduction." Fink, *Hegel*, p. 41; U. Claesges, *Darstellung des erscheinenden Wissens: Systematische Einleitung in Hegels Phänomenologie des Geistes, Hegel-Studien*, Beiheft 21 (1981): 68. Both recognize the crucial turn in paragraph 9, and Fink locates the major themes of paragraphs 1–8 but does not see the corresponding themes in paragraphs 9–16. Claesges recognizes that the two sections are generally parallel but does not spell out the substantive themes and consequently does not see the complementary relations of the two sections.

14. For a fuller discussion of this point, see Labarrière, *Structures*, p. 36.

15. *HW*, p. 119. This interpretation of the "Introduction" by Heidegger is clearly one of the most profound discussions of the *Phenomenology* available. In many ways, however, it is peculiar. In general Heidegger argues that the *Phenomenology* represents the end of metaphysics in which the *theion* or god that hitherto served as the highest ground appears finally in its parousia as absolute subjectivity. The *Phenomenology* in this sense is understood as the final and complete manifestation of what Heidegger characterizes as the onto-theo-logical essence of metaphysics and the West. Such an interpretation, which we might characterize as phenomenological or ontological, contrasts with the traditional epistemological reading. While broadly ontological, the interpretation presented here seeks to show the necessary and unavoidable conjunction of ontology and epistemology that underlies Hegel's thought.

16. Hyppolite argues in this light that the *Phenomenology* rejects transcendental idealism and begins like Schelling's *Bruno* with the assertion of the absolute. Hyppolite, *Genesis*, p. 5. While the *Phenomenology* does reject transcendental idealism, it is not therefore a mere deduction from a presupposed absolute. Nor does it abandon Cartesian skepticism as Heidegger argues. *HW*, p. 119. Hegel's assertion of the absolute in the "Introduction" and throughout the *Phenomenology* is hypothetical or conditional, and his apparent faith reveals itself on closer examination as a deep although perhaps not complete skepticism.

17. *Ph*, 3:70. For an alternative interpretation of this phrase and the "Introduction" as a whole, see Fink, *Hegel*, pp. 23–57. Fink understands Hegel's project in the *Phenomenology* as the education of everyday consciousness in fundamental ontological problems.

18. Heidegger argues that Hegel's assertion of the identity of the true and the absolute is totally ungrounded. *HW*, p. 124. This does not mean in his view that it is false but that, as the fundamental insight of Hegel's thought, it cannot be demonstrated. As Fink adds, this means that there is no special region of the absolute that is by its very nature superior to the other realms of human life and activity. Fink, *Hegel*, p. 39. The absolute is rather the Being of beings, which allows all else to be as it is. This phenomenological or ontological interpretation, however, neglects Hegel's attempt to show the conjunction of absolute knowledge and all other forms of knowing and thus neglects the whole realm of mediation between the absolute and all ordinary forms of consciousness.

19. The meaning of this "presentation of appearing knowledge" is far from clear. Werner Marx and Jacob Loewenberg suggest that it is the retrospective presentation of the development of natural consciousness to science that is meant to show natural consciousness how it is bound up with science. W. Marx, *Hegel's Phenomenology*, p. 28; and Jacob

Loewenberg, *Hegel's Phenomenology: Dialogues on the Life of the Mind* (LaSalle, Ill.: Open Court, 1965), p. 16. In a less traditional manner Fink argues that this presentation (*Darstellung*) is not merely a way of knowing but a way of Being itself, the way in which the absolute establishes itself in and through representation (*Vorstellung*), that this *Dar-stellung* is thus a *demonstratio* of the identity of the true and the absolute, i.e., of truth and Being. Fink, *Hegel*, pp. 27, 41, 45–47. The *Phenomenology* in this sense is a presentation of what Heidegger in a similar vein calls the "itinerarium mentis in Deum." *HW*, p. 132. It hardly seems necessary, however, to draw such a sharp distinction between the epistemological and ontological in Hegel's thought, especially since Hegel himself continually sought their reconciliation.

There is also considerable debate about the correct translation of "appearing knowledge" (*erscheinenden Wissen*). Arnold Miller and John Findlay believe it ought to be rendered 'phenomenal knowledge,' since it is concerned with knowledge of the phenomena. Hegel, *Hegel's Phenomenology of Spirit*, trans. Arnold Miller, with a forward and analysis by John Findlay (Oxford: Oxford University Press, 1977), passim. Loewenberg argues more convincingly that it must be understood as "apparent knowledge," since it is both evident and specious. Loewenberg, *Hegel's Phenomenology*, p. 10. This seems correct as far as it goes but fails to capture the participial character of *erscheinenden* and thus misses or obscures the developmental character of "appearing knowledge" that connects it to absolute knowledge or science. Hegel recognized as early as 1802 that "reason is but one" and that all past knowledge must in some sense be embodied in the present. Hegel, "Ueber das Wesen der philosophischen Kritik," in *Werke*, 2:172. W. Marx has argued that this view of reason owes much to the genetic methodology of Fichte and Schelling. W. Marx, *Hegel's Phenomenology*, xviii.

20. For a fuller discussion of this point, see Hyppolite, *Genesis*, pp. 7–8.

21. There is much debate about the meaning of this notion of natural consciousness. Relying on the "Preface," W. Marx asserts that "*qua* natural, consciousness has its 'inorganic nature,' which, as its historical situation, directly determines it." W. Marx, *Hegel's Phenomenology*, p. 13; see also pp. 5, 31, 33, 51. This, however, leads him to the assertion that the process of development in the *Phenomenology* is the process by which consciousness overcomes its naturalness. Such an interpretation, however, places Hegel too close to the Enlightenment, on one hand, and Marx, on the other, and fails to recognize the necessity for the *reconciliation* of freedom and nature.

Heidegger characterizes natural consciousness as inauthentic, nonphilosophical consciousness, the pre-ontological consciousness of the 'they' that determines the actual spirit of an age. *HW*, pp. 118,135,137,163,186. Hyppolite in a similar vein characterizes it as "common consciousness," while Claus Scheier and others argue that it ought to be understood as a circumlocution for modern philosophy. Hyppolite, *Genesis*, p. 16; Claus-Artur Scheier, *Analytischer Kommentar au Hegels Phänomenologie des Geistes: Die Architektonik des erscheinenden Wissens* (Freiburg: Alber, 1980), p. 3.

22. The character of this "history" has been much debated. Kojève argues throughout his brilliant but problematic *Introduction* that this history is the concrete history of humanity. In contrast, Hyppolite suggests that it is not an account of world-history but an application of the genetic method of Fichte and Schelling for tracing the development of consciousness to the absolute, an itinerary of the soul on the model of the *Émile* or *Wilhelm Meister*. Hyppolite, *Genesis*, pp. 9–12. He is joined by Walter Kaufmann who compares the *Phenomenology* to *Wilhelm Meister*, or like Josiah Royce, Ernst Bloch, or Merold Westphal to *Faust*. Walter Kaufmann, *Hegel: A Re-interpretation* (Garden City: Doubleday, 1966), pp. 115–25; Ernst Bloch, *Tübinger Einleitung in die Philosophie*, 2 vols. (Frankfurt am Main: Suhrkamp, 1963–64), 1:84–114; Merold Westphal, *History and Truth in Hegel's Phenomenology* (Atlantic Highlands, N.J.: Humanities Press, 1976), p. 14. Judith Shklar sees the *Phenomenology* as a tragedy on the model of *Oedipus*. Judith Shklar, *Freedom and Independence: A Study of the Political Ideas of Hegel's Phenomenology of Mind* (Cambridge: Cambridge University Press, 1976), pp. 10; 70–71. Loewenberg wants to see this history as a series of ultimately comic roles played by an essentially histrionic absolute spirit, while Scheier and

Miller discern an allusion to the stations of the cross in Hegel's presentation. Loewenberg, *Hegel's Phenomenology*, pp. 18–20; Sheier, *Analytischer Kommentar*, p. 10; Miller, trans., *Hegel's Phenomenology*, p. 49. While the interpretation here draws attention to another "model," it is important to recognize that such analogical appeals are ultimately insufficient in themselves as a means for understanding the *Phenomenology*. Hegel drew upon the wealth of Western history and literature, and there are consequently resonances between the *Phenomenology* and many other works, but the *Phenomenology* itself ultimately has only itself as its model and must be understood on its own terms.

    23. There is little agreement among commentators about the precise meaning of Hegel's notions of doubt and despair. Schelling had argued earlier that transcendental idealism began with universal doubt, and it has often been assumed that Hegel adopted this reasoning. Hyppolite argues, however, that Hegel begins not with doubt but with common consciousness, which accepts the given and indeed *is* the given. Hyppolite, *Genesis*, p. 121. W. Marx argues on the contrary that it is necessary for doubt to become despair in order to dissolve all the modes of givenness that characterize natural consciousness. W. Marx, *Hegel's Phenomenology*, p. 51. Heidegger argues that *natural consciousness* does not despair at all and that this despair is really philosophical skepticism, the seeing (*skepsis*) that arises out of doubt and that characterizes the historicity of history. *HW*, pp. 139–41. This idea of "despair," was of central importance to the so-called existential interpretation of the *Phenomenology*, especially in the hands of Alexandre Koyré and Jean Wahl, both of whom greatly influenced Hyppolite. See Alexandre Koyré, "Rapport sur l'état des études hégéliennes en France," in *Verhandlungen des ersten Hegelkongresses vom 22. bis 25. April 1930 im Haag*, ed. Baltus Wigersma (Tübingen: Mohr, 1931; Haarlem: Willinz, 1931), pp. 80–105; Jean Wahl, *Le Malheur de la conscience dans la philosophie de Hegel*, 2d ed. (Paris: Presses Universitaires de France, 1951).

    24. *Ph*, 3:73. W. Marx argues convincingly that every interpretation of the *Phenomenology* must start with the fact that Hegel conjoins an educational history with the development of a series of forms, every stage of which is determined by a particular relationship of universal spirit or the absolute to the individual. W. Marx, *Hegel's Phenomenology*, p. 30. The recognition of this dual task reveals the insufficiency of an interpretation such as Scheier's that attempts to understand the series of forms merely as moments of absolute knowledge or science without reference to their political or pedagogical significance. Scheier, *Analytischer Kommentar*.

    25. The *Phenomenology* is thus in one sense a return to the ancient conception of dialectic. See *GP*, 18:457–59. This way of doubt and despair, however, ultimately departs from Socratic dialectic, which in Hegel's view was unable to construe itself as science and ended only in aporiae or demonic restraint. Hegelian dialectic necessarily construes itself as science. The consequence of this dialectic is thus not a thorough, restraining skepticism that honors the superior knowledge of the god but the completion and perfection of knowing in and as absolute knowledge and the *Science of Logic*. For an excellent discussion of the role of ancient dialectic in Hegel's thought, see Hans-Georg Gadamer, *Hegel's Dialectic*, trans. P. C. Smith (New Haven: Yale University Press, 1976), pp. 5–34.

    26. Plato *Phaedo* 76a; *L*, 5:49.

    27. What does it mean, however, to speak of the end of history? In what sense does history come to an end for Hegel? Kojève has argued perhaps as forcefully as anyone that this end must be understood literally as the end and thus exhaustion of all human possibilities. This does not mean of course that after Hegel nothing occurs, which would be absurd, but rather that because man's historical tasks have been completed neither work nor struggle gives rise to anything new. The post-Hegelian world from this perspective resembles the world of Nietzsche's last man, a world of stagnation upset perhaps by the ineffective efforts of tyrants and madmen to bring about change and by the occasional but historically insignificant flashing of an individual genius. All in all, however, this world is fundamentally fixed and unchanging. However compelling such a vision, it is by no means clear that it is Hegel's view of the matter. In fact, Hegel argues in the *Philosophy of History* that the New World has a future that

is fundamentally different from that of the Old World and thus not conditioned or delimited by it nor derivable from it. Hegel's claim is not that all human activity ceases but that the sequential development of all human possibilities is complete. Man can understand the absolute truth about himself and his world and thus can overcome the bifurcation that has characterized his being from the very beginning. It is not clear, however, that Hegel believes that this reconciliation is itself dissolved by the dialectical essence of consciousness itself, casting man once again into contradiction and alienation. The *Phenomenology* in this light is something more than the record of the dialectical voyage of the human spirit; it is the bark to which sailors may cling when their ship has gone down in "the night of self-consciousness"; it is a hieroglyph of vanished reason for "a new world and a new spirit." *Ph*, 3:590–91.

28. Hyppolite, *Genesis*, p. 15.

29. Much has been made of this notion of death by Wahl, Heidegger, and Hyppolite. Hyppolite even asserts that the *Phenomenology* as a whole is a meditation upon death. Hyppolite, *Genesis*, pp. 17, 18, 31. This is fairly typical of the existential interpretation of *Phenomenology* that fastens upon the unhappy consciousness and portrays it as the determinative section of the work. This leads to the conclusion that the essence of Hegel's thought is the notion of negativity and that this negativity is not merely cognitive but also and fundamentally existential. Kojève also sees the problem of death as central to Hegel's thought but interprets it on the basis not of the unhappy consciousness but of the master-slave relationship. According to Kojève, it is this relationship (and the attendant life and death struggle) that in its various guises characterizes all historical epochs. That the twentieth century should find the essence of the *Phenomenology* in the notion of struggle and death is perhaps understandable, but such a view ultimately distorts Hegel's thought: the dialectical for Hegel is always conjoined to the speculative; death and negation seem to characterize human history from every limited, historical perspective, but absolute science recognizes that for every death there is a new birth and that *Aufhebung* is preservation as well as destruction.

30. *Ph*, 3: 138–45.

31. *Ph*, 3: 75, 591.

32. This method is not merely a technique but first and foremost a path, as Fink convincingly argues. Fink, *Hegel*, p. 44.

33. In this sense, as Scheier points out, Hegel seems to accept the Fichtean dualism of I and not-I as his beginning, i.e., as the fundamental characteristic of consciousness and thus also as its underlying problem. Scheier, *Analytischer Kommentar*, pp. 21–23. Consciousness thus comes to understand itself by comparison to its world and its world by comparison to itself. Fink, following Hegel's distinction in the *History of Philosophy*, sees the first as the task of antiquity and the second as the task of modernity. Fink, *Hegel*, pp. 52–53.

34. Hegel refers to these participants as "us." The use of this 'us' and its referent has been much debated. For a comprehensive consideration of this question, see Kenley Dove, "Hegel's Phenomenological Method," *Review of Metaphysics* 23 (1970): 615–41.

35. As Fink indicates, it is the history of self-testing (skeptical) consciousness that passes in front of this pure contemplation. Fink, *Hegel*, p. 55. It would be incorrect to assume, however, that this history was an object distinct from absolute consciousness. It is, in fact, its ownmost being: absolute consciousness is contemplation as introspective retrospection.

36. This dialectical movement is seen by many as the thetic essence of consciousness or experience, what W. Marx refers to as the unfolding of the self and what Labarriere calls the self-movement of the content. W. Marx, *Hegel's Phenomenology*, pp. 46, 86; Labarriere, *Structures*, p. 48. Heidegger and Fink understand dialectic as the conversation of consciousness with itself, in which consciousness is understood as the unity of the thetic and the logical. *HW*, pp. 155, 160, 169–70; Fink, *Hegel*, p. 49. Hyppolite goes even further to describe it as the relationship of common or natural consciousness and transcendental consciousness. Hyppolite, *Genesis*. p. 16. All of these thinkers try to think dialectic as the way of being of the absolute, i.e., they try to conceive the appearance of knowledge or history out of the unity of the

I and the not-I or the identity of identity and non-identity. They all thus understand the absolute fundamentally as an *activity*. Such an interpretation is of course plagued by the problem that has always beset identity-philosophy of deriving multiplicity from unity. They ultimately rely, however, upon the fact or experience of self-consciousness, which seems to be such a multiplicity within unity. Despite its difficulties and shortcomings such an interpretation of Hegel is, however, clearly superior to Findlay's denigration of the idea of dialectic altogether as a method in Hegel's thought. John Findlay, *Hegel: A Re-examination* (New York: Macmillan, 1958), pp. 58–82. The absolute cannot be constructed or created by natural consciousness and any attempt to do so is thus fundamentally misguided.

37. Many have suggested in this light that the *Phenomenology* has to be understood as a theodicy. See Scheier, *Analytischer Kommentar*, p. 11; Stephen Crites, "The Golgotha of Absolute Spirit," in Merold Westphal, ed., *Method and Speculation in Hegel's Phenomenology* (Atlantic Highlands, N.J.: Humanities Press, 1982), pp. 47–55; Nicolai Hartmann, *Die Philosophie des deutschen Idealismus*, 2 vols. (Berlin and Leipzig: de Gruyter, 1923–29), 2:24; Justus Schwarz, "Die Vorbereitung der Phänomenologie des Geistes in Hegels Jenenser Systementwürfen," *Zeitschrift für deutsche Kulturphilosophie* 2 (1936): 138; Reinhart Maurer, *Hegel und das Ende der Geschichte: Interpretation zur Phänomenologie des Geistes*" (Stuttgart: Kohlhammer, 1965), pp. 48, 73–84.

38. Kojève sees this as the proof that Hegel's method is not really dialectical but phenomenological in a Husserlian sense, i.e., that it is "empirical" or "positivistic." Kojève, *Introduction*, pp. 460–71. Hegel abandons dialectic as a method in Kojève's view because the real historical dialectic has come to an end. Consequently, Hegel in his view is the first auditor-historian-philosopher. Not only does such an interpretation rest upon the problematic assumption of the actual end of history but it also overlooks the thetic and especially synthetic activity present in speculation.

39. This is the underlying significance of Hegel's statement, "I think it [truth] dwells in every authentic consciousness, in all religions and in all philosophies, but . . . our present point of view has been to understand its development." Hegel to Duboc, 30 July 1822. Hegel, *Briefe*, 2:329.

40. It is in this sense that Heidegger characterizes phenomenology as the self-collection of spirit. *HW*, p. 185.

Chapter 4

1. *Ph*, 3:591. There is a long-standing debate whether the *Phenomenology* is an account of historical development or only an account of the epistemological development of consciousness that employs historical examples to illuminate an essentially abstract metaphysical argument. For a thoughtful discussion of this debate, see Maurer's *Hegel und das Ende der Geschichte*. Maurer comes to the conclusion that while Hegel opens philosophy up to history his fundamental intention is theological and not historical. While generally sensible this argument fails to sufficiently recognize Hegel's attempt to coordinate the development of consciousness or the absolute with the actual historical development of humanity. His critique of Kojève's overly historical reading of Hegel, however, is a sound corrective.

2. *PG*, 12:20.

3. *Ph*, 3:325–27, 498–502, 505, 507, 512, 522, 545, 547, 578–83, 590–91. Labarrière and Lukàcs both note similar divisions although they explain them differently. Labarrière, *Structures*, p. 37; Lukàcs, *The Young Hegel*, pp. 466–536. Lukàcs ties these three stages to the divisions of the *Encyclopaedia* as subjective spirit, objective spirit, and absolute spirit. This is clear-sighted. He goes astray, however, in his assumption that Hegel is thus interested in discovering the laws of history. Hegel is rather interested in showing the development and presence of the absolute in all its historical forms. Like many others,

Hyppolite argues that the first division (chapters 1–5) is an ahistorical abstraction from spirit, which is alone historical. He likewise notes many gaps with reference to actual history. Hyppolite, *Genesis*, pp. 35–38. Most of the gaps are the result of the tripartite character of the development and are thus only apparent. Others are the result of Hegel's inability to achieve a perfect coordination of phenomenology and actual history.

    4. *Ph*, 3:82.

    5. Ibid., pp. 137–39, 143–44. Satisfaction is ultimately found only in another soul, i.e., in the recognition that one is a self-conscious individual. Individual soul as self-consciousness is thus driven into society in pursuit of its own satisfaction and reconciliation with itself.

    6. *PG*, 12:34, 36–40. Manfred Riedel has presented perhaps the strongest counterargument in his thoughtful *System und Geschichte: Studien zum Historischen Standort von Hegels Philosophie* (Frankfurt am Main: Suhrkamp, 1973), pp. 58, 99–117. He correctly sees the tension between Hegel and Hobbes but is less cognizant of the tension between Hegel and Rousseau.

    7. *PG*, 12:45–46.

    8. Ibid., p. 30.

    9. *Ph*, 3:326. Hegel's debt to Montesquieu, Rousseau, and Herder in this matter is manifest. W. Marx has even argued that 'substance' in the *Phenomenology* means the ethical substance or ethical life of a people. W. Marx, *Hegel's Phenomenology*, p. 54.

    10. *PG*, 12:55. This concrete reconciliation in and as the state is of course discussed at length in the *Philosophy of Right*. *PR*, 7:398–512.

    11. *PG*, 12:56–57.

    12. Ibid., p. 71; see pp. 68–69, 73.

    13. Ibid., p. 70; see pp. 72–73.

    14. Ibid., p. 57. As Hyppolite points out, Schelling had already discovered the basis for the historical reconciliation of freedom and necessity as the absolute in the union of the conscious and the unconscious, but history was for him always the history of nature and he was thus unable to come to terms with the concrete and particular human things because of his Spinozistic beginning. Hyppolite, *Genesis*, p. 28.

    15. *PG*, 12:76, 106.

    16. Hegel's conception of history must not be confused with that of Schelling. Not only is history always the history of nature for Schelling but it is always a development toward the reestablishment of an original but lost unity of man with nature and the divine. Hegel, on the contrary, recognizes the original unity not as a "golden age" to which one might want to return but as the crassest of unities, the unity of nature devoid of spirit, a regime of animal passions. Hegel indeed explicitly denies the existence of the original spiritual unity postulated by Schelling and the Romantics. Ibid., pp. 78–79.

    17. *GP*, 20:454–55. Absolute science as a secularization of religion is in one sense an answer to the contradiction Rousseau sees between the religion of man (Christianity) and the religion of the citizen (the civic religions of antiquity).

    18. Ibid., p. 460.

    19. Löwith understands this solution as the combination of Christian eschatology and the Greek conception of cosmic circularity. Löwith, *Meaning in History*, pp. 52–59.

    20. *L*, 5:70; see also *Ph*, 3:589–90.

    21. *Ph*, 3:590–91.

    22. W. Marx is thus correct in one sense—that natural consciousness must give up its naturalness to become absolute knowledge. This entails the surrender of its form as consciousness as well, since it thereby becomes pure knowing. W. Marx, *Hegel's Phenomenology*, p. 35. Since pure knowing, however, is likewise pure being, this naturalness is in a sense resurrected, although on a more fundamental or primordial level.

    23. *L*, 5:83, 100, 111.

24. Ibid., p. 74. Hegel had already developed this concept of identity as early as 1801 and its genesis is clearly bound up with the genesis of the absolute in Hegel's thought. See *D*, 2:113–16. See also Mauer, *Hegel*, p. 48. For a discussion of the beginning of the *Logic* and Hegel's method, see Dieter Henrich's thoughtful *Hegel im Kontext* (Frankfurt am Main: Suhrkamp, 1967), pp. 73–94.

25. *L*, 6:24–25. On the "Logic of Essence," see Henrich, *Hegel im Kontext*, pp. 95–156.

26. *L*, 6:269–75.

27. David Friedrich Strauss, *Das Leben Jesu*, 2d ed., 2 vols. (Tübingen: Osiander, 1835–36), 2:734–37; Fackenheim, *The Religious Dimension in Hegel's Thought*. Löwith tries to show that Hegel understands himself in this "theological" manner. See his "Aktualität und Inaktualität Hegels," in Heede, ed., *Hegel-Bilanz*, pp. 9–11. Ludwig Feuerbach, *Werke in sechs Bänden*, ed. Hans Martin Saß, 6 vols. (Frankfurt am Main: Suhrkamp, 1975), 3:51; Lukàcs, *The Young Hegel*, pp. 13–16, 31–32, 74–89. The history of the Left and Right Hegelians has been portrayed by Löwith in his *Von Hegel zu Nietzsche*.

28. Marx and Engels, *Marx-Engels-Werke*, supplementary vol. 1:571–73.

29. Johann Eduard Erdmann, *Die Entwicklung der deutschen Speculation seit Kant*, 2 vols. (Leipzig: Vogel, 1848–53), 2:853; Feuerbach, *Werke*, 5:32. This objection was often raised by traditional Christianity, which saw Hegel as a promulgator of atheism. See Peter Robbins' fine *The British Hegelians, 1875–1925* (New York: Garland, 1982), pp. 26–37.

30. Although a few interpreters such as McTaggart adopted Hegel's cosmology, most twentieth-century scholars have sided with Kojève, who asserted that is wasn't even necessary to refute Hegel's philosophy of nature anymore. Maurer has argued, however, that Hegel's philosophy of history is crucially dependent upon a teleological conception of nature. Reinhart Maurer, "Die Aktualität der Hegelschen Geschichtsphilosophie," in Heede, ed., *Hegel-Bilanz*, pp. 155–91.

31. Dilthey, *Gesammelte Schriften*, 4:249–51. Maurer points out that this position was also taken by Jung, Litt, Haering, Barth, and Plenge among others. Maurer, *Hegel*, p. 69.

32. See Maurer, *Hegel*, p. 25.

33. Löwith, *Meaning in History*, p. 53.

34. *E*, 8:128. For a concise discussion of this problem, see Hans Friedrich Fulda's "Unzulängliche Bemerkungen zur Dialektik" and the following discussion in Heede, ed., *Hegel-Bilanz*, pp. 231–82. On the contradiction of freedom and natural necessity in particular, see Emil Angehrn, *Freiheit und System bei Hegel* (Berlin: de Gruyter, 1977), pp. 57–58, 409, 449; and Wilhelm Seeberger, *Hegel oder die Entwicklung des Geistes zur Freiheit* (Stuttgart: Klett, 1961), pp. 598–99.

35. On this question see the Hook-Avineri exchange in Walter Kaufmann, ed., *Hegel's Political Philosophy* (New York: Atherton, 1970), pp. 59–76; and Avineri, *Hegel's Theory*, pp. 34–36.

36. See Riedel, *System*, p. 116. On this question also see the illuminating discussion of Hegel's political philosophy in Heede, ed., *Hegel-Bilanz*, pp. 214–29.

37. Stanley Rosen sees this as the result of Hegel's rejection of the Platonic-Aristotelian notion of the intuition of determinate form. Such noetic intuition is in his view replaced by sensuous intuition that never reaches the whole. Stanley Rosen, *G. W. F. Hegel: An Introduction to the Science of Wisdom* (New Haven: Yale University Press, 1974), pp. 266–67.

Chapter 5

1. Hegel, *Werke*, 2:432–33.

2. Nietzsche, *Werke: Kritische Gesamtausgabe*, ed. G. Colli and M. Montinari (Berlin: de Gruyter, 1967–), div. V, 2:159.

3. See Otto Pöggeler, "'Historicity' in Heidegger's Late Work," *Southwestern Journal of Philosophy* 4 (1973): 56–57; and his *Der Denkweg Martin Heideggers* (Pfullingen: Neske, 1963), p. 28. Pöggeler's sympathetic discussions of Heidegger offer perhaps the clearest and most thoughtful explication available of his thought. His unique access to many unpublished manuscripts, especially those from the years before *Being and Time*, renders his work both authoritative and indispensible.

4. To what extent Heidegger can be considered a phenomenologist remains unclear. For a good introduction to this question, see Herbert Spielberg's fine *The Phenomenological Movement: A Historical Introduction*, 2 vols. (The Hague: Nijhoff, 1960), 1:271–357. For Heidegger's own account, see Martin Heidegger, *Zur Sache des Denkens* (Tübingen: Niemeyer, 1969), pp. 81–90 (hereafter cited as *SD*); and his letter to Richardson in William Richardson, *Heidegger: Through Phenomenology to Thought* (The Hague: Nijhoff, 1963), pp. VIII–XXIII.

5. Martin Heidegger, *Séminaire tenu par le Professeur Martin Heidegger sur la Differenzschrift de Hegel* (Paris: by Roger Munier, 1968), p. 13 (hereafter cited as *Th68*). It would be a mistake to see this concern with history as Spenglerian or as analogous to the thought of the central European Marxist movement, as George Steiner has argued in his more or less biographical *Martin Heidegger* (New York: Viking, 1978), pp. 74–75, 148. Heidegger's concern is not with political or social history but with the history of metaphysics or philosophy.

6. For a thorough analysis of this "magnificent torso," see J. L. Mehta's comprehensive *The Philosophy of Martin Heidegger* (Varanasi: Banaras Hindu University Press, 1967), pp. 88–341; Mark Blitz's thoughtful *Heidegger's "Being and Time" and the Possibility of Political Philosophy* (Ithaca: Cornell University Press, 1982); and Pöggeler's, *Denkweg*, pp. 46–66. In this chapter, *Sein* and *Dasein* are translated as shown, *Seiende(n)* as 'being(s)'.

7. Hans Georg Gadamer, *Wahrheit und Methode*, 4th ed. (Tübingen: Mohr, 1975), p. 243.

8. See Martin Heidegger, *Séminaire tenu au Thor en septembre 1969 par le Professeur Martin Heidegger* (Paris: by Roger Munier, 1969), p. 28 (hereafter cited as *Th69*).

9. The significance of this so-called turn (*Kehre*) in Heidegger's thought has been perhaps the most debated point in the entire secondary literature. Since it was announced by Heidegger himself in his *Letter on Humanism*, scholars have debated whether it is a turn to a new sort of thinking that is incompatible with Heidegger's earlier thought and especially *Being and Time* (Löwith, Arendt, Schulz, Ott), or whether it is a return to the original themes that motivated his thought (Pöggeler, Fürstenau, Seidel). For a comprehensive consideration of this question and debate, see Orlando Pugliese, *Vermittlung und Kehre: Grundzüge des Geschichtsdenkens bei Martin Heidegger* (Freiburg: Alber, 1965).

10. Martin Heidegger, *Nietzsche*, 2 vols. (Pfullingen: Neske, 1961), 2:143–47 (hereafter cited as *N*).

11. *N*, 2:142, 145; *Th68*, p. 8.

12. *N*, 2:144.

13. *HW*, pp. 81, 85, 102; *N*, 2:468.

14. *N*, 2:461–62.

15. Martin Heidegger, *Vorträge und Aufsätze* (Pfullingen: Neske, 1954), p. 72 (hereafter cited as *VA*); *Einführung in die Metaphysik* (Tübingen: Niemeyer, 1953), pp. 77–82 (hereafter cited as *EM*).

16. Friedrich Nietzsche, *The Will to Power*, trans. and ed. Walter Kaufmann and R. J. Hollingdale (New York: Random House, 1967), p. 550, also see *N*, 1:426.

17. *N*, 1:46.

18. *VA*, p. 80. In other contexts Heidegger identifies technology (*Technik*) with culture. See *N*, 2:76. Reinhart Maurer has insightfully pointed out that technology for Heidegger becomes the metaphysics of our times. R. Maurer, *Revolution und 'Kehre': Studien zum Problem gesellschaftlicher Naturbeherrschung* (Frankfurt am Main: Suhrkamp, 1975), p. 26.

19. *VA*, p. 22; *HW*, pp. 102–3; *Th69*, p. 44; Martin Heidegger, "Ansprache zur Heimatabend," in *700 Jahre Stadt Meßkirch* (Meßkirch, 1969), p. 40; Martin Heidegger to Kojima, 18 August 1963, in *Begegnung, Zeitschrift für Literatur, bildende Kunst, Musik und Wissenschaft* 1, no. 4 (1965): 5. It should be noted that Heidegger's critique of technical organization is at least implicitly a critique of Weber's conception of a rational bureaucratic administration as well as the rational social science or sociology that underlies it.

20. This theme was developed more fully by the Frankfurt School (especially Marcuse and Habermas) and others such as Jacques Ellul. See Martin Heidegger, "Nur ein Gott Kann uns retten," in *Der Spiegel*, no. 23 (1976): 206 (hereafter cited as *Sp*); Maurer, *Revolution*, p. 9; and Otto Pöggeler's thorough *Philosophie und Politik bei Heidegger* (Freiburg and Munich: Alber, 1972), pp. 115–20.

21. Heidegger, "Ansprache," p. 41.

22. *VA*, pp. 80–81; *HW*, p. 237.

23. Martin Heidegger, *Was Heisst Denken?* (Tübingen: Niemeyer, 1954), p. 104 (hereafter cited as *WD*); "Ansprache," p. 38; *N*, 2:386–87.

24. *N*, 1:538; *HW*, p. 87.

25. *VA*, pp. 90–92; *N*, 2:278; *HW*, p. 103.

26. *WD*, pp. 31, 65.

27. *Martin Heidegger. Zum 80. Geburtstag von seiner Heimatstadt Meßkirch* (Frankfurt am Main: Klostermann, 1969), pp. 24–25.

28. *WD*, p. 11; see also *Sp*, p. 206.

29. Martin Heidegger, "Aufzeichnungen aus der Werkstatt," *Neue Zürcher Zeitung*, 27 September 1959.

30. *Sp*, p. 206; Martin Heidegger, *Platons Lehre von der Wahrheit. Mit einem Brief über den "Humanismus"* (Bern: Francke, 1947), pp. 88–89 (hereafter cited as *PL*); "Dankansprache," in *Ansprachen zum 80. Geburtstag 1969 in Meßkirch* (Meßkirch, 1969), p. 34.

31. For Heidegger's remarks on America and Americanism, see *N*, 2:487; *WD*, p. 10; *TH68*, p. 28; *TH69*, pp. 34–35, 44; *Sp*, p. 212; *SD*, p. 64; *VA*, p. 29; Martin Heidegger, "Ansprache," p. 40; "Zeichen," *Neue Zürcher Zeitung*, 21 September 1969; *Der Satz vom Grund* (Pfullingen: Neske, 1957), p. 202 (hereafter cited as *SG*).

32. *Th69*, p. 35; *N*, 2:145; *PL*, p. 88.

33. *N*, 1:442.

34. Martin Heidegger, *Vier Seminare* (Frankfurt am Main: Klostermann, 1977), p. 125 (hereafter cited as *VS*).

35. For Heidegger's remarks on Marxism, see *N*, 2:145; *Th69*, p. 29; *WD*, p. 101; Heidegger, "Zeichen," p. 51; *VS*, p. 131.

36. *EM*, pp. 35–36.

37. *N*, 2:145–46, 254.

38. *N*, 2:309; *VA*, pp. 91–94. It must be noted of course that Heidegger himself was for a brief time during his tenure as rector of Freiburg University a member of the Nazi party. This attachment and its significance for the interpretation of Heidegger's thought has understandably been a subject of tremendous controversy. Many have argued that Heidegger's emphasis on nihilism prepared the way for Nazism and that he himself would have been satisfied with a dictatorial, although not a totalitarian, regime (Löwith, Rosen, Schwan); others that he shared the Nazi distaste for liberalism without being in sympathy with their ideology or political methods (Blitz, Pöggeler) and in fact was a critic and opponent of the regime from 1934 on (Pöggeler, Palmier). See Karl Löwith, *Heidegger: Denker in dürftiger Zeit* (Frankfurt am Main: Fischer, 1953); Stanley Rosen, *Nihilism: A Philosophical Essay* (New Haven: Yale University Press, 1969); Alexander Schwan, *Politische Philosophie im Denken Heideggers* (Cologne: Westdeutscher Verlag, 1965); Blitz, *Heidegger's Being and Time*; Pöggeler, *Philosophie und Politik*; Jean-Michel Palmier, *Les Écrits politiques de Heidegger* (Paris: Herne, 1968).

Relevant documents may be found in Rosen, Palmier, and in Guido Schneeberger's *Ergän-zungen zu einer Heidegger-Bibliographie* (Bern: Suhr, 1960); as well as Heidegger's *Spiegel* interview, his *EM*, and his *Die Selbstbehauptung der deutschen Universität* (Breslau: Korn, 1933). Karsten Harries' short "Heidegger as a Political Thinker" *Review of Metaphysics* 29, no. 4 (June 1976): 642–49, also sheds some light on this subject.

While this subject cannot be treated at length here, some few remarks are necessary. That Heidegger saw something appealing in National Socialism can hardly be denied. Even in 1935 after he had left the party and had argued that the works being peddled as the philosophy of National Socialism "have all been written by men fishing in the troubled waters of 'values' and 'totalities,'" he could still speak of "the inner truth and greatness of this movement (namely the encounter between world technology and modern man)." *EM*, p. 152. He thus apparently saw something in Nazism that seemed to come to grips with the problem of technology and thus with nihilism. He asserts as much in his *Spiegel* interview, adding that those then in power were too unskilled in thinking to bring about such a reconsideration of human life. *Sp*, p. 214. What Heidegger apparently had in mind by such an encounter with world technology was a communal reconsideration of human existence. Such a consideration, however, presupposes that the question of man's own Being becomes the center of human life. It is perhaps in this light that Heidegger's brief attachment to Nazism and his role as rector ought to be understood, i.e., as an attempt to transform Nazism into a new philosophically directed investigation of human life. His speech, *The Self-Assertion of the German University* in fact presents such an argument.

Of course it might be objected that a man of Heidegger's intelligence must have seen that such a transformation was impossible. To assume, however that the events of the late 1930s and 1940s were the necessary and unavoidable consequence of the Nazi seizure of power is to fall victim to one of the most insidious forms of historicism. That they were a possibility was certainly clear to many and among them Heidegger. He apparently hoped, however, despite the difficulties and dangers of such an attempt, that the regime might be given a philosophical basis and thereby avoid the racism and romanticism that later manifested themselves in such an unspeakable way. His *Self-Assertion* ends with a quotation from Plato, "Everything great stands in the storm." This passage occurs in the sixth book of the *Republic* after the recognition of the necessary corruption of philosophic natures in the ordinary city and as Socrates moves into a discussion of the manner in which the good city can come into being, i.e., "how a city can take philosophy in hand without being destroyed. For surely everything great stands in the storm" (497d). Socrates then goes on to discuss the character of education in the regime ruled by the philosopher-king. Apparently, Heidegger hoped in the chaos, the storm of the moment, to establish a system of education and ultimately thereby a regime based upon philosophy rather than the instinctualism of the Nazis. As rector he was able to begin this transformation of education in Freiburg. This was cut short, however, by his resignation when it became clear to him that even his educational reforms would not be tolerated, let alone his hopes for a political transformation. That the possibility of failure was great was undoubtedly clear to him as the *Republic* passage indicates. Whether this attempt was the result of political naiveté, Nazi fanaticism, or civic courage is thus difficult to determine. We will have the opportunity to consider this question further below.

39. *N*, 2:343.

40. This does not mean, however, as Richardson has argued, that Heidegger attempts to ground metaphysics. Richardson, *Heidegger*, p. 628. Nor is he interested in a Hegelian *Aufhebung* of metaphysics but seeks instead to reveal an entirely new tradition and hence an entirely new meaning for metaphysics. Both Maurer and Mehta see this point more clearly. See Maurer, *Revolution*, p. 35; and Mehta, *Heidegger*, pp. 393–98.

41. For what is perhaps the clearest and most straightforward discussion of Heidegger's history of metaphysics, see Jean Wahl's *Sur L'Interpretation de l'histoire de la métaphysique d'après Heidegger* (Paris: Centre de Documentation Universitaire, 1951).

42. George Seidel goes astray on this point in his otherwise sound *Martin Heidegger and the Pre-Socratics: An Introduction to His Thought* (Lincoln: University of Nebraska Press, 1964), p. 44.

43. Maurer and Gurvitch thus go astray in their interpretation of Heidegger's thought as dialectical. Each revelation of Being is spontaneous and not the effect of preceding causes or the synthesis of preceding contradictions. Maurer, *Revolution*, pp. 49–50; Georges Gurvitch, *Les Tendances actuelles de la philosophie allemande: E. Husserl-M. Scheler-E. Lask—M. Heidegger* (Paris: Vrin, 1930; reprint ed., 1949), pp. 228–30. Gurvitch's chapter on Heidegger contains an excellent critique of his thought.

44. Martin Heidegger, *Aristotles, Metaphysik Theta 1–13* (Frankfurt am Main: Klostermann, 1981), p. 24 (hereafter cited as *Ar*).

45. What is surprising about this configuration is the striking resemblance to Nietzsche's Dionysian-Apollinian dualism. The Dionysian element seems to reappear in Heidegger as the idea of the nothing, the abyss, and the question of Being, while the Apollinian element appears as being, answer, and appearance.

46. *EM*, pp. 47–48.

47. *HW*, p. 304.

48. *EM*, pp. 120–21.

49. *EM*, p. 146.

50. *EM*, p. 117; Martin Heidegger, *Erläuterungen zur Hölderins Dichtung* (Frankfurt am Main: Klostermann, 1944), p. 111 (hereafter cited as *HD*).

51. *HD*, pp. 61, 73. Heidegger here too takes his clue from Hölderlin. See Werner Marx's excellent *Heidegger and the Tradition*, trans. Theodore Kisiel and Murray Greene (Evanston: Northwestern University Press, 1971), p. 235.

52. *HD*, p. 83; see also p. 111.

53. *HW*, p. 34; *EM*, pp. 78–79, 100–103, 126–27.

54. *EM*, p. 117.

55. *Martin Heidegger, Heraklit* (Frankfurt am Main: Klostermann, 1979), pp. 11–13.

56. *EM*, p. 48. See also Pöggeler, *Denkweg*, p. 206.

57. See Aristotle *Metaphysics* 1003a20, 1028a10–20, 1030a18–20; Categories 1b25–26.

58. Martin Heidegger, "Vom Wesen und Begriff *Phusis*: Aristotles Physik B 1," *Il Penserio* 3 (1958): 153.

59. *EM*, p. 111; *VA*, p. 255; Martin Heidegger, *Sein und Zeit*, 14th ed. (Tübingen: Niemeyer, 1977), p. 2 (hereafter cited as *SZ*); Pöggeler, *Denkweg*, p. 199.

60. On the Sophists, see *EM*, pp. 48, 80; Heidegger, "Aristotles Physik," pp. 153–55.

61. *WD*, p. 52.

62. *PL*, pp. 5–52; *N*, 1:180, 230; 2:14–15, 225, 458.

63. *N*, 2:458.

64. *PL*, p. 38.

65. *Martin Heidegger, Vom Wesen des Grundes* (Halle: Niemeyer, 1929), pp. 56–57 (hereafter cited as *WG*); *PL*, pp. 40–41, 48; *N*, 1:196.

66. *WD*, p. 7.

67. *N*, 2:228, 409.

68. *SZ*, p. 3; *Th68*, p. 11; *Ar*, pp. 43–44.

69. *VA*, pp. 15–19, 167; *N*, 1:205, 214; see Plato *Symposium* 205b.

70. *EM*, pp. 43–45; *Ar*, p. 39.

71. *N*, 2:412.

72. *PL*, p. 62. See also Peter Fürstenau, *Heidegger: das Gefüge seines Denkens* (Frankfurt am Main: Klostermann, 1958), p. 129.

73. *EM*, p. 31.

74. *EM*, p. 80.

75. According to Pöggeler, Heidegger argued in his early lectures that original Christianity represented an antimetaphysical way of thinking that came to terms with the concrete facticity of life, that lived time rather than living in time. Pöggeler, *Denkweg*, pp. 37–38, 193–94; "Being as Appropriation," *Philosophy Today* 19, no. 1–4 (Spring 1975): 19.

76. *WG*, pp. 40–43; Pöggeler, *Denkweg*, pp. 39–44.

77. *N*, 2:413–21; *Ar*, p. 46.

78. Martin Heidegger, *Phänomenologie und Theologie* (Frankfurt am Main: Klostermann, 1970), pp. 15, 32.

79. Western history is thus both eschatological and self-same. See *HW*, p. 311; W. Marx, *Tradition*, pp. 165–67; and Löwith, *Heidegger*, p. 60.

80. Heracleitus 123, Diels, *Fragmente*, 1:79; *EM*, p. 87.

81. *VS*, p. 144; Martin Heidegger, *Was ist Metaphysik?* 5th ed. (Frankfurt am Main: Klostermann, 1944), p. 107 (hereafter cited as *WM*).

82. Martin Heidegger, "Ernst Cassiere: Philosophie der symbolischen Formen, z. Teil: Das mythische, Denken," *Deutsche Literaturzeitung* 5 (1928): 1002, 1009; *HW*, p. 104.

83. *HW*, p. 104; *N*, 2:362.

84. *N*, 2:251.

85. *N*, 2:355; Martin Heidegger, *Vom Wesen der Wahrheit* (Frankfurt am Main: Klostermann, 1943), p. 17 (hereafter cited as *WW*).

86. See *VA*, pp. 251–52; Hesiod *Theogonia* 217–23.

87. Parmenides 8, in Diels, *Fragmente*, 1:120; *N*, 2:382.

88. *SZ*, pp. 384–85.

89. *SZ*, pp. 226–27; *HW*, 70–77.

90. Otto Pöggeler, "Heidegger's Neubestimmung des Phänomenbegriffs" (paper presented at the meeting of the German Phenomenological Society, Munich 1979), p. 7. See Bible, Eph. 1:8–11, 21; 3:3–4, 9–12; Augustine *Confessions* 9.3–14.

91. Pöggeler, "Being as Appropriation," pp. 19–20.

92. *SZ*, p. 427, n.1. Rosen's assertion that there is no eternity in any sense in Heidegger's thought but only pure possibility and his analogous assertion that Being is pure process both rest upon a conception of eternity as presence. Rosen, *Nihilism*, pp. 97–98, 124. Heidegger is concerned with that which is the source of possibility and process but which is itself beyond both.

93. Mehta argues in this light that Heidegger's notion of truth as revelation or disclosure is more Judaic than pagan. Mehta, *Heidegger*, p. 492n.

94. This is apparently what Heidegger means to capture in his notion of appropriation (*Ereignis*). See Pöggeler's important "Being as Appropriation."

95. Martin Heidegger, *Zur Seinsfrage* (Frankfurt am Main: Klostermann, 1956), p. 7. See *WG*, p. 21; and Jacques Derrida, *Of Grammatology*, trans. Gayatri Chakraworty Spivak (Baltimore: Johns Hopkins University Press, 1974), p. 23. Derrida characterizes Heidegger's articulation of this "null point" with "Being" as the final writing of an epoch.

96. This idea of nothingness belongs to a closely related cluster of concepts Heidegger employed at various periods in his work including 'finitude,' 'transcendence', 'nihilism', 'difference', 'ontological difference', 'Being', and 'chaos'. See Mehta, *Heidegger*, pp. 346–51; and Henri Birault's thoughtful "Heidegger and the Thought of Finitude," *Revue internationale de philosophie* 52 (1960): 135–62.

97. *WM*, p. 100; Heidegger, *Selbstbehauptung*, p. 12. Heidegger claimed sometime later that "questioning is the piety of thinking." *VA*, p. 44. While he continued to emphasize this decisive importance of questioning in his later work, he recognized as well that such a questioning presupposes and is predicated upon the experience and apprehension of

questionality itself. Thus, he concludes that "questioning is not the authentic gesture of thinking, but rather hearing the promise of that which should come into question." Martin Heidegger, *Unterwegs zur Sprache* (Pfullingen: Neske, 1959), p. 180 (hereafter cited as *US*).

98. *VA*, p. 259. The question of History and its relation to history was a central concern of Heidegger's thought. See *SZ*, pp. 19–21, 234–35, 332, 375–79, 395–96, 436; *N*, 2:26–27, 110, 206, 483; *VA*, pp. 32, 80, 95; *HW*, p. 76; *SG*, p. 52; *WD*, p. 104; and especially "Aus einer Erörterung der Wahrheitsfrage," *Zehn Jahre Neske Verlag* (Pfullingen: Neske, 1962), pp. 19–23.

99. *N*, 2:26–27.

100. *N*, 2:386.

101. Heidegger, "Zeichen," p. 51; *N*, 2:18.

102. *N*, 1:476; 2:262.

103. *EM*, p. 28. Heidegger's two ways bear a striking and unmistakeable resemblance to the two ways of Parmenides. For a discussion of the similarity of their methods see Seidel, *Pre-Socratics*, p. 118.

104. *EM*, p. 32.

105. *EM*, p. 154.

106. *SG*, p. 107; *VA*, p. 227; Heidegger, *Aus der Erfahrung des Denkens* (Pfullingen: Neske, 1954), p. 19 (hereafter cited as *ED*).

107. See *N*, 2:388.

108. *WD*, pp. 114, 146; *HW*, pp. 95, 334, 337–40; *EM*, pp. 124, 129.

109. For a fuller discussion of this point, see Seidel, *Pre-Socratics*, pp. 12–20.

110. *N*, 2:392.

111. *VA*, p. 90.

112. *VA*, p. 177.

113. *N*, 2:393.

114. See *WD*, p. 13.

115. *HW*, pp. 249–50.

116. *HW*, p. 336.

117. *WW*, pp. 13, 15; *VA*, p. 258. Derrida goes too far when he asserts that Heidegger abandons ontology, i.e., the relation of Being and being, in favor of Being as such after the *Introduction to Metaphysics*. Derrida, *Grammatology*, p. 22. It is true that Heidegger is thereafter concerned with ontology only in terms of the history of Being, but this is also a concern with the *difference* of Being and being, i.e., with their negative relationship to one another.

118. *SG*, p. 171; *WG*, p. 59.

119. Martin Heidegger, *Schellings Abhandlung über das Wesen der menschlichen Freiheit (1809)*, ed. Hildegard Freick (Tübingen: Niemeyer, 1971), pp. 100–101. Freedom for Heidegger belongs to a cluster of terms that includes 'truth' (*alētheia*), 'openness' (*Lichtung*), and 'world' (*Welt*). For a general discussion of their interrelationship, see Mehta, *Heidegger*, pp. 355–71, 504.

120. *VA*, p. 149.

121. It is an exaggeration to see this as a utopian harmony of man and world or man and things as Fürstenau argues. Fürstenau, *Heidegger*, p. 169. It cannot be denied that the images of the *Feldweg* and the concept of the fourfold lend themselves to such an interpretation and thus might lead one to wonder whether Heidegger was not perhaps a romantic or a utopian, but they are better understood as poetic attempts to articulate not an experiential but an ontological reality.

122. See Gerhard Krüger's critical "Martin Heidegger und der Humanismus," *Studia Philosophica* 9 (1949): 121–22.

123. See W. Marx, *Tradition*, p. 169, 253. On the superiority of ancient

thought, see Löwith, *Heidegger*, pp. 7, 67–68, 72; Blitz, *Heidegger's Being and Time*; and Lazlo Versényi, *Heidegger, Being, and Truth* (New Haven: Yale University Press, 1965).

124. This is argued rather convincingly by Maurer, *Revolution*, pp. 52–55.

125. For an excellent discussion and critique of Heidegger's understanding of Plato, see William A. Galston's "Heidegger's Plato: A Critique of *Plato's Doctrine of Truth*," *Philosophical Forum* 13, no. 4 (Summer 1982), pp. 371–84.

126. See Richardson, *Heidegger*, p. 631.

127. Löwith considers these at length and particularly with respect to Heidegger's Nietzsche interpretation. Löwith, *Heidegger*, pp. 77–110.

128. See Heinrich Ott's thoughtful *Denken und Sein: Der Weg Martin Heideggers und der Weg der Theologie* (Zollikon: Evangelischer Verlag, 1959), p. 117.

129. Löwith has made this argument as forcefully as anyone. Löwith, *Heidegger*, pp. 69–72.

130. Whether and to what extent this sort of interpretation necessarily has the character of violence as W. Marx has suggested will be considered below. W. Marx, *Tradition*, p. 108.

131. Löwith, *Heidegger*, p. 60.

132. See W. Marx, *Tradition*, pp. 169, 246–48; Gurvitch, *Tendances*, p. 232.

133. As Blitz points out, however, the ontological usage is still dependent upon the commonsense meaning of the term. Blitz, *Heidegger's Being and Time*, p. 205.

134. For an excellent discussion of this problem, see Fürstenau, *Heidegger*, pp. 171–79. He shows how Heidegger's concern with Being and human Being obscures the bodily unity of nature, natural multiplicity, and the variety of realms of human life. This lack of mediation also makes it difficult, if not impossible, to determine what constitutes authentic choice. See Rosen, *Nihilism*, p. 100.

135. See W. Marx, *Tradition*, p. 245.

136. This point is argued convincingly by Blitz, *Heidegger's Being and Time*, p. 253.

137. Heidegger does say that each people comes to be only through a struggle with other peoples, but it is certainly unfair to league Heidegger with Carl Schmitt merely on this basis, as Schwan tries to do. *EM*, p. 117; *N*, 1:185, 361; Schwan, *Politische Philosophie*, p. 92. Blitz asserts more soberly that the distinction of peoples is too significant. Blitz, *Heidegger's Being and Time*, pp. 205, 255–58. On the meaning of 'people' for Heidegger, see Pöggeler, *Philosophie and Politik*, pp. 23–25; and John Sallis, ed., *Heidegger and the Path of Thinking* (Pittsburg: Duquesne University Press, 1970), p. 26.

138. See Schwan, *Politische Philosophie*, pp. 144–45, 164–66; and Maurer, *Revolution*, p. 43. For a more sympathetic interpretation of this idea of *Gelassenheit* or letting-be, see Mehta, *Heidegger*, p. 520.

139. See György Lukàcs, *The Destruction of Reason*, trans. Peter Palmer (Atlantic Highlands, N.J.: Humanities Press, 1980); Ernst Bloch, *Erbschaft dieser Zeit* (Zürich: Oprecht & Helbing, 1935); Henri Lefèbvre, *L'Existentialisme* (Paris: Sagittaire, 1946); M. Merleau-Ponty, *Les Aventeures de la dialectique* (Paris: Gallimard, 1955); and Theodor Adorno, *Jargon der Eigentlichkeit. Zur deutschen Ideologie* (Frankfurt am Main: Suhrkamp, 1964).

140. Gurvitch sees this as the necessary consequence of the supremacy of the practical over the theoretical in Heidegger that harkens back to Fichte and the late Schelling. Gurvitch, *Tendances*, pp. 228, 232–33. Löwith believes it is the result of a misunderstanding of history. Löwith, *Heidegger*, pp. 48–53.

141. See W. Marx, *Tradition*, p. 248.

142. Rosen likens Heidegger's thought in this sense to poetic prophecy. Rosen, *Nihilism*, p. 39.

143. See Blitz, *Heidegger's Being and Time*, p. 222.

144. *ED*, p. 17. Schwan argues in this vein that the notion of the necessity of

error does away with all responsibility. Schwan, *Politische Philosophie*, p. 106. W. Marx suggests that this indicates that science offers a better, truer path. W. Marx, *Tradition*, pp. 249–51.

      145. Ott argues forcefully that Heidegger's history of Being presupposes Being as a mythic historical power. Ott, *Denken und Sein*, p. 106. Fürstenau sees this mythic power replacing social-cultural powers and the old idea of nature. Fürstenau, *Heidegger*, pp. 180–82. Rosen sees this whole strain of thought as an attempt to manifest a *deus absconditus*, while Löwith understands it as a Kierkegaardian attempt to found a new religion. Rosen, *Nihilism*, p. 87; Löwith, *Heidegger*, pp. 36, 59.

      146. This of course is much disputed. See Mehta, *Heidegger*, p. 6.

Bibliography

Adorno, Theodor. *Jargon der Eigentlichkeit: Zur deutschen Ideologie*. Frankfurt am Main: Suhrkamp, 1964.
———. *Negative Dialektik*. Frankfurt am Main: Suhrkamp, 1966.
Angehrn, Emil. *Freiheit und System bei Hegel*. Berlin and New York: de Gruyter, 1977.
Arendt, Hannah. *Between Past and Future: Six Exercises in Political Thought*. New York: Viking, 1961.
———. *The Life of the Mind*. 2 vols. New York and London: Harcourt Brace Jovanovich, 1978.
Avineri, Shlomo. *Hegel's Theory of the Modern State*. Cambridge: Cambridge University Press, 1972.
Baker, Keith. *Condorcet: From Natural Philosophy to Social Mathematics*. Chicago: University of Chicago Press, 1975.
Barnes, Harry. *A History of Historical Writing*. Norman: University of Oklahoma Press, 1937.
Beck, Lewis White. *A Commentary on Kant's Critique of Practical Reason*. Chicago: University of Chicago Press, 1960.
Bennet, Jonathan. *Kant's Dialectic*. Cambridge: Cambridge University Press, 1960.
Bernadette, Seth. *Herodotean Inquiries*. The Hague: Nijhoff, 1969.
Beyer, Wilhelm Raimund. *Hegel Bilder: Kritik der Hegel Deutung*. Berlin: Akademie, 1967.
Birault, Henri. "Heidegger et la pensée de la finitude." *Revue Internationale de Philosophie* 52 (1960): 135–62.
Blitz, Mark. *Heidegger's "Being and Time" and the Possibility of Political Philosophy*. Ithaca: Cornell University Press, 1982.
Bloch, Ernst. *Erbschaft dieser Zeit*. Zürich: Oprecht & Helbing, 1935.
———. *Subjekt-Objekt: Erläuterungen zu Hegel*. 2d ed. Frankfurt am Main: Suhrkamp, 1972.
———. *Tübinger Einleitung in die Philosophie*. 2 vols. Frankfurt and Main: Suhrkamp, 1963–64.
Bloch, Marc. *Feudal Society*. Translated by L. A. Manyon. 2 vols. Chicago: University of Chicago Press, 1961.
Braniss, Christian Julius. *Die Wissenschaftliche Aufgabe der Gegenwart als leitende Idee im Akademischen Studium*. Breslau: Maske, 1848.
Burg, Peter. *Kant und die Französische Revolution*. Berlin: Duncker & Humblot, 1974.
Claesges, Ulrich. *Darstellung des erscheinenden Wissens*. Hegel-Studien. Beiheft 21 (1981).

Collingwood, Robin George. *Essays on the Philosophy of History.* Edited by William Debbins. Austin: University of Texas Press, 1965.

———. *The Idea of History.* Oxford: Clarendon, 1946.

Croce, Benedetto. *What Is Living and What Is Dead of the Philosophy of Hegel.* Translated by Douglas Ainslie. London: MacMillan, 1915.

Derrida, Jacques. *Of Grammatology.* Translated by Gayatri Chakraworty Spivak. Baltimore: Johns Hopkins University Press, 1974.

Diels, Hermann. *Die Fragmente der Vorsokratiker.* Edited by Walter Kranz. 6th ed. 3 vols. Berlin: Weidmann, 1959–62.

Dilthey, Wilhelm. *Gesammelte Schriften.* Leipzig: Teubner, 1914–.

Dove, Kenely. "Hegel's Phenomenological Method." *Review of Metaphysics* 23 (1970): 615–41.

Düsing, Klaus. *Das Problem der Subjektivität in Hegels Logik. Hegel-Studien.* Beiheft 15 (1976).

Erbse, Hartmut, ed. *Festschrift Bruno Snell.* Munich: Beck, 1956.

Erdmann, Johann Eduard. *Die Entwicklung der deutschen Speculation seit Kant.* 2 vols. Leipzig: Vogel, 1848–53.

Fachenheim, Emil. *The Religious Dimension in Hegel's Thought.* Bloomington: Indiana University Press, 1967.

Fanon, Frantz. *The Wretched of the Earth.* Translated by Constance Farrington. New York: Grove, 1965.

Feick, Hildegard. *Index zu Heideggers Sein und Zeit.* Tübingen: Niemeyer, 1961.

Feist, Hans. *Der Antinomiegedanken bei Kant und seine Entwicklung in den vorkritischen Schriften.* Borna-Leipzig: Noske, 1932. (Dissertation, Berlin, 1932.)

Feuerbach, Ludwig. *Werke in sechs Bänden.* Edited by Hans Martin Saß. 6 vols. Frankfurt am Main: Suhrkamp, 1975.

Findlay, John. *Hegel: A Re-examination.* New York: Macmillan, 1958.

Fink, Eugen. *Hegel: Phänomenologische Interpretation der "Phänomenologie des Geistes."* Frankfurt am Main: Klostermann, 1977.

Fränkel, Ernst. *Geschichte der griechen Nomia agentis.* Strassburg: Trübner, 1910.

Fränkel, Hermann. *Dichtung und Philosophie des frühen Griechentums.* Munich: Beck, 1962.

Franklin, Julian. *Jean Bodin and the Sixteenth Century Revolution in the Metholodogy of Law and History.* New York: Columbia University Press, 1963.

Frings, Manfred, ed. *Heidegger and the Quest for Truth.* Chicago: Quadrangle, 1968.

Fulda, Hans Friedrich. *Das Problem einer Einleitung in Hegels Wissenschaft der Logik.* Frankfurt am Main: Klostermann, 1965.

Fulda, Hans Friedrich, and Henrich, Dieter, eds. *Materialien zu Hegels 'Phänomenologie des Geistes'.* Frankfurt am Main: Suhrkamp, 1973.

Fürstenau, Peter. *Heidegger: Das Gefüge seines Denkens.* Frankfurt am Main: Klostermann, 1958.

Gadamer, Hans-Georg. *Hegel's Dialectic.* Translated by P. Christopher Smith. New Haven: Yale University Press, 1976.

———. *Wahrheit und Methode.* 4th ed. Tübingen: Mohr, 1975.

Galston, William. "Heidegger's Plato: A Critique of Plato's Doctrine of Truth." *Philosophical Forum* 13, no. 4 (1982): 371–84.

———. *Kant and the Problem of History.* Chicago: University of Chicago Press, 1975.

Gardiner, Patrick. *Theories of History.* New York: Free Press, 1959.

Gentile, Giovanni. "Il concetto dello Stato in Hegel." In *Verhandlungen des 2. Hegelkongresses vom 19. bis 22. Oktober 1931 in Berlin.* Edited by Baltus Wigersma. Tübingen: Mohr, 1932; Haarlem: Willinz, 1932. Pp. 121–34.

Görland, Ingtraud. *Die Kantkritik des jungen Hegel.* Frankfurt am Main: Klostermann, 1966.

Grene, Marjorie. *Martin Heidegger.* London: Bowes & Bowes, 1957.

Gueroult, Martial. "Hegels Urteil über die Antithetik der reinen Vernunft." In *Seminar: Dialektik in der Philosophie Hegels.* Edited by Rolf-Peter Horstmann. Frankfurt am Main: Suhrkamp, 1978. Pp. 261–91.

Günther, Maluschke. *Kritik und Absolute Methode in Hegels Dialektik. Hegel-Studien.* Beiheft 13 (1974).

Gurvitch, Georges. *Les Tendances actuelles de la philosophie allemande: E. Husserl-M. Scheler-E. Lask-M. Heidegger.* Paris: Vrin, 1930; reprint ed., 1949.

Habermas, Jürgen. *Theorie und Praxis.* Neuwied and Berlin: Luchterhand, 1963.

Haering, Theodor. *Hegel: Sein Wollen und sein Werk. Eine chronologische Entwicklungsgeschichte der Gedanken und der Sprache Hegels.* 2 vols. Leipzig: Teubner, 1929 and 1938; reprint ed., Aalen: Scientia, 1963.

Hager, Achim. *Subjektivität und Sein: Das Hegelsche System als ein geschichtliches Stadium der Durchsicht auf Sein.* Freiburg: Alber, 1974.

Harries, Karsten. "Heidegger as a Political Thinker." *Review of Metaphysics* 29, no. 4 (June 1976): 642–49.

Harris, H. S. "Hegel and the French Revolution." *Clio* 7 (1977): 5–18.

———. *Hegel's Development: Toward the Sunlight.* Oxford: Clarendon, 1971.

Harris, W. T. "Kant's Third Antinomy and His Fallacy Regarding the First Cause." *Philosophical Review* 3 (January 1894): 1–13.

Hartmann, Nicolai. *Die Philosophie des deutschen Idealismus.* 2 vols. Berlin and Leipzig: de Gruyter, 1923–29.

Haym, Rudolph. *Hegel und seine Zeit. Vorlesungen über Entstehung und Entwicklung, Wesen und Werth der Hegel'schen Philosophie.* Berlin: Gärtner, 1857; reprint ed., Hildesheim: Olms, 1962.

Heede, Reinhard, and Ritter, Joachim, eds. *Hegel-Bilanz: Zur Aktualität und Inaktualität der Philosophie Hegels.* Frankfurt am Main: Klostermann, 1973.

Hegel, Georg Wilhelm Friedrich. *Briefe von und an Hegel.* Edited by Johannes Hoffmeister and Friedhelm Nicolin. 4 vols. Hamburg: Meiner, 1969–79.

———. *Hegel's Phenomenology of Spirit.* Translated by Arnold V. Miller with a Forward and Analysis by John N. Findlay. Oxford: Oxford University Press, 1977.

———. *Phänomenologie des Geistes.* Edited by Georg Lasson and Johannes Hoffmeister. Hamburg: Meiner, 1952.

———. *Werke in 20 Bänden.* Edited by Eva Moldenhauer and Karl Markus Michel. Frankfurt am Main: Suhrkamp, 1970–71.

Heidegger, Martin. "Ansprache zum Heimatabend." In *700 Jahre Stadt Meßkirch.* Meßkirch: Acker, 1962. Pp. 34–35.

———. *Aristotles, Metaphysik Theta 1–3.* Frankfurt am Main: Klostermann, 1981.

———. "Aufzeichnungen aus der Werkstatt." *Neue Zürcher Zeitung,* 27 September 1959.

———. *Aus der Erfahrung des Denkens.* Pfullingen: Neske, 1954.

———. "Aus einer Erörterung der Wahrheitsfrage." In *Zehn Jahre Neske Verlag.* Pfullingen: Neske, 1962. Pp. 19–23.

———. "Dankansprache." In *Ansprachen zum 80. Geburtstag 1969 in Meßkirch.* Meßkirch: Acker, 1969. Pp. 33–36.

———. *Einführung in die Metaphysik.* Tübingen: Niemeyer, 1953.

———. *Erläuterungen zu Hölderlins Dichtung.* Frankfurt am Main: Klostermann, 1944.

———. "Ernst Cassiere: Philosophie der symbolism Formen, z. Teil: Das mythische Denken." *Deutsche Literaturzeitung* 5 (1928): 999–1012.

———. *Der Feldweg.* Frankfurt am Main: Klostermann, 1953.

———. "Grundsätze des Denkens." *Jahrbuch für Psychologie und Psychotherapie* (1958): 33–41.

———. "Hegel und die Griechen." In *Die Gegenwart der Griechen in neueren Denken. Festschrift für Hans-Georg Gadamer zum 60. Geburtstag.* Edited by Dieter Henrich. Tübingen: Mohr, 1960. Pp. 43–57.

———. *Hegels Phänomenologie des Geistes.* Frankfurt am Main: Klostermann, 1980.

———. *Heraklit.* Frankfurt am Main: Klostermann, 1979.

———. *Holzwege.* Frankfurt am Main: Klostermann, 1950.

————. *Nietzsche*. 2 vols. Pfullingen: Neske, 1961.

————. "Nur ein Gott Kann uns retten." *Der Spiegel*, no. 23 (1976): 193–219.

————. *Phänomenologie und Theologie*. Frankfurt am Main: Klostermann, 1970

————. *Platons Lehre von der Wahrheit. Mit einem Brief über den "Humanismus."* Bern: Francke, 1947.

————. *Der Satz vom Grund*. Pfullingen: Neske, 1957.

————. *Schellings Abhandlung über das Wesen der menschlichen Freiheit (1809)*. Edited by Hildegard Feick. Tübingen: Niemeyer, 1971.

————. *Sein und Zeit*. 14th ed. Tübingen: Niemeyer, 1977.

————. *Die Selbstbehauptung der deutschen Universität*. Breslau: Korn, 1933.

————. *Seminaire tenu au Thor en september 1969 par le Professeur Martin Heidegger*. Paris: By Roger Munier, 1969.

————. *Seminaire tenu par le Professeur Martin Heidegger sur la Differenzschrift de Hegel*. Paris: By Roger Munier, 1968.

————. *Unterwegs zur Sprache*. Pfullingen: Neske, 1959.

————. *Vier Seminare*. Translated by Curd Ochwadt. Frankfurt am Main: Klostermann, 1977.

————. *Vom Wesen des Grundes*. Halle: Niemeyer, 1929.

————. *Vom Wesen der Wahrheit*. Frankfurt am Main: Klostermann, 1943.

————. "Vom Wesen und Begriff *Phusis*: Aristotles Physik B 1." *Il Penserio* 3 (Milan 1958): 131–56, 265–90.

————. *Vorträge und Aufsätze*. Pfullingen: Neske, 1954.

————. *Was heisst Denken?* Tübingen: Niemeyer, 1954.

————. *Was ist das—die Philosophie?* Pfullingen: Neske, 1956.

————. *Was ist Metaphysik?* 5th ed. Frankfurt am Main: Klostermann, 1949.

————. "Zeichen." *Neue Zürcher Zeitung*, 21 September 1969.

————. *Zum 80. Geburtstag von seiner Heimatstadt Meßkirch*. Frankfurt am Main: Klostermann, 1969.

————. *Zur Sache des Denkens*. Tübingen: Niemeyer, 1969.

————. *Zur Seinsfrage*. Frankfurt am Main: Klostermann, 1956.

Heimsoeth, Heinz. *Atom, Seele, Monad*. Wiesbaden: Steiner, 1960.

————. "Zum Kosmotheologischen Ursprung der Kantischen Freiheitsantinomie." *Kant-Studien* 57 (1966): 206–29.

Helferich, Christoph. *Georg Friedrich Wilhelm Hegel*. Stuttgart: Metzler, 1979.

Henrich, Dieter. *Hegel im Kontext*. Frankfurt am Main: Suhrkamp, 1967.

————. "Leutwein über Hegel." *Hegel-Studien* 3 (1965): 39–77.

Hinske, Norbert. "Kants Begriff der Antinomie und die Etappen seiner Ausarbeitung." *Kant-Studien* 56 (1965): 485–96.

Hoffmeister, Johannes, ed. *Dokumente zu Hegels Entwicklung*. Stuttgart: Fromman, 1936.

Hölzle, Erwin. *Das alte Recht und die Revolution*. Munich: Oldenbourg, 1931.

Huppert, George. *The Idea of Perfect History*. Urbana: University of Illinois Press, 1970.

Hyppolite, Jean. *Genesis and Structure of Hegel's Phenomenology of Spirit*. Translated by Samuel Cherniak and John Hekman. Evanston, Illinois: Northwestern University Press, 1974.

————. *Studies on Marx and Hegel*. Translated by John O'Neill. New York: Basic Books, 1969.

Kaltenbrunner, Gerd-Klaus, ed. *Hegel und die Folgen*. Freiburg: Rombach, 1970.

Kant, Immanuel, *Gesammelte Schriften*. Edited by the Königlich Preussischen Akademie der Wissenschaften. Berlin: Reimer, 1900–.

————. *Kants Prolegomena*. Edited by Benno Erdmann. Leipzig: Voss, 1878.

————. *Kritik der reinen Vernunft*. Hamburg: Meiner, 1926.

Kaufmann, Walter. *Hegel: A Re-interpretation*. Garden City, N.Y.: Doubleday, 1966.

Kaufmann, Walter, ed. *Hegel's Political Philosophy*. New York: Atherton, 1970.

Kelly, Donald. *Foundations of Modern Historical Scholarship*. New York: Columbia University Press, 1970.

Kelly, George Armstrong. *Idealism, Politics and History: Sources of Hegelian Thought.* Cambridge: Cambridge University Press, 1969.

Keuck, Karl. *Historia. Geschichte des Wortes und seiner Bedeutung in der Antike und in den romanischen Sprachen.* Emsdetten: Leuchte, 1934. (Dissertation, Münster, 1934.)

Kieswetter, Hubert. *Von Hegel zu Hitler: Eine Analyse der Hegelschen Machtstaatideologie und der politischen Wirkungsgeschichte des Rechtshegelianismus.* Hamburg: Hoffman & Campe, 1974.

Kojève, Alexandre. *Introduction à la lecture de Hegel.* Paris: Gallimard, 1947.

Koselleck, Reinhart. *Vergangene Zukunft: Zur Semantik Geschichtlicher Zeiten.* Frankfurt am Main: Suhrkamp, 1979.

Koyré, Alexandre. "Rapport sur l'état des études hégéliennes en France." In *Verhandlungen des ersten Hegelkongresses vom 22. bis 25. April 1930 im Haag.* Edited by Baltus Wigersma. Tübingen: Mohr, 1931; Haarlem: Willinz, 1931. Pp. 80–105.

Krüger, Gerhard. "Martin Heidegger und der Humanismus." *Studia Philosophica* 9 (1949): 93–129.

Labarrière, Pierre-Jean. *Structures et mouvement dialectique dans la Phénomenologie de l'esprit de Hegel.* Paris: Aubier-Montaigne, 1968.

Lauer, Quentin. *A Reading of Hegel's Phenomenology of Spirit.* New York: Fordham University Press, 1976.

Lefébvre, Henri. *L'Existentialisme.* Paris: Sagittaire, 1946.

Leibniz, Gottfried Wilhelm, Freiherr von. *Philosophische Schriften.* 7 vols. Edited by C. J. Gerhard. Berlin: Weidmann, 1875–90; reprint ed., Hildesheim: Olms, 1960.

Leumann, Manu. *Homerische Wörter.* Basel: Reinhardt, 1950.

Loewenberg, Jacob. *Hegel's Phenomenology: Dialogues on the Life of the Mind.* LaSalle, Ill.: Open Court, 1965.

Löwith, Karl. *Heidegger: Denker in dürftiger Zeit.* Frankfurt am Main: Fischer, 1953.

———. *Meaning in History.* Chicago: University of Chicago Press, 1949.

———. *Nature, History, and Existentialism and Other Essays in the Philosophy of History.* Edited by Arnold Levison. Evanston, Ill.: Northwestern University Press, 1966.

———. "Philosophische Weltgeschichte?" In *Stuttgarter Hegel-Tage 1970.* Edited by Hans-Georg Gadamer. Bonn: Bouvier, 1974. Pp. 3–27.

———. *Von Hegel zu Nietzsche. Der revolutionäre Bruch im Denken des neunzehnten Jahrhunderts.* Zürich and New York: Europa, 1941.

Lübbe, Hermann. "Bibliographie der Heidegger-Literatur 1917–1955." *Zeitschrift für philosophische Forschung* 11 (1957): 401–52.

Lukàcs, György. *The Destruction of Reason.* Translated by Peter Palmer. Atlantic Highlands, N.J.: Humanities Press, 1980.

———. *The Young Hegel: Studies in the Relations between Dialectics and Economics.* Translated by Rodney Livingstone. Cambridge, Mass.: M.I.T. Press, 1975.

Maluschke, Günther. *Kritik und Absolute Methode in Hegels Dialektik. Hegel-Studien*, Beiheft 13 (1974).

Marcuse, Herbert. *Hegels Ontologie und die Theorie der Geschichtlichkeit.* Frankfurt am Main: Klostermann, 1932.

———. *Reason and Revolution: Hegel and the Rise of Social Theory.* London: Oxford University Press, 1955.

Marquard, Odo. *Schwierigkeiten mit der Geschichtsphilosophie.* Frankfurt am Main: Suhrkamp, 1973.

Marx, Karl, and Engels, Friedrich. *Marx-Engels-Werke.* Edited by Manfred Kliem et al. Berlin: Dietz, 1956–.

Marx, Werner. *Hegel's Phenomenology of Spirit*. Translated by Peter Heath. New York: Harper & Row, 1975.

———. *Heidegger and the Tradition*. Translated by Theodore Kisiel and Murray Greene. Evanston, Ill.: Northwestern University Press, 1971.

Maurer, Reinhart. *Hegel und das Ende der Geschichte: Interpretation zur Phänomenologie des Geistes*. Stuttgart: Kohlhammer, 1965.

———. *Revolution und 'Kehre': Studien zum Problem gesellschaftlicher Naturbeherrschung*. Frankfurt am Main: Suhrkamp, 1975.

Mehta, J. L. *The Philosophy of Martin Heidegger*. Varanasi, India: Banaras Hindu University Press, 1967.

Meinecke, Friedrich. *Historicism: The Rise of a New Historical Outlook*. Translated by J. E. Anderson. London: Routledge & Kegan Paul, 1972.

Merleau-Ponty, Maurice. *Les aventeures de la dialectique*. Paris: Gallimard, 1955.

Michelet, Carl Ludwig. *Hegel, der unwiderlegte Weltphilosoph*. Leipzig: Duncker & Humblot, 1870; reprint ed., Aalen: Scientia, 1970.

Momigliano, Arnaldo. *Studies in Historiography*. New York: Harper & Row, 1966.

Negt, Oskar. *Aktualität und Folgen der Philosophie Hegels*. Frankfurt am Main: Suhrkamp, 1970.

Neske, Günther, ed. *Erinnerung an Martin Heidegger*. Pfullingen: Neske, 1977.

Nicolin, Friedhelm. "Zum Titelproblem der Phänomenologie des Geistes." *Hegel-Studien* 4 (1967): 114–23.

Nicolin, Günther, ed. *Hegel in Berichten seiner Zeitgenossen*. Hamburg: Meiner, 1970.

Nietzsche, Friedrich. *Werke: Kritische Gesamtausgabe*. Edited by Giorgio Colli and Mazzino Montinari. Berlin: de Gruyter, 1967–.

Norman, Richard. *Hegel's Phenomenology: A Philosophical Introduction*. London: Sussex University Press, 1976.

O'Brien, George Dennis. *Hegel on Reason and History: A Contemporary Interpretation*. Chicago: University of Chicago Press, 1975.

Ott, Heinrich. *Denken und Sein: Der Weg Martin Heideggers und der Weg der Theologie*. Zollikon: Evangelischer Verlag, 1959.

Palmier, Jean-Michel. *Les Écrits politique de Heidegger*. Paris: Herne, 1968.

Pelczynski, Z. A., ed. *Hegel's Political Philosophy: Problems and Perspectives*. Cambridge: Cambridge University Press, 1971.

Pocock, J. G. A. *The Ancient Constitution and the Feudal Law*. New York: Norton, 1957.

Pöggeler, Otto. "Being as Appropriation." *Philosophy Today* 19, no. 2/4 (1975): 16–42.

———. *Der Denkweg Martin Heideggers*. Pfullingen: Neske, 1963.

———. *Hegels Idee einer Phänomenologie des Geistes*. Freiburg: Alber, 1973.

———. "'Historicity' in Heidegger's Late Work." *Southwestern Journal of Philosophy* 4 (1973): 53–73.

———. "Perspectiven der Hegelforschung." In *Stuttgarter Hegel-Tage 1970*. Edited by Hans-Georg Gadamer. Bonn: Bouvier, 1974. Pp. 79–102.

———. *Philosophie und Politik bei Heidegger*. Freiburg: Alber, 1972.

Pöggeler, Otto, ed. *Heidegger Perspectiven: zur Deutung seines Werkes*. Cologne: Kiepenheuer & Witsch, 1969.

Popper, Karl Raimund. *The Open Society and its Enemies*. 4th ed. 2 vols. Princeton: Princeton University Press, 1963.

———. *Poverty of Historicism*. London: Routledge & Kegan Paul, 1957.

Pugliese, Orlando. *Vermittlung und Kehre: Grundzüge des Geschichtsdenkens bei Martin Heidegger*. Freiburg: Alber, 1965.

Richardson, William. *Heidegger: Through Phenomenology to Thought*. The Hague: Nijhoff, 1963.

Riedel, Manfred. "Natur und Freiheit in Hegels Rechtsphilosophie." *Hegel-Studien*, Beiheft 11 (1974): 365–82.

————. *System und Geschichte: Studien zum historischen Standort von Hegels Philosophie*. Frankfurt am Main: Suhrkamp, 1973.

Riedel, Manfred, ed. *Materialien zu Hegels Rechtsphilosophie*. 2 vols. Frankfurt am Main: Suhrkamp, 1975.

Ritter, Joachim. *Hegel und die Französischen Revolution*. Frankfurt am Main: Suhrkamp, 1965.

Ritter, Moriz. *Die Entwicklung der Geschichtswissenschaft an den führenden Werken Betrachtet*. Munich and Berlin: Oldenbourg, 1919.

Robbins, Peter. *The British Hegelians, 1875–1925*. New York and London: Garland, 1982.

Rosen, Stanley. *G. W. F. Hegel: An Introduction to the Science of Wisdom*. New Haven: Yale University Press, 1974.

————. *Nihilism: A Philosophical Essay*. New Haven: Yale University Press, 1969.

Rosenkranz, Karl. *G. W. F. Hegels Leben*. Berlin: Duncker & Humblot, 1844; reprint ed., Darmstadt: Wissenschaftliche Buchgesellschaft, 1977.

Rosenzweig, Franz. *Hegel und der Staat*. 2 vols. Munich and Berlin: Oldenbourg, 1920; reprint ed., Aalen: Scientia, 1962.

Rousseau, Jean Jacques. *Oeuvres Complètes*. Edited by Bernard Gagnebin and Marcel Raymond. Paris: Gallimard, 1959–.

Sallis, John, ed. *Heidegger and the Path of Thinking*. Pittsburg: Duquense University Press, 1970

Saß, Hans Martin. *Heidegger-Bibliographie*. Meisenheim am Glan: Hain, 1968.

Scheier, Claus Arthur. *Analytischer Kommentar zu Hegels Phänomenologie des Geistes: Die Architektonik des erscheinenden Wissens*. Freiburg: Alber, 1980.

Schelling, Friedrich Wilhelm Joseph von. *Sämmtliche Werke*. 14 vols. Stuttgart and Augsburg: Cotta, 1856.

Schnädelbach, Herbert. *Geschichtsphilosophie nach Hegel: Die Problem des Historismus*. Freiburg: Alber, 1974.

Schneeberger, Guido. *Ergänzungen zu einer Heidegger-Bibliographie*. Bern: Suhr, 1960.

Schwan, Alexander. *Politische Philosophie im Denken Heideggers*. Cologne and Opladen: Westdeutscher Verlag, 1965.

Schwarz, Justus. "Die Vorbereitung der Phänomenologie des Geistes in Hegels Jenenser Systementwürfen." *Zeitschrift für deutsche Kulturphilosophie* 2 (1936): 127–59.

Seeburger, Wilhelm. *Hegel oder die Entwicklung des Geistes zur Freiheit*. Stuttgart: Klett, 1961.

Seidel, George. *Martin Heidegger and the Pre-Socratics: An Introduction to His Thought*. Lincoln: University of Nebraska Press, 1964.

Shell, Susan. *The Rights of Reason: A Study of Kant's Philosophy and Politics*. Toronto: University of Toronto Press, 1980.

Shklar, Judith. *Freedom and Independence: A Study of the Political Ideas of Hegel's Phenomenology of Mind*. Cambridge: Cambridge University Press, 1976.

Siegel, Carl. "Kants Antinomielehre in Lichte der Inaugural-Dissertation." *Kant-Studien* 30 (1925): 67–86.

Smith, Norman Kemp. *A Commentary to Kant's "Critique of Pure Reason."* London: Macmillan, 1918.

Spielberg, Herbert. *The Phenomenological Movement: A Historical Introduction*. 2 vols. The Hague: Nijhoff, 1960.

Steiner, George. *Martin Heidegger*. New York: Viking, 1978.

Strauss, David Friedrich. *Das Leben Jesu*. 2d ed. 2 vols. Tübingen: Osiander, 1835–36.

Strauss, Leo. *Natural Right and History*. Chicago: University of Chicago Press, 1953.

Taylor, Charles. *Hegel*. Cambridge: Cambridge University Press, 1975.

Tocqueville, Alexis de. *Democracy in America*. Translated by George Lawrence. Garden City, N.Y.: Doubleday, 1969.

Troeltsch, Ernst. *Gesammelte Schriften von Ernst Troeltsch*. 4 vols. Tübingen: Mohr, 1912–25; reprint ed., Aalen: Scientia, 1961.

Versenyi, Lazlo. *Heidegger, Being, and Truth*. New Haven: Yale University Press, 1965.

Voltaire, François Marie Arouet de. *Dictionnaire philosophique.* Edited by Julien Benda and Raymond Naves. Paris: Garnier, 1967.

Vycinas, Vincent. *Earth and Gods: An Introduction to the Philosophy of Martin Heidegger.* The Hague: Nijhoff, 1961.

Wahl, Jean. *Le Malheur de la conscience dans la philosophie de Hegel.* 2d ed. Paris: Presses Universitaires de France, 1951.

————. *Sur L'Interpretation de l'histoire de la métaphysique d'après Heidegger.* Paris: Centre de Documentation Universitaire, 1951.

Weiss, Helene. *Kausalität und Zufall in der Philosophie des Aristotles.* Basel: Falken, 1942.

Werner, Karl. *Giambattista Vico als Philosoph und gelehrter Forscher.* Vienna: Braumüller, 1881.

Westphal, Merold. *History and Truth in Hegel's Phenomenology.* Atlantic Highlands, N.J.: Humanities Press, 1979.

Westphal, Merold, ed. *Method and Speculation in Hegel's Phenomenology.* Atlantic Highlands, N.J.: Humanities Press, 1982.

Windelband, Wilhelm. *Geschichte der neueren Philosophie.* 3d ed. 2 vols. Brietkopf & Härtel, 1878–80.

Yovel, Yirmiahu. *Kant and the Philosophy of History.* Princeton: Princeton University Press, 1980.

Index

213